FIND A
SAFE PLACE

Also by Alex Lazzarino and E. Kent Hayes
BROKEN PROMISE

FIND A
SAFE PLACE

Alex Lazzarino

E. Kent Hayes

McGRAW-HILL BOOK COMPANY

New York • St. Louis • San Francisco
Toronto • Mexico • Hamburg • London • Sydney

1 2 3 4 5 6 7 8 9 D O C D O C 8 7 6 5 4

ISBN 0-07-036782-5

Library of Congress Cataloging in Publication Data

Lazzarino, Alex.
    Find a safe place.
    1. Abandoned children—United States—Case Studies. 2. Socially
handicapped children—United States—Case studies. 3. Boys—United
States—Case studies. 4. Broken homes—United States—Case studies.
5. Juvenile detention homes—United States. I. Hayes, E. Kent, 1937-
II. Title.
HV881.L39 1984   364.3'6'0926   83-27552
ISBN 0-07-036782-5

Book design by Marea Epes.

Contents

Authors' Note

This story is based on actual case histories from among the hundreds of thousands of dependent, neglected children we have worked with and observed over the past twenty years in nearly every state in the nation.

More than a million children are incarcerated in this country every year, and approximately half are not even accused of a crime. Others are sentenced for "status offenses," acts for which adults cannot be prosecuted—truancy, curfew violations, and the like. Irrespective of the cause, more than eighty percent of the children in jail are there because they have no adults to care for them.

This is the story of four such boys. They were not criminals, but they were remanded to an institution created for hard-core delinquents—a setting that is, by its very design, a hostile and destructive environment.

We chose to dramatize the experiences of these boys because of their determination to survive and capacity to adapt to a system that has rendered them helpless. We marvel at their tenacity, and we rejoice in the indomitability of spirit that is characteristic of so many children in similar circumstances. Moreover, the lives of these four boys were touched by caring people—professionals and volunteers alike—who were dedicated to providing appropriate care for children. The institutions themselves—from juvenile courts and state hospitals to small-town jails and big-city detention homes— are also portrayed in a manner that depicts the evils that can result from the best of intentions.

Authors' Note

This story is set in Mid–America of the 1960's. Above all, do not fall into the trap of believing that the problems are regional or that conditions have improved. Our jails across the country are filled with children with neurological disorders and youngsters crying out for nothing more than parental affection, and even in this day of sophisticated psychological testing it is not unusual to find deaf and mute children confined to mental wards of state hospitals. If anything, conditions have deteriorated: facilities condemned for human habitation are reopened as juvenile detention centers; children are heavily drugged to substitute for the professional treatment that is unavailable; and funding for their care is the first to be cut in times of economic stress.

More than a dramatization of four case histories, this story depicts the ways in which the courts, caseworkers, police departments, governmental agencies, and juvenile institutions are struggling with the changes that need to take place if the hundreds of thousands of dependent and neglected children in this country are to survive.

It is to their strength, and to the inspirational courage of the children, that this book is dedicated.

The authors

. . . and to Joe and Anne Lazzarino,
and the Reverend Clare and Lois Hayes,
who provided a safe place.

BOOK 1:

Three in Crisis

BOOK I:

Three in Crisis

PART 1: *Matt, 1961–1963*

Chapter One: Matt, 1961–1963

The surrounding mountains were still buried in deep snow, but spring had finally come to the basin. Northern Wyoming summers are notoriously brief, but the late spring snows of 1961 had ensured that the summer would be shorter than usual.

It was going to be a bad season for the small number of dry farmers. It would also be tough on Dan McFadden, one of the last of the itinerant horsemen in the high plains. It would be impossible for him to break horses for the mountain ranchers until the snow melted from the high passes. The spring roundups would be delayed, but once the work began, there would be no respite for Dan and his son until August.

The McFadden name had been synonymous with horsemanship in the basin ever since 1907, when a band of Blackfeet taught Dan's father, still a boy at the time, to trap wild mustangs and break them for market. Five years later Oren McFadden trailed a Nez Percé raiding party for more than two hundred miles, returning home a month later with the Appaloosa stallion that was to sire the finest strain of horses ever seen in the basin.

Dan McFadden had reared Matt in the family tradition, so as they waited for the mountain passes to open, he devoted himself to honing the bronco-busting skills of his twelve-year-old son. "Get his head up! Dammit, Matt, get his head up!" he shouted as the rank gelding twisted and bucked across the length of Frank Johnson's corral with the young boy clinging like a burr to the horse's back. The excitement and concern in Dan's voice seemed to carry for miles in the brisk air, reverberating off the surrounding mountains and echoing back across the valley.

"No! No!" Dan screamed as horse and boy skittered dangerously close to the fence. "Yank him! Yank him out!"

Suddenly the horse twisted in toward the fence, lowering its head to the left and swinging its rump viciously to the right, dislodging the boy and tossing him into a graceful headlong arc that contrasted sharply with the clumsy landing that followed.

Dan spurred his bay forward, but the anxiety in his face vanished as his son rolled over in the dust, laughingly spitting dirt. "Stupid knothead didn't even see the fence," Matt sputtered as he propped himself on his elbows and grinned up at his father.

The mischief returned to Dan's eyes as he sat back in his saddle and watched the boy struggle to his feet with an exaggerated grimace. "He's a dumb one, all right," Dan said chidingly, nodding toward the gelding, who was already grazing contentedly through the lower rail. "He doesn't even know how bad his butt is gonna hurt tomorrow."

Matt returned his father's grin and said, "Wait till morning. That buckjumper will be lucky to straighten up at all."

Dan chuckled sarcastically. "We better call it quits. That poor horse has had enough punishment for one day."

The two unsaddled their mounts and headed for the pickup, Matt slapping the dust from his clothes as they walked.

"Damn if you can't raise more dust than one of those Kansas twisters," Dan said teasingly.

Matt straightened up and slammed his hat flush into his father's midsection, eliciting a surprised "Oof!" and a counterattack that sent them both tumbling and laughing into the high grass.

The twelve-year-old boy, at five feet ten inches, was already as tall as his father and, at 150 pounds, was 10 pounds heavier, but he was no match for the wiry strength of a man who had been breaking horses and wrestling stock for almost all of his thirty-nine years. Nonetheless, Dan permitted his son to maneuver him into a headlock that would have been impossible to break, except for Matt's vulnerability to tickling.

Matt was oblivious of his father's intentions. "Give?" the boy panted, tightening his grip around Dan's neck and digging his heels into the soft ground for greater leverage.

"Not yet," Dan grunted, jabbing two gnarled and wriggling fingers into his son's ribs.

"No fair!" Matt shrieked, rolling over disjointedly as the attack persisted. Dan came off the ground, pounced on the boy's chest, and poked two fingers into the left side of his son's sensitive neck. Matt clamped his head down on the wriggling fingers, leaving the right side of his neck vulnerable to the thrust of Dan's bristled chin.

"I give! I give!" Matt shrieked helplessly as the hysteria drained his strength.

"Not *yet* you don't," Dan growled. "I owe you twelve for your birthday, plus one more for good luck." Then he scraped his unshaved chin along the tender skin of the boy's neck, eliciting a mixed reaction of excruciating laughter, pathetic pleas, and stamping feet.

"That's *one.*"

"No, Dad! Please! No more!"

"That's *two,*" he said, twitching his chin again.

"Yeoow! No fair!"

"That's *three,*" Dan intoned, but he shifted his weight subtly to decrease his leverage and make it easier for the boy to throw him off.

Matt sensed the advantage and kicked his feet as high as he could; then he slammed them down to lift his midsection, tossing his father off. He rolled quickly across Dan's chest and pinned his wrists to the ground.

"Give?"

"Again?" Dan groaned, tensing his arm muscles for a counter-attack.

Matt sensed trouble and was immediately conciliatory. "Okay, truce?" he asked hopefully.

Dan's neck muscles tightened as he appeared to strain against his son's grip; then he relaxed his head and arms and grunted, "Truce."

Matt tumbled away from his father and mumbled gruffly, "Just in time. I was trying not to hurt you," and the two lay head to head, breathing deeply, chuckling contentedly, and staring up into the cloudless June sky.

"I still owe ya," Dan warned with menacing affect.

"How come?"

"It's your birthday, that's how come. I gotta give you *something*."

"Why don't you just give me that new saddle? And call it even?"

"'Cause you've never set a saddle long enough to justify the expense, that's why."

"Ha!" the boy taunted, rolling over to stare into his father's upside-down face. "Just because I have to break the boneheads that are too tough for you!"

"Get lost," Dan said derisively. "You were riding better that first summer we came back from Chicago . . . and you were only four years old"

"I always *was* a fast learner, wasn't I?"

Dan smiled abstractedly and thought back to Chicago. Oren had coerced Dan into enrolling at the University of Wyoming on the pretext that a degree in animal husbandry would be important to their partnership. Oren died two years later, and Dan learned that he had sold off the remaining land to finance the college expenses. Filled with grief and anger, Dan broke cleanly with his past by switching to journalism and taking a job as a copy editor for an advertising firm in Chicago.

Two years later Lori died giving birth to Matt, and Dan's life again came apart. He employed a series of housekeepers to take care of the baby, and he threw himself into his work, jumping at every chance to leave the apartment. As soon as young Matt began to recognize and respond to his father, however, Dan's reluctance to leave him began to grow, and he revived his long-buried memories of growing up on the ranch with Oren. One evening, returning from work on the elevated train, Dan made up his mind, and two weeks later he and his three-and-a-half-year-old son were on their way back to the land that had been settled by the boy's great-grandfather, more than sixty years earlier.

Dan's thoughts were unceremoniously interrupted by pieces

of grass being dribbled onto his face. "You asleep?" Matt asked.

"No. I think I'm dead."

"Good! I can just bury you right here." And the laughing boy tore up massive clumps of grass with both hands and tossed them gleefully, with dirt still clinging to the roots, all over his father's chest, chanting, "Pore ol' Dan McFadden . . . died without a friend to mourn him . . . just 'cause he wouldn't buy his son a saddle for his birthday."

Dan rolled over and quickly sprang to his feet with a menacing gesture that sent Matt scrambling sideways out of reach. "Okay, joker, that settles it. For your birthday present, I'm going to let you wash these clothes."

"That's all right with me," Matt taunted him from a distance. "This is about the time of year you usually wash up anyway."

"Very funny. You're getting to be a regular smart-ass in your old age, aren't you?" Dan grinned as he brushed the grass and dirt from his jacket and said, "Let's get on home. Martha's probably brought over your birthday cake by now, and this year I'd like to get to it before your raccoon."

"Last one to the truck's a candy-ass," Matt said challengingly in a singsong voice as he sprinted ahead.

"Hey! Watch your language." Dan scolded him angrily, stopping the boy in his tracks.

Matt was suddenly contrite. "Sorry, Dad. I was only joking."

"Come over here," Dan commanded.

Matt was stunned by his father's uncharacteristic outburst and was unable to move as Dan slowly approached him, limping slightly from too many years of jousting with uncooperative mustangs. "Well, it's not very funny," Dan said sternly. His eyes were squinted and his lips compressed in anger until he came abreast of his son; then suddenly his grin erupted again, and he sprinted for the truck, running ahead of Matt, blocking the boy off with his body. "Last one to the truck's a *what?*"

"No fair," Matt laughed, trying to push his father out of the way, finally succeeding in reaching around him to touch the truck in a dead heat with him.

Dan doubled over in laughter, trying to catch his breath as

he shuffled toward the door of the truck. He climbed behind the wheel, still gasping for air, and leaned against the backrest with a happy groan.

"Push over, old-timer." Matt was holding the door open. "You said I could start driving on my birthday."

Dan started to protest but realized it would be useless. He simply shook his head and grinned as he slid across the seat, wondering where the years had gone.

The butterflies in Matt's stomach belied his outward bravado. Until then his driving had been restricted to starts and stops around their cabin, most of the time under Dan's strict supervision but sometimes on his own, contrary to his father's wishes. But this was the real thing. True, the road between Frank Johnson's corral and the McFadden cabin was dirt all the way, and the only activity they might encounter between the corral and home would be at the Johnson house, but this was real enough. Matt wanted desperately to pull away from the corral smoothly, but the old truck bucked and stalled in first gear. Matt hurriedly shifted to second, and their heads popped back as the gears engaged.

"Easy does it," Dan said softly.

Matt knew he was on trial. He had the greatest father in the world, but no father wants to admit his son is growing, and the surest sign of that happening is the first time his son drives.

"You're drifting too far to the right, son. Keep it on the dirt." Dan's voice was soft and reassuring, but his head and eyes were riveted straight ahead, as he tried to conceal his nervousness and his furtive glances at the speedometer.

Matt tried to appear cool and confident. "Nice day." His voice cracked dryly.

"Yep."

"Not too many antelope for this time of year, huh?" *What the hell did that mean?*

"Better shift to third, son."

Suddenly Matt was aware of the high-pitched whine of the engine overworking. "Right. I was just keeping it in second on this hill," he said, shifting quickly and smoothly.

"Right."

Matt was sitting so rigidly that his only concessions to gravity seemed to be his feet on the floorboard and his white-knuckled fists on the steering wheel. In third gear, however, the old truck rolled smoothly, and Matt relaxed. As they approached the Johnson house, he entertained a fleeting urge to run over the mailbox for the sheer pleasure of watching Fat Frank turn apoplectic. Matt grinned to himself as he pictured the outraged and ill-tempered rancher jumping up and down and cursing while Martha—she preferred *Aunt* Martha—fretted and sobbed in the background. She did that a lot, but this time she would have good reason.

But when Fat Frank unexpectedly stepped off his porch, Matt veered off the road, away from the mailbox, in a show of extreme caution. Frank gestured to Matt, then realized it was not Dan behind the wheel and repeated the gesture to the man in the passenger seat. He simply nodded and jerked his thumb in the air, but it was so out of place for their perpetually sour employer that Matt attached great significance to it. Dan waved back, and Matt smiled nervously, wondering what was going on.

They had driven out of the hollow and around the bend leading to the final hill overlooking their cabin when the meaning of Frank's signal struck Matt. *The saddle!* Dad had asked Frank to keep the saddle hidden; then, when Marth—*Aunt* Martha delivered the birthday cake, Frank would set the saddle up on the pile of logs near the front door. Matt did not want to spoil the surprise, so he struggled to appear impassive and was glad he hadn't run over Fat Frank's mailbox. He snatched a quick look at his father, but Dan's eyes were focused on the top of the hill, as always, waiting for the first glimpse of the mountain peaks that would soon appear. Matt thought about the saddle and tried to remain calm, but the color drained from his face, and he squirmed on the seat.

As they approached the crest of the hill, the mountains in the background loomed into full view. Dan always slowed the truck to absorb the panorama, so when they reached the top, Matt, in a special gesture of love, brought the pickup to a complete stop. He seemed to understand that his father, struggling with the pain of relinquishing the childhood of his only son, was filled with melancholy.

The snow-covered mountains were framed by a deep blue

sky, and a thin line of clouds divided the top half from the bottom. Immediately below the line of clouds, the slopes were covered with thick forests of pine trees, broken only by occasional out-croppings of pink and purple shale. Farther down the mountain, where the snow had melted, the aspens were beginning to leaf out, and at the very base stood their weathered two-room shack.

Matt cut the engine, and Dan smiled his thanks. *Eight years . . . it can't be possible.* "I know I've told you this story a thousand times," Dan said softly, "but you were hardly four years old the first time we came over this hill together."

Matt nodded indulgently.

"We had stopped by the Johnsons' on the way out, and Frank said the cabin was in such bad shape even the drifters had moved out." Then, as though an explanation were necessary, he said defensively, "Don't forget, it was empty for seven years."

"Yeah, but I helped you fix it up," Matt said, encouraging Dan to continue.

"Roof slats were missing, the doors were hanging off their hinges, and every window was broken," Dan said, shaking his head, remembering how he and Oren had cut, chiseled, and fitted each board into place soon after Dan's mother had died, almost thirty years ago.

"You and I camped out for a couple of nights," Dan continued. The bigness of the country had frightened Matt, but when nightfall compressed their world into a crackling campfire, Martha's chicken and biscuits, and warm blankets, the four-year-old boy had dried his tears, cuddled comfortably against his father, and found contentment.

"I tried to get you to play by yourself while I fixed up the place," Dan said with a grin, "but you were into everything. Finally, I gave you a hammer and carried you up to the roof with me. You were a pain then, but you know, we've kinda been working together ever since, haven't we?"

Matt sensed that his father was close to tears and became uncomfortable until Dan rapped him on the shoulder and said brightly, "The hell with all that. Let's get down there and see if we can't rustle you up a birthday present."

The old truck bounced down the hill, but Matt was too excited to care about such formalities as roadbeds. He scanned the front yard for his new saddle, but there was nothing on the pile of wood except the old hatchet. Maybe he had made a mistake, maybe he was getting another collection of arrowheads or, worse, some new school clothes. *Please . . . not that.*

"Better pull up right here," Dan said. "There's not room enough in the kitchen for the pickup."

Matt stopped and jumped out of the truck, expectantly scanning the side yard for some clue.

"What's wrong with your eyes?"

Matt looked questioningly at his father. "What do you mean?"

"They look like they're about to pop outta your head. What're they looking for?"

"You know."

Dan untied his neckerchief. "I know they're looking for your present, but I mean what's the present they're looking for exactly?"

"You know."

"Come here. Let me tie this thing over your face," Dan said, stretching out his sweaty neckerchief.

Matt sniffed at it, wrinkled his nose, and said, "How about if I just close my eyes?"

"Turn around. I got a better idea." As soon as Matt complied, Dan reached up to the boy's broad-rimmed, high-domed hat and jammed it down over his eyes.

"Yeouch!" Matt yelped. "My ears!"

"I don't care about your ears. It's those big *eyes* I'm thinking about." Dan moved around in front of his son to be certain the hat was down far enough; then he bent over and peered upward. "You can still see, can't you?" Matt nodded. "Well, just tilt your head forward, and I'll lead you."

Dan tugged at Matt's shirt, and the boy stepped forward tentatively, his chin buried in his chest and his arms already flailing at the air in front of him. "You got it all figured out, don't you?" Dan asked.

"I sure hope so."

"You think it's that fancy saddle, right?"

Matt shrugged his shoulders noncommittally, but there was an expectant grin on his half-hidden face.

"That fancy Mexican job with the silver conches and hand-tooled latigos and stirrups, right? Is that what you're hoping for?"

"I wouldn't mind," Matt said coyly, playing along with the game.

Dan led Matt around the corner of the cabin, stopped him, and turned him around. "Lift up that hat and look at me," he said gravely.

Matt's grin evaporated when he looked into his father's somber face.

"Son, you know we can't afford that kind of a saddle. Why, we don't even own our own horses. Besides, we're *working* hands, not dudes. They'd laugh you clear outta the basin with a rig like that."

Matt was suddenly ashamed. He shrugged his shoulders and said, "That's okay, Dad. I was only kidding."

Dan placed his hands on his son's shoulders and consoled him. "The saddle I bought for you is *honest*. It's not fancy, but it'll get the job done."

Matt forced a smile.

"Now, if you'll turn around, you'll see it about fifteen steps in front of you."

Matt turned slowly, expectantly, and he saw the honest saddle his father had described, but it was strapped to a black and white Appaloosa that gleamed magnificently in the afternoon sun. The boy was too stunned to move. When he turned back to his father, there were tears in his eyes and his voice was tremulous. "Juniper?" he whispered. "Juniper?"

Suddenly there were tears in Dan's eyes, too. He smiled crookedly and nodded. "She's all yours, pal."

"Oh, Dad." Matt reached out and hugged his father roughly, unable to suppress his sobbing until Dan succeeded in pushing him off toward the tethered horse. Matt's first steps were uncertain, but he broke into a run and threw himself against the animal, wrapping his arms around its neck. One more look at his beaming father, and Matt reached down to untie the tether, vaulted onto Juniper's back, and sprinted across the meadow.

*　　*　　*

Sleep was out of the question for both of them that night. Nor did they bother to light the kerosene lamps. They sat in front of the fire, Dan in his chair and Matt sprawled on the braided oval rug. "Whose turn was it to cook tonight?" Dan asked sluggishly.

"Have another piece of cake."

"I'm up to here with cake. I just want to know which one of us missed his turn."

"You said you would tell me about Juniper, Dad."

"Don't try to change the subject. It was *your* turn, wasn't it?"

"I had it brought in."

"The hell you did. Chocolate cake? That's not what I call a nourishing meal."

Matt laughed sarcastically. "Look who's talking. What did you serve last night?"

"Beef! I made us a beef dinner last night," Dan said ingenuously. "What's wrong with that?"

"In the first place, it was beef *jerky,* and in the second place, you didn't make it last night. We *both* made it last September."

"Right," Dan said self-righteously, "so it's your turn to cook tomorrow."

Matt shook his head ruefully, smiling to himself in the dim light. "Okay, tell me about Juniper."

Dan reached for his pipe and started tamping the tobacco. That was a sure sign that he was going to tell another story about old Jeremiah or Grandpa Oren, and Matt was delighted. For as long as he could remember, their winter evenings had been spent in front of the fire either doing homework or telling the old tales. Matt much preferred the latter.

"Do you remember when Juniper was born?" Dan asked.

"Sure. About three years ago. Mr. Johnson called you over in the middle of the night."

"*Exactly* three years ago. Matter of fact, it was you who named her, wasn't it?"

Matt shrugged. "By the time I got to the shed that night you and Mr. Johnson had finished off a whole jug of that homemade gin of his, and I said the place smelled like juniper berries. The name just kind of stuck."

"Well, your grandpa Oren was the first white man to bring an Appaloosa into this whole basin." Dan paused for effect. "It was 1911 or so. He was no more than eighteen or nineteen years old, but he had already been trapping and breaking wild horses for a couple of years . . . all mangy stuff . . . nothing fit for breeding, except an occasional palomino mare or two."

Dan struck a match to his pipe, and Matt reached for some cushions to make himself more comfortable. There was no such thing as a short story once his father had got started.

"Anyway, that spring Pa went into the hills after a new batch of those buckjumpers, but the winter had been so mild they were already way up in the mountains, clear to hell and gone. He finally put together a string of a dozen or so, one more shabby than the other, but he made up his mind to stick it out until he found one horse he could use for breeding, even if it took all summer. My pa was a tough old geezer . . . and *stubborn*, believe me. I remember one time—"

Matt recognized the danger signal and sat up straight. "Juniper, Dad."

"Huh?"

"What about Juniper?"

"I was just getting to that," Dan said reproachfully. "Your grandpa Oren was just about ready to give up the whole deal when a half dozen of the most beautiful animals he had ever seen came trotting right into his camp."

Matt had a feeling he was about to hear another fairy tale. "Dad," he said with some suspicion, "is this going to be another 'Coggly-Woo' story?"

"No, *I'm telling you*, he'd never seen anything like it. Some of them were white, with little black spots over their entire bodies, and some of them were black, with big white patches on their necks and rumps. They were built like Arabians, but they were spotted . . . and no more than fourteen hands."

"And they just walked into Grandpa's camp?" Matt asked incredulously.

"Yeah, and every one of them had a mean-looking Indian on his back. Their entire bodies were painted purple, and white, and red."

Matt grinned. "The horses?"

"No, smart-ass, the *Indians*. Scared the bejingers outta Pa, too."

This time Matt laughed out loud. Dan had graduated from college, had worked in a Chicago advertising house, and had personally tutored Matt in a range of academic disciplines that had extended from ancient Indian petroglyphics to the classical literature and philosophy of the Western world. Nevertheless, given the chance to talk about horses or the old times, he quickly reverted to the idiom of a crotchety cook on a cattle drive.

"Anyway, your grandpa knew right off what was happening. The Indians had to be Nez Percé because they was . . . *were* . . . the only ones who still painted up. They're *still* the meanest—"

"Dad."

"Okay . . . Pa spoke to them in sign language and offered to trade his entire string of broomtails for just one of those Appaloosas, and they agreed. That is, they agreed to *half* the deal—the part about taking Pa's horses."

Matt clapped and laughed delightedly, and Dan warmed to the task.

"He tracked those devils clean into Idaho, and to hear him tell it, you'da thought it was all the way to China. More'n a month! But by God, he found 'em."

Dan struck another match, but Matt was caught up in the story and impatient. "What happened then?" he urged.

Dan affected a look of surprise. "Whaddya mean? Pa just waited for night and cut out with the biggest Appaloosa stud he could find." He leaned back in his chair and indicated by his silence that the story was over.

"Is that it?" Matt asked. "You mean he *stole* one of their horses?"

"He *traded*. Those people were roasting his horses for food, so he just traded even—twelve of his mustangs for one Appaloosa. Seemed fair at the time."

"So he rode him all the way back home?"

"Well, it wasn't *quite* that easy, son. Some army boys . . . cavalry . . . took out after him, but that horse climbed the mountains like a goat and ran the flats like an antelope. Pa knew right then he had his stud."

Matt persisted. "What about Juniper?"

"Well, your grandpa Oren had a string of four or five palominos for Titanic to service—"

"Titanic?"

"That's what he named him. At first he named him Outlaw because of the way the cavalry had chased them, but then he heard about this *unsinkable* ship, and he figured that name fit better." Dan chuckled, and Matt braced for another side excursion. "The following year the *Titanic* sunk, and Pa—those Blackfeet had made him a little superstitious—Pa almost changed the name back to Outlaw, but the name had already stuck."

By this time Matt was beginning to deduce the remainder of the story. "So Titanic sired the Appaloosas in this area, is that what you're saying?"

"You could put it that way . . . if you were in a hurry," Dan said petulantly, "but there's more to the story."

"I'm not surprised."

"Okay, I'll tell it quick. Seven or eight years later, in 1918, there was a drought that wiped out all the farms in Wyoming and Montana. It stretched into 1919, and most of the cattle were destroyed, too. That's when Grandpa's two sisters left the ranch for St. Louis. Anyway, by 1920 the whole range looked like it was carpeted with dead animals, but through it all, your grandpa Oren held on to Titanic. He turned out every other animal, but he held on to that horse. When the drought finally broke, he started up again, but this time he bred Titanic to Arabians mainly, and *that's* the line you see today. And Juniper is a direct descendant of old Titanic."

Matt was genuinely impressed. "Wow," he breathed. "When did Grandpa finally get rid of them? I mean, how come we don't have any others?"

Dan's eyes clouded over. "Grandpa and I . . . we had kind of a disagreement. He knew he was dying . . . didn't say a word . . . Later I found out he had sold everything . . . except this cabin . . . to send me to college." Dan rubbed his eyes with the back of his hand and said with finality, "It's really getting late, son. We better call it a night."

*   *   *

The weather during the week that followed was dominated by a chinook, a warm breeze from the southwest that was certain to melt the snow in the high passes. Matt was despondent because his father would soon be heading for the mountain ranches, leaving him behind to finish school. He longed for the old days, when he was too young to be left alone and Dan had to take him along to complete the semester in the field.

Matt had plotted and schemed for a way to accompany his father. He had come directly home from school every day to help Dan break the remaining horses in Frank Johnson's string, and Juniper was quickly learning to be an effective cow pony. Matt was feeling sorry for himself, convinced that neither he nor his horse would be getting a fair chance to prove his worth.

Dan noticed the change. "What's wrong with you, boy. Lose your best girl?"

"Naw, I don't have a girl."

"Maybe that's the problem." Dan grinned.

Matt shook him off impatiently. "I just want to go out with you this time. Juniper and I could be a big help." Matt was suddenly talking faster. "There's only three more weeks of school, and Miss Mason—"

"Hold on," Dan said sternly. "That's the biggest bunch of crap I've ever heard out of you."

Matt pursed his lips and looked down.

"I'm already a month late getting started."

Matt turned away, not wanting to hear that he would be in the way, but Dan reached for his shoulder and turned him around. "Damn if you don't have a headful of water. Turn it off, will ya? What I *started* to say is . . . there's no way I can do it by myself."

Matt looked up and shook his head in disbelief, his eyes pleading for confirmation.

"Whatever gave you the idea that I wasn't putting you to work?"

"You mean it, Dad?"

"We leave on Saturday."

"And school?"

"I talked to your Miss Mason this morning. Starting Satur-day, *I'm* the new Miss Mason."

With mist in his eyes, Matt did something that most boys have usually forgotten by the time they are twelve: He hugged his father around the neck and kissed him on the cheek.

Chapter Two

The summer of 1961 fulfilled its promise. Matt and Dan traveled among the mountain ranches, breaking horses at a record pace. Word of Matt's proficiency began to precede them, and by the end of the summer ranchers were dragging their own sons out to witness the spectacle of a twelve-year-old broncobuster holding his own with the best of them.

They finished their work in late July, almost three weeks ahead of schedule and just in time to ride into the mountains to harvest the gentian roots that would serve as the basis for Dan's Indian horse remedies in the cold months of winter. They set out from home, Matt aboard Juniper and Dan riding one of Frank Johnson's old Morgans.

They rode through Avalanche Pass and camped on Broken Man Mountain, on the edge of a blue lake that reflected the tall green pines on the hillside and the golden peaks beyond. The shoreline was overgrown with cattails, and Dan took advantage of the situation to tell another story.

"Your great-grandfather Jeremiah used to cut the reeds from this very place," he said. "He'd bundle them up and carry them all the way back, and the women used to weave them into mats and chair seats." Dan chuckled. "The old boy used to chop off the roots and cart off the reeds. He did that for years, until some old Shoshoni ridiculed him for throwing away the best part."

Matt reached into the marshy vegetation and pulled out a cattail for closer scrutiny. "It all looks bad to me."

Dan separated the reed and swished the base of the plant

through the clear water. "It's the roots," he said, handing them to his son. "They'd dry them out in the sun and grind them up for flour."

Matt never ceased to wonder at the wealth of information his father possessed, and he looked forward to the second night out, when they would camp by the old mine shaft and spend the day exploring the tunnels. Life with Dan was full of discovery, and Matt knew it would be a sad day for both of them when it came time for him to return to school.

Matt was an exceptional student, and when the winter blizzards isolated them, Dan also became a great teacher. The two spent the long winter evenings talking or reading by the fire, arguing about whose turn it was to do which household chore, and generally becoming the closest of friends.

Perhaps too much so. Dan began to worry about his son's uninterest in youngsters his own age. He tried to broach the problem in different ways: "You know, son, we'd have plenty of room if you should decide to bring a friend home for the weekend. I'll sleep out here and give you guys the bedroom."

"Naw, there's no one I'm friends with."

"How come?"

"Most of the guys are just interested in cars and girls. They're drippy."

"Which ones? The cars, the girls, or the guys?"

"All of them." Matt seemed uninterested in the topic.

"Isn't there anyone at school you like?"

"Only Miss Mason. This is my third year with her, and she's about the only person I like to talk to."

"What about sports? You're big enough for basketball or football."

"We play six-man flag football sometimes during gym. It's fun, but the other kids seem so . . . young." Matt looked up at his father and said, "Don't worry about me, Dad. I enjoy being around older people. I like the way they joke around, and I like the stories they tell. Most of all, I kind of like the way they . . . you know . . . respect me. Like last summer at the Nelson

Ranch . . . after I rode that hammerhead of theirs . . . all the men laughed and beat me on the back. *That* was fun."

"Okay. I just thought I'd mention it. Actually I guess it was the same way for me when I was your age."

The summer of 1962 passed in much the same way as the previous year, except Matt was less of a curiosity on the circuit. He was two inches taller than his father by that time, but he and Dan were built alike: sinewy bodies devoid of excess fat, legs slightly bowed, thick hands and fingers, and heavily muscled necks and shoulders. Matt was now six feet tall and weighed 170 pounds, and Dan had learned not to wrestle with him anymore. His voice deepened, his skin seemed perpetually tanned, and he was generally regarded as an intelligent, well-read, gentle boy of thirteen, but one with the strength and temper to be reckoned with as a man. He suffered through all the moods and pains of adolescence, except he never felt the need to put down his father, who had become his best and only friend.

They enjoyed a brief fling at some of the local rodeos that popped up at roundup time, and they enjoyed additional successes as they learned to function as a team. They quit only for their annual trek into the mountains.

One day, in the fall of 1962, Matt commented on a change he had perceived in Frank Johnson. "He was always a grouchy old slob," Matt said, "but he's getting worse than ever. Is something wrong, Dad?"

Dan chuckled gleefully. "It's Juniper."

"How come?"

"Old Frank made a bad deal, and he'd like to back out of it."

Matt showed his concern. "You mean, take Juniper back?"

"There's no way he can do that," Dan assured him. "When Frank sold him, I agreed to break sixty horses for him over the next three years. We've already broken forty-five, and Frank gets himself all worked up every time he sees your filly work. Best damned cow horse in the basin. Don't worry about Frank, son. He'll get over it."

Matt was not so certain. "How many more do we have to break?"

"No problem. Come spring, it'll take us less than two weeks." Dan lifted a business ledger from the shelf and flipped through the pages. "Fifteen more . . . here's the paper we signed."

Matt looked out at the black clouds moving in from the north with the first heavy snowfall of the season and thought, *I sure wish it was spring.*

It was one of those on-again, off-again winters. Two days of sunshine and three days and nights of howling blizzards. Shirt sleeve days and arctic nights. There was talk of running electrical lines out to the McFadden cabin, but the speculation generated no excitement because Matt and Dan preferred the mellow light of the kerosene lamps, and both had long since mastered the art of cooking on a wood stove. If the idea held any allure, it was on those frigid mornings when Matt had to venture out to the pump for water or break through the ice in the trough so Juniper could drink. In his mind, the only luxury that electricity would afford was a pump for indoor plumbing.

It was a dull winter, too. Matt used his own money to buy one of those new augers for ice fishing, and it worked very well through November, when the ice was no thicker than eight inches. He would enthusiastically set out six lines, having effortlessly and flamboyantly drilled separate holes for each, but his father always stuck to the old way of chopping a single hole with the old double-bladed ax.

Matt never tired of teasing him: "Better hurry, old man, the season ends in March," or, "You're not so dumb. By the time you chop through that ice, the fish will be a lot bigger." Every tirade concluded with cackling laughter and more heckling about Dan's someday entering the sixteenth century.

By Christmas, however, the ice was more than two feet thick, and Matt's new auger was about as useless as a bent spoon. The two of them shared a single hole that only the old ax could open, but mostly Matt sat in the pickup and sulked.

All the signs—the velvet covering on the deer's horns, the

color of the elks' coats, and the thickness of the range animals' hair—had indicated it would be a relatively mild winter, so Matt and Dan harvested only enough game to supply them through a short season. In September they had hung two antelope in the tiny shed behind their cabin, in October they added a deer, and in late November they brought in a cow elk that they shared with the Johnsons, much to Matt's dismay. By the end of February, however, they were reduced to grinding up the tougher cuts or marinating the meat for days.

Matt was so impatient for spring that he began to complain incessantly, especially about the wild meat around which every home meal and school lunch was constructed. The early arrival of the chinooks, however, brightened his outlook considerably, and when the first shipment of horses finally arrived at the Johnson Ranch, he was ecstatic.

He was eager to settle his account with Frank Johnson, convinced in his own mind that the irascible rancher was waiting for the slightest excuse to reclaim Juniper. "How about it, Dad? He's got eight horses up there."

"Not yet. The ground's still frozen. We'll split a hoof."

And on another day: "How about it, Dad? He just got in another shipment."

"Not yet. You'll bust your butt."

By the middle of March Matt had almost despaired of spring, but he arrived home from school one day to find his father oiling their tack and stretching the ropes. For the first time in six months he was confident he would save his horse.

As usual, Dan dreaded the start of a new season. He would be all right after the first few days, but the mere thought of again submitting his body to the punishment of breaking horses reawakened the dormant pain of every injury he had ever sustained. He spent more and more time inspecting the stock, testing his gear, and doing whatever else might delay the inevitable moment when that first bronc would jar his bones and stretch every muscle to the tearing point.

When the time finally arrived, the two of them stood inside

the corral, and Matt sensed his father's reluctance to cut out the first horse. "Maybe you're just getting old," he said chidingly as they strapped on their spurs.

"Maybe I'm getting *smart.*"

"I doubt that."

"Doesn't matter"—Dan shrugged—"either way . . . this is no business for smart old men." Then he walked forward and arched his lariat deftly over the head of one of the milling broncs.

Dan's qualms disappeared with the first jolt. He rode as though he were in midsummer form, instinctively shifting his weight in the stirrups when the horse spun, raising his heels high over the horse's shoulders when he bucked, raking his spurs across the animal's flanks when it grew too tired to jump, and finally cackling with satisfaction when the horse trotted smoothly out of its frenzy.

Satisfied that the lot was a manageable one, Dan permitted Matt to try his skill on the third horse of the day. The boy expertly roped a big bay mare and tethered her while his father secured the saddle. The ride that followed was not particularly exciting, but Dan glowed with pride and pleasure by the time his son rode the bay to a halt and vaulted from the saddle. He was truly a man now. Three months short of his fifteenth birthday, he was already more than six feet tall. His deep-set brown eyes and perpetually tanned face made him look older than he was, but he would lose some of those years as soon as the summer sun had bleached his sandy hair. At that moment, though, the unbridled excitement in his face betrayed his youth.

"How about one more?" the boy suggested confidently, appearing to swagger a little.

"No need," Dan answered. "After that ride *Simon LeFrank* went right home and tore up the foreclosure papers."

"Let's do it," Matt urged. "I feel real good."

A slight shiver coursed through Dan's shoulders as a cold gust of wind whipped the dust across the corral. He looked back at the black clouds beginning to shroud the mountain peaks to the north and said, "Your fleece jacket is in my saddlebag. Why don't you put it on first? . . . It'll be snowing in a couple of hours."

"Shoot, Dad! No horse is going to take me *that* long."

"*Shoot, Paw,*" Dan drawled, twisting his mouth idiotically and mimicking the uneven extremes in the adolescent voice of the excited boy, "ain't been a broomtail borned I cain't bring down!"

Matt usually had a quip for any occasion, but he was embarrassed about his adolescence in general and his changing voice in particular. Teasing about it was hitting below the belt. He cringed slightly and returned to the question in carefully modulated tones. "How about it? You getting goosey?"

Dan laughed and bowed at the waist, gesturing broadly toward the milling herd. "Be my guest."

Matt shook his rope loose, lengthened the loop, and, advanced on the horses, his spurs jangling softly in the loose dirt. He swung his arm and flicked the lariat around a three-year-old gelding that stood a full hand taller than any others in the corral. The gelding showed no signs of fear. It stood its ground, resisted the pressure of Matt's rope, and glowered down at the approaching boy with defiance.

Dan's expectant smile faded as the other horses scattered and revealed Matt's selection. It was a horse he had not noticed before. Then he found himself walking toward the gelding, abreast of his son, as though in a dream, without knowing how he got there. Somehow Matt's fleece jacket was in his hand. "Put this on," he ordered curtly. "You're going to need it." His somber tone left no room for discussion, so Matt did as he had been told.

Dan saddled the tall gelding with extra caution, closely examining the deep and ragged scars that covered the withers and marked the animal as a born fighter. When he finally spoke, the dryness in his throat reflected his anxiety. "This is a rank animal, son. You'd better let me take him."

Matt mistook the intensity in his father's voice for excitement, and he was so pleased to see Dan back in the groove that he agreed without saying a word. He loved to see his father ride, and he sensed that something special was about to happen.

As soon as Dan was firmly seated, he nodded once, and Matt released the tether, but the horse did not move. Then its nostrils flared, its ears flattened, and its skin twitched all over. Suddenly the gelding exploded straight up from the ground with a terrifying shriek, and as Matt backed hurriedly toward the corral fence, he realized that he was about to see an exciting exhibition of horse-manship.

Dan's rhythm was absolutely perfect, shifting his weight from pommel to stirrups, from his back to his legs, virtually anticipating every leap, every lunge, and every spin in the horse's arsenal. The defiance in the animal's eyes gave way to terror when it finally appeared that it would not rid himself of its rider.

The gelding dashed and bucked toward the fence, determined to scrape the man off its back as a last resort, but Dan heaved against the reins and forced it away. Suddenly the gelding threw itself sideways, lunging out of control, and viciously crushed the rider's leg between the tether post and a thousand pounds of frenzied horseflesh, shattering Dan's knee and fracturing his tibia. He felt no pain, but when the fearsome animal whirled back toward the fence, Dan was unable to balance himself in the stirrups. He was flung from the horse and into the railing with an impetus that broke his neck and killed him instantly.

Matt realized his father was dead as soon as he hit the ground. The thud, the loud crack, the body spasms, the blank stare. The boy's immediate instinct was to go for help, but there was nowhere to go and no one to help.

Matt and his dad had had each other, and there was nothing else.

Chapter Three

Matt lost track of time as he knelt cradling his father's body in the sandy corral. He didn't realize he was crying until his tears splashed on the dead man's face, re-forming the smooth layers of dust into tiny splotches of mud on Dan's cheeks. Matt tenderly wiped his father's face; then he gently placed his right hand over the vacant eyes, forcing himself to accept the final truth by drawing down the eyelids with a painful sob.

The sun had set by the time Matt picked up the small, limp body and started out of the corral. His Appaloosa whinnied apprehensively, but it had never entered the boy's mind to surrender his burden to a horse. Instead, he walked blindly across the ridge toward the Johnson house, taking no notice of the swirling spring snow or the cold air sweeping down from the range. The lifeless body in his arms bore no resemblance to the cocky, tough little man who had spent his life loving, caring, and giving.

As Matt walked, his mind filled with unconnected images of his father and their life together.

You gotta mud-pond that critter, son.

Aw, Dad, that's no fun. Porky's done so much time in the danged mud pond, he's getting duck's feet.

So're you, but that don't make a damn. If you wanna learn to bust broncs, you gotta do it in the mud pond.

Matt had not resorted to a mud pond in the five years since that incident, but if there had been a mud pond that day, his dad would still be alive. Dan had had a premonition that something was going to happen. . . . *This is a rank animal, son. You'd better let me take him. . . .* The cold shivers . . . *Put this on. . . . You're going to need it.* Why hadn't they mud-ponded that gelding? *It's too cold yet. Be patient. The ground is hard enough to bust your butt.* Goddamn the mud pond anyway.

Matt was thirteen again, and they had just completed their work at Ike Jorgenson's ranch, barely two weeks into the summer. *C'mon, Pop, they're gonna think we're scared.*

I don't care what they think, Matt. Breaking horses is our profession; rodeo is only a sport. It's stupid to take any more chances than we have to.

I won't get hurt calf roping. There's even a girl entered . . . Jewell Soderholm.

The opportunity for Matt to be with other youngsters had been one that Dan could not deny, so he grudgingly gave his consent and cheered from the rails as Matt pulled down his high-domed hat determinedly and followed the calf from the chute with lariat whistling. Matt lassoed the calf, dismounted quickly, and chased the bawling animal around the corral as Juniper, untrained in the art, trotted behind, instead of backing away and keeping the rope taut.

Dan had laughed as hard as anyone else as the flushed and embarrassed boy finally caught up with the calf, flipped it, and tied off three legs. *Let's hear it for a determined young man and his playful pony, folks . . . thirty-eight seconds.*

The laughter of the crowd had still burned in his ears ten minutes later, when the announcer added the ultimate insult: *Let's hear it for pretty little Jewell Soderholm, folks . . . sixteen seconds.*

After two days of obligatory teasing Dan had agreed to prac-tice team roping and bulldogging. When Matt's skills as a hazer finally matched Dan's abilities as a dogger, the two took a blue ribbon and the $25 first prize, and Matt felt no compunction to continue.

Matt lowered the body to the ground to wipe away the snow that was beginning to accumulate on his father's cold face. *Put this on. You're going to need it.* He looked down at Dan's torn denim jacket and succumbed to an inexplicable urge to tidy it up. He pulled down the sleeves to cover the shirt cuffs, and he stuffed the torn breast flap into the pocket when he discovered that the button was missing.

They had few material things to show for their life together. Their worldly possessions consisted of the battered pickup, the contents of their tiny two-room cabin, and Matt's Appaloosa. At fifteen years of age Matt could not remember a time when they were not living on someone else's ranch or breaking other people's horses. Their life had been simple, but it had been enriched by love, companionship, laughter, and tears. His father had been the core of that world, and now everything that mattered was gone.

Matt covered the mile and a half to the Johnson house without remembering a single step of the arduous journey. He kicked at the heavy front door, and Frank Johnson was suddenly silhouetted against the lights from within. "What the hell happened, boy?" he asked, flipping his cigar into the night and reaching for the body in a single movement.

Matt recoiled from the rancher's grasp. "My father's dead. Where should I put him?"

"Well, *goddamn*, boy, what the hell happened?" Fat Frank demanded angrily.

Matt's body began to tremble violently, and Johnson reached out to snatch the corpse from the boy's arms as he collapsed to the floor, gasping for breath, sobbing deeply from exhaustion and grief.

When Martha Johnson recovered her composure, she tried to comfort the boy, finally urging him to his feet and guiding him to the back bedroom, past the sofa where his father had been placed and covered with a white sheet.

"Now you just lay down there and rest. Frank and I will take care of everything," she said, as if she could bring his dad back to life or give Matt a pill that would burn out the throbbing pain in his head. He staggered toward the bed but fell to his knees before he got there.

"That's right, son, you just pray," Martha intoned. "God will help you through this. Prayer always helps." She pulled the door shut without realizing that Matt had passed out on the floor.

*   *   *

Find a Safe Place

Matt came to in the darkness and lay motionless on the cold floor, hoping desperately that he had just awakened from a bad dream, but the muffled bickering in the front room brought him back to reality, and a new panic seized him as he realized that they were arguing about his dad. They might have taken him away already. Perhaps he would never see his father again. Forcing his aching muscles to respond, Matt lifted himself from the cold floor and cautiously made his way through the darkness, groping for the door. The light from the living room cast long shadows in the hall, but he could see well enough to make his way silently toward the front room.

Matt stopped short to identify the newcomer, who was insisting in a gravelly voice, "Well, dammit, Frank, you *are* stuck. He was killed on *your* place, breakin' *your* horses."

"Don't give me that crap, Lew," Johnson said angrily. "The county buries people all the time."

Matt placed the voice: Lew Walters, the sheriff.

"Dan McFadden was a friend of yours," the sheriff said with disgust. "How can you ask the county to bury your friend in the goddamn paupers' field?"

"Because he's layin' right there without a nickel to his name, that's why," Johnson responded heatedly. "Dan had friends all over this basin, but that didn't stop him from being a saddle bum. Let some of his other *good friends* dig up the cash for a fancy funeral."

Martha Johnson asked cautiously, "What about the boy, Sheriff?"

"And that's another thing," Frank blurted indignantly. "That kid ain't my problem, and you ain't gonna stick me with problems that ain't mine. You get them both out of here tonight."

"Please, Frank, he's only a boy. He could—"

"You stay out of this, Martha," Frank demanded. "Let the sheriff do his job. They got places for kids like that."

Lew Walters sighed and resigned himself to a distasteful task. "There's a home up in Harrison County," he said softly to no one in particular. "It takes time, but I'll put Matt up in the jail till they can take him. I'll call welfare first thing in the morning."

Matt could not move. They had no idea that he had heard

them, and if he could keep himself from screaming, he meant to keep it that way. He peeked through the crack in the door and saw the sheriff zipping up his puffy down jacket.

"I'll be back with the ambulance in an hour," he said. "I'll take them both off your hands at the same time."

"One more thing before you go, Sheriff," Frank Johnson said. "I'm putting you on notice right now that I intend to take possession of Dan's cabin first thing in the morning."

"What the hell for?" Walters asked.

"I bought the McFadden place, sixteen . . . eighteen years ago—"

"Nineteen," Martha corrected timidly.

"Nineteen years ago . . . but old Oren McFadden kept a life interest in the shack for himself and Dan. Now they're both dead, and the place is mine. I'm gonna disinfect the son of a bitch and rent it to a *regular* family."

Lew Walters struggled to restrain his anger and contempt as he stared hard at Frank Johnson. Finally, he shrugged and turned toward the door. "That's not up to me. I'll be back in an hour."

Matt turned slowly and returned to the bedroom in a daze. All this time he had been concerned about his father and what they would do with him, but that wasn't really his father out there on the couch. It was just a body, and kind of scary at that. For the first time he confronted the real problem and reconstructed the conversation:

They got places for kids like that . . . There's a home up in Harrison County . . . I'll put him up in the jail till they can take him.

Matt thought about the children from the Harrison County Orphanage and remembered seeing them when he and his dad had been up there breaking horses two years earlier. There seemed to be no life in the drugged children. Their faces were blank, and they huddled together like sheep in a snowstorm.

What's wrong with them, Dad? Are they retarded or something?

Dan's voice was sad. *Nothing a good home and a little honest living couldn't cure. Children are like little animals . . . they will shrivel up and die without love.*

Matt vowed that he would never become a part of that home. He quietly returned to the empty living room, made certain no one was about, and hurried to the table where the contents of Dan's pockets had been emptied. He reached for the billfold, searching for the $180 that Harry Olson had paid Dan the day before. The money was gone. Matt tore the wallet apart, looking for a secret compartment, but it soon became clear that Frank Johnson had been there before him.

Matt struggled with the urge to find the potbellied rancher and kick him into submission, but he bolted for the door instead. There was no moon to break the darkness, but Matt had no trouble finding his way. He left a clear trail in the fresh snow, and the cold air made it difficult to breathe, but Matt was oblivious of pain as he covered the three miles to the cabin.

The Appaloosa had returned on her own and was standing at the corral gate. Juniper could travel days without food or rest, and she could outperform any jeep and most goats in the mountains. She usually played coquettish games with Matt whenever he tried to catch her, but tonight she came up to him without a chase. Matt picked up her dragging reins and vaulted effortlessly onto her bare back. Then he urged her gently toward the dark cabin. He saddled and fed her before entering the cabin, determined to be prepared for a long chase after he had accomplished the task of protecting his dad's belongings from the desecration of Frank Johnson.

Matt emptied the winter larder of beef jerky and smoked fish, rolled a change of clothes into his sleeping bag, and strapped it all to the saddle. He took his father's rifle from the peg, found a box of cartridges, and stopped to gaze around the room for the final time. His eyes filled with tears. Dan's beloved books, the old photographs of Oren, Oren and Dan, and Dan and Matt pasted beneath the hand-drawn McFadden family tree, the arrowheads and semiprecious stones—all the artifacts of their entire life together. Matt walked to his father's room and saw Dan's church suit stretched over a hanger, partially concealed by the long underwear hanging from the same peg. Then he dug into the bottom drawer of Dan's dresser and found his grandfather's pocket watch, which was to have been passed down to him in due course. The metal attached to the tarnished chain bore the inscription "To

Daniel McFadden . . . A man I am proud to have as my son . . . Love, Pa."

Matt snapped open the metal cover and once again saw the tiny picture of his beautiful mother. He threw the watch on the bed in anger; then he emptied the contents of the Coleman lantern all over the floor, sobbing uncontrollably.

He struck a wooden match and stood in the doorway as the flames erupted, illuminating his face bathed in tears. Suddenly he burst back into his father's bedroom and snatched the gold pocket watch from the burning bed. He stuffed it into his jeans as he ran from the smoke-filled room.

Matt led the spooked Appaloosa from the burning building before mounting her. He sat watching the fire consume the cabin until he saw the lights of Sheriff Walters' jeep winding its way down the road. Then he spurred Juniper into a gallop and melted into the snowy night.

It took ten minutes to reach the top of the ridge and another five to locate the trail leading to the south pass. He would be safe as long as he stayed off the main roads. Frank Johnson was too fat and lazy to follow, and Matt had never seen Lew Walters on a horse.

After two hours of slowly picking his way through the dark timber, he came to the only place within a hundred miles where the trail would cross a highway. He reined Juniper to a halt and strained for the sounds of approaching vehicles in the snowstorm.

It suddenly occurred to the boy that he had no idea where he was going. The purpose and direction of the last four hours had been to escape his shattered world and those who would destroy him. Whenever he stopped moving, he realized anew that there was no one left to care about him, to solve problems with, to talk to, or to laugh with. An empty loneliness seemed to grip and tear at every part of him. *To hell with a plan. The main thing is to keep moving.*

He nudged Juniper with his knees, and they came out of the timber onto the road. Suddenly he was blinded by a pair of head-lights beamed at him from a parked car.

"Get off the horse, boy . . . and keep your hands away from that rifle." Sheriff Walters stepped out of the darkness and advanced on Matt with a pair of handcuffs gleaming in the glare of the lights.

Chapter Four

Lew Walters led Matt to a cell and locked the door before removing the handcuffs through the bars. "You've gotten too big to take chances," he mumbled without being asked. Then he walked to his desk on the far side of the room and said in a louder voice, "Just as well take off your coat, boy. The way I see it, you won't be going anywhere for a long time." Finally, the sheriff sat down and began to scribble his report on a yellow legal pad.

Deputy Sanner arrived at midnight and received his instructions. "Type this up, Charlie," Walters said, handing him one of the yellow sheets. "Then get him to sign it."

"No problem, Lew." Charlie read the report and glanced at the silent boy slumped over on the cot. "Sounds like quite a night," he said, rolling a fresh sheet of paper into the old typewriter as the sheriff headed for the bunk in the back room.

Charlie pecked away laboriously for more than an hour, frequently cursing his mistakes, tearing the paper from the typewriter, and starting all over again. When he finally completed the job, he approached Matt's cell with a satisfied expression. "Sign this," he ordered. "Read it first; then sign it."

"What is it?" Matt asked tonelessly, taking the sheet of paper through the bars.

"Your confession, hotshot. Just sign it so we can all get some sleep."

May 30, 1963
I, Matthew Loren McFadden, did on this day steal and

abscond with Frank Johnson's Appaloosa mare—value $2,800. On this same day I did deliberately burn down a home owned by Frank Johnson—value $4,000.

Matthew Loren McFadden

Matt's face flushed, and he shouted, "*No! That's stupid!*" Then he wadded the paper and flung it against the wall with a wild shriek.

"Don't do that!" Charlie shouted, unlocking the door and rushing in to restrain the boy, who had fallen to his knees and was furiously pounding his fists on the concrete floor. The deputy threw his arms around Matt and rolled over on top of him in the hope of calming his hysteria.

Instead, Matt pounded on the deputy's shoulders with his bleeding and mutilated fists, screaming, "That was *my* horse!" In his frenzy the boy summoned the strength to catapult the deputy off him and against the back wall of the cell. Then Matt jumped on him and wrestled him down again, pounding the deputy's head into the floor and shouting, "Juniper is *mine!* I'll kill her first! I'll *kill* her!"

Matt's head snapped sideways, his eyes watered, and he wasn't even sure where he had been hit. He had seen only a flash of something long, and black, and round, and suddenly the rage flickered out and was replaced by blessed sleep.

"You all right, son?"

Matt recognized the coarse voice and had a general idea of where he was, but if he was right about the voice, why did it sound so kind? He opened his eyes and squinted up at the craggy face. There was a dripping towel in Lew Walters' hand.

"Don't move too fast. Your head will hurt."

"It already does."

"Not so bad as it would if you tried to move around. Doc will be here soon."

"What happened?"

Charlie Sanner walked over, his head wrapped in a cold towel. "You mean before or after you tried to force my head through twelve inches of concrete real estate?" he asked, forcing a laugh.

"After."

"The sheriff had to sap you. You were out of your head." Then Charlie laughed and had to press the wet towel against the resulting pain in his head. "I've had complaints about my typing before, but you were ridiculous."

Matt was suddenly aware of a numbness in his hands and the pains that stretched all the way to his shoulders.

"You might've broken something in your hands," Walters offered. "You were punching out the floor."

Matt nodded once.

"Just take it easy. Doc will be here soon," Walters repeated soothingly. "He was out lambing for the Criswells, but he'll be here soon."

The remainder of Matt's first night in jail was filled with a bombardment of strange new sensory stimuli. The sheriff returned to his cot in the back room as soon as Dr. Tatum treated and wrapped Matt's bruised and bleeding fists and assured the sheriff that the blow to Matt's head was no more serious than the boy had experienced countless times in the years he had been working wild horses with his father.

Nonetheless, Charlie Sanner's nerves remained on edge. He was a tall, thin young man in his late twenties. His dark hair was closely cropped over the collar and ears, but a long wisp of straight black hair drooped perpetually over his forehead, giving him a boyish appearance. His sallow complexion and the deep concern in his eyes that night, however, made him look older than he was.

Matt sat quietly on his bunk, his back against the bars separating him from the next cell, his knees drawn up to his chest, his arms crossed over his knees, and his head resting on his forearms. He tried to think. He tried not to think. *Quiet as a tomb.* For the first time he fully understood the meaning of the phrase. No one spoke, but the squeak of Charlie's swivel chair reverberated around the steel and concrete room like the screak of untuned violins, and his footsteps echoed like the slow ticking of a giant clock in the void of outer space every time he walked across the room to check on Matt.

Sometime after midnight Crazy Jake Conger was escorted to the second cell, which also served as the town's drunk tank. He was a regular patron of the jail, and he seemed pleased to be there again. He staggered about happily, singing bawdy songs punctuated with lusty belches and joking with Charlie, his "innkeeper." At first Matt welcomed the diversion, even permitting himself a tentative smile, but soon the raucous tunes turned into drunken mutterings and finally into guttural snoring that expelled the noxious fumes of alcohol and stale cigarettes with every breath.

Crazy Jake occasionally pushed himself from the cot with a loud groan and rushed to the toilet at the back of the cell. There he threw his head into the porcelain bowl and heaved up his insides with a painful roar.

Crazy Jake was now a clearly offensive diversion for Matt, and he wished again for the solitude that had prevailed earlier in the evening.

Frank Johnson appeared the following morning to sign the formal complaints for arson and horse theft. In response to Lew Walters's irate cross-examination, Johnson demanded, "Whose side are you on anyway, Lew? . . . I told you, I let the kid have the horse two years ago, but it wasn't paid up yet. They still had twelve more head to break before it belonged to them. He stole *my* horse! I'd be willing to pay for the work they did, but the horse is *mine*." The rancher then lowered his voice and said confidentially, "I heard what happened here last night, Lew. I figured all along the kid might jump his track."

Lew Walters pushed himself up and glared ominously at the bloated man. "If you don't get out of my sight, I'm going to turn him loose on you, Frank."

Matt spent the first day of his confinement trying to organize his thoughts and emotions, but the lack of sleep and loss of appetite disorganized his thought processes even further. Matt felt anger toward his father for dying and leaving him alone, and he hated

Frank Johnson for somehow making it all happen. When there was nowhere else to go with those feelings, Matt began to direct his hatred and aggression inward, toward himself.

He decried the cockiness in him that had compelled him to push his father into breaking that final horse after Dan had suggested they quit for the day. *How about one more?. . . I feel real good.* Then he lamented his insolence for the insulting challenge: *How about it, old man? You getting goosey in your old age? Can't you keep up with me anymore?* In fact, he had not been nearly that reproachful toward his father, but that's how it must have sounded to Dan, and it suited Matt's purposes to remember it that way.

The boy's irrational introjection at first created a restlessness that caused him to pace his cell in extreme agitation. Any attempts by the anonymous daytime deputies to calm him elicited angry outbursts that persuaded them to leave him alone, which, in turn, resulted in a further deterioration into moodiness and despair.

Matt slept fitfully that second night, awaking with a start whenever the images of Dan's vacant eyes or cold skin appeared. He continued to refuse to eat, and much of the second day he spent slipping in and out of consciousness, tortured by the loud crack of his father's broken neck and tormented by the enormousness of his loss and the emptiness of his life.

Whenever he managed to force himself into moments of lucidity, he would awake and stare about his cell, astonished to find himself behind bars, wondering for an instant why and how he had got there.

Martha Johnson came to see him late in the afternoon of the second day. She stood trembling outside his cell and spoke to him through the bars while he lay on his cot and gave no indication that he could hear her. But her voice brought him back to a full awareness of reality.

"I'm so sorry about all of this, Matthew," she said, weeping. "No one wanted it to turn out this way. It all happened so suddenly." She pressed her hands against her lips and waited for a response.

Matt sat up and glared at her, and she sobbed, "Don't look at me that way. I've always liked you . . . right from the first day . . . you were just a baby. I took you your first meal . . . and a birthday cake every year . . . don't you remember?''

"My father never let me forget," Matt growled. "He told me if anything ever happened, I should go to you for help. He said you were our friends."

"He was right," Martha said quickly, encouraged to have Matt talking. "Don't you remember? Frank gave you the tent . . . the sleeping bags . . . everything you needed. Don't you remember?''

Matt walked toward her and stood close to the bars. "Then why am I in jail, Mrs. Johnson?"

Martha reached through the bars and gently caressed the exposed fingers protruding from Matt's bandaged fist. Then she pressed her forehead against the steel and began to cry. "You're a man now," she finally whispered, struggling to compose herself. "Perhaps you can understand. Frank has changed. When you and your father came back that first time, I was . . . expecting. But right after that I lost the baby . . . and Frank changed. . . .'' Then she stood erect and stared straight into his eyes. "He's all I have, Matthew . . . I'm sorry."

As the evening passed, Matt's thinking became increasingly disorganized. It had been simple to hate himself, and it had been perfectly natural to externalize his grief by substituting Frank Johnson as the object of his venomous feelings, but Martha had somehow managed to dilute the intensity of those perceptions. Strangely there was no longer any comfort in hating Fat Frank so much when even his own wife knew what an insidious bastard he was.

Matt was completely incapable of evaluating his external world objectively, and he could not differentiate between reality and his internal self-recriminations. His uneasiness, perplexity, apprehension, and anger were symptomatic of the depression and melancholia that finally spawned a solution.

Matt quietly tore his sheet into strips and fashioned a crude rope. He stood on his bunk and tied one end to the water pipe and the other around his neck. Then he stepped off the bunk, and a searing pain coursed through his head and neck. Before losing consciousness, he heard someone screaming, but he knew it was not coming from him.

Chapter Five

The first sensation Matt experienced as his mind floated toward consciousness was one of empty despair. Then his brain echoed with disconnected thoughts: *No one will listen to me. . . . Juniper is mine. . . . My father is dead. . . . I'm alone. . . . You're getting goosey. . . . He's dead.* Then he felt the pressure on his nostrils, and he realized that his mouth was being held open and someone was blowing air into his lungs. His eyelids fluttered, and he tried to turn his head, but a sharp pain shot through his neck and shoulders, eliciting a piercing groan.

"He's coming to. You can stop now."

Matt opened his eyes and saw Sheriff Walters gently urging Charlie Sanner up off the floor. Charlie's face was contorted with anger and flushed by the struggle to breathe life back into the boy's body. "You goddamn crazy bastard!" he hissed, trying to catch his own breath.

"Lighten up, Charlie," Walters ordered, dropping to his knees next to Matt. "Don't try to talk," he said gently to the boy. "Your voice won't work for a while. You're gonna have a hell of a rope burn, but I don't think you busted anything bad."

Charlie continued to rage in anger and frustration, but there were tears in his eyes as he shrieked, "If that stupid rope of yours hadn't broken, you'd be *dead*! You hear me? *Dead!*"

Lew Walters ignored his deputy and said, "Let's see if you can sit up, Matt." He slid his arms under the boy's shoulders and said, "I'll help you a little, but let me know if there's any pain."

Matt's face twisted in pain as he struggled off the floor, and Charlie scampered out of the cell. "I'll get the doc," he said.

"Hold it!" Walters ordered, stopping Charlie in his tracks. "Let's see if we can keep the doc out of this for right now."

Charlie looked questioningly at the sheriff and said, "The kid needs help."

"Maybe," Walters responded. "Let's just wait a few minutes." The two men raised Matt into a sitting position as the boy rubbed his throat to alleviate the pain and ease his breathing.

Charlie listened to the labored wheezing and pleaded, "He sounds awful, Lew. Let me get the doc."

Walters sat on the bunk next to Matt and kept his arm around the boy's shoulders for support. "Relax, Charlie. Give it a few more minutes." As soon as he was satisfied that Matt was out of danger, he pulled up a stool and sat in front of him, looking directly into his eyes. "I'll leave it up to you, boy. There's nothing else Doc can do for you except give you a couple of aspirins and call in the shrink from Sheridan. He'll fly in, wrinkle his nose, and send you to the state hospital. The kids' wards are always filled up, but you're big enough to go to the adult ward, with the permanent-type crazies. In six months you'll be a basket case for sure, and the chief shrink will say, 'See, I knew he was nuts all along.' Is that what you want?"

Matt was unable to speak, but the urgent tightening of his grip on the sheriff's wrist was answer enough.

None of them slept that night, nor did they speak. When Charlie's tour ended at eight o'clock in the morning, he walked to Matt's cell and said, "I'm gonna get cleaned up, but I'll be back. We gotta talk."

Matt stared vacantly at the deputy but gave no indication that he had heard. He just wanted to be left alone to try to sort out his reasons for doing such a dumb thing.

Charlie returned after lunch, but he was no longer morose and haggard. Instead, he seemed buoyant and enthusiastic, although he averted his eyes from the ring of angry blisters bubbling up along the rope burn around Matt's neck. His arms were filled with books. "You know where I've been?" he said lightly as he balanced his load in one arm and unlocked the cell door. "I've been talking to your teachers, and they don't think you're nearly as stupid as I do."

He entered the cell and deposited the books on Matt's bunk, pointedly leaving the cell door ajar. "Matter of fact," he continued, "they think you're kinda bright. Don't know's I'd go that far"— he chuckled,—"but I'll give them the benefit of the doubt." Charlie then walked to his desk and rolled his swivel chair into the cell, again leaving the barred door open. "In any event, you've been pitying yourself too long," he said, sitting down with a grunt, "and you sure as hell don't get that from all the McFaddens *I've* been hearing about all my life."

Matt looked up sharply but did not comment. "That's right," Charlie continued expansively, "I know a lot about the Mc-Faddens. Your daddy was a few years older than me, but we used to laugh about it a lot. My great-grandfather was running five thousand head when old Jeremiah McFadden staked out his piddling six hundred acres. You could ride for a month, in those days, and never get off land belonging to the Sanners, or old Dutch Keefer, or Dice Warren. Then the government started giving land away to drifters, gamblers, cowboys, sodbusters, and anyone else who wanted it, and there was nothing but trouble. Every spring there was a race to grab off unbranded calves to stock the little ranches, so the big boys hired themselves a fellow by the name of Tom Horn and some so-called range detectives to shoot up the little guys."

Then Charlie leaned back and waited, fully aware that Matt was intimately familiar with the history of the Johnson County War and the part his ancestors had played in it. "And it would have worked," he continued, "except for the fact that people like your great-grandfather, old man Jeremiah, were too tough to give up. You never would have caught that old buzzard tying a sheet around his neck when things got tough. You can bet your ass on that.

"And your grandfather," Charlie continued, "he was younger than you when his old man died and left him to take care of his mamma and two sisters. Did he give up?" Charlie persisted in spite of the fact that Matt seemed not to be listening. "Hell, no, he didn't. The Indians taught him to dry-farm and catch horses. . . . What was his name? . . . Orville McFadden!"

Still unable to speak, Matt instinctively shook his head and silently mouthed "Oren," and Charlie grinned. "That's right . . . *Oren* McFadden. How could I forget?"

Matt looked up, realizing he had been tricked, and suppressed a grin.

The smile faded from Charlie Sanner's face as he reached forward to clutch Matt's wrists. "It's not going to be easy, Matt," he said earnestly. "You've got a long way to go, but you can make it. Just never forget who you are. You have *roots* here . . . real breeding. . . . Your people fought hard for everything, and they never gave up. . . . Don't forget that. When it gets tough for you, just remember who you are."

Matt looked up at the deputy and wanted to tell him that last night was a stupid mistake that he would not repeat. He wanted to say it, but the hoarseness and soreness in his throat were too great, so he just nodded.

"That's good," Charlie said. Then he stood and began to pace thoughtfully, searching for the right words. "Now we have some sad business. Today's the funeral . . . this afternoon. Do you feel up to it?"

Matt was caught by surprise. He had almost put his father's death out of his mind and felt guilty about it. It took him a moment to reconstruct the events of the past three days. Then he nodded again.

Charlie clapped him on the shoulder and said, "Good boy. I'll come get you when it's time." The deputy started to lock the door behind him, but hesitated. "One more thing. Are you ready to start eating again?"

Matt looked up, and his brow furrowed in surprise. Of course he was.

"How about a milk shake?"

Matt opened his eyes wider to convey his interest.

"Strawberry? Mr. Colter's making them with fresh straw-berries."

Matt flared his nostrils and wrinkled his nose.

"Chocolate? . . . Good! I'll be back in ten minutes." Charlie was tempted to reinforce Matt's progress by leaving the cell door unlocked, but he decided in a flash that it might be too soon to trust the boy, so he quickly turned the key and left.

Matt found it difficult to swallow the thick, creamy milk shake, but it tasted so good that the pain seemed secondary. He was working on his second when Charlie unlocked the door and announced, "Time to hit it. We got a long ride."

Charlie led Matt across the room but stopped him at the front door. "One more thing," he said, reluctantly brandishing his handcuffs. "I got no choice, kid."

The boy pulled back reflexively as the handcuffs were snapped to his wrists, right above the mittenlike bandages covering his fists. He stared down at the chained steel bracelets incredulously as Charlie led him to the waiting patrol car.

Charlie maintained a steady stream of lighthearted patter to counteract Matt's confusion and agitation. Matt finally looked up when they approached the cemetery, but Charlie drove past it and out of town, heading north toward the mountains.

"Some of the boys chipped in for a stone, and they talked Frank Johnson into letting us bury Dan in the old family plot on the ranch," Charlie volunteered. "Nice fella, old Frank."

Charlie's sarcasm did not escape the boy, but he was relieved that his father was being taken care of properly. He had given the matter no thought, but he was relieved anyway. He had forgotten all about the old graveyard, but it seemed right that Dan's body would be put there with old Jeremiah, Grandpa Oren, and the other McFaddens.

Now that all the arrangements had been made, Matt was sorry he had agreed to attend the funeral. He thought back to the almost forgotten time, six years earlier, when his dog had to be put to sleep after it had been wounded by a careless hunter. *No use crying about Gruesome, son. He's gone. The real Gruesome's somewhere else.* Now Dan was somewhere else, too, and it was not the cemetery.

"Looks like old Frank went all out," Charlie said. They were driving past the Johnson ranch house, and there were long tables with food and drink in the front yard.

Matt remembered Rowdy Macfee's funeral and how all the

neighboring mountain ranchers had come together for a big feast afterward. He was surprised anyone would have gone to the trouble for his father and even wondered how they had found out about his death. As the patrol car passed the house, several women interrupted their preparations to stare at them.

"Looks like a few folks will be there," Charlie said.

Just past the Johnson house, Charlie took the left fork leading to the tiny cemetery, and Matt was grateful that he would not have to view the charred remains of their old cabin. As they approached the top of the ridge, Matt found himself waiting for the mountain peaks to loom up, just as his father had always done. He had always chided Dan for observing the ritual, but when the mountains finally appeared, he stared in wonder, as though seeing them for the first time, suddenly fearing that he might never see them again.

The graveyard sat on a knoll, surrounded by a picket fence. The entire valley beneath the knoll was crowded with pickup trucks and cars—mostly pickup trucks—and there was a school bus. The people walking along the dirt road leading to the cemetery parted for the patrol car, and as he and Charlie passed slowly through the crowd, Matt saw the sad faces of his dad's old friends from throughout the basin and mountain ranches. Matt recognized many of them: Harry Olson and Ike Jorgenson were there; Cash Warren was wiping his eyes beneath his glasses; old Colonel Keefer had already buried too many of his friends to cry, but his mournful expression reflected his sorrow. Frank Johnson had called his father a saddle bum, but the grief in the eyes of those lining the path all the way to the open grave eloquently disputed that assessment.

Matt's attention then focused on a group of twenty young people who stood silently watching the approaching patrol car with mixed expressions of bewilderment and curiosity. Matt had never known his classmates very well, so their presence surprised and unnerved him.

They were accompanied by Miss Mason, a tall, thin woman in her mid-forties, who had been Matt's social studies teacher for the past three years and the one person he had come to know well in the entire school. Miss Mason had a reputation for being exacting, formal, and stern, disapproving of the indulgences enjoyed by most young people. She respected Matt for his intelligence and dedication to hard work, and a warm relationship had developed between them over the years. It suddenly occurred to Matt, however, that he had never seen the prim woman outside the classroom, and she seemed out of place standing on the hillside, unmindful of the strands of brown hair protruding from the bun at the back of her head. At the sight of Miss Mason, Matt strained at the handcuffs and spontaneously brought both hands to his neck to button his shirt over the blistered rope burns.

Charlie observed Matt's reaction silently as he parked the car near the fence and walked around to open Matt's door. The boy seemed to stare right through the deputy's body, his eyes filled with confusion and shame. Charlie turned toward the staring faces of the crowd. Then he looked down at Matt's clenched fists straining against the handcuffs, cutting off the circulation to his hands. He said softly, "It doesn't make any difference what *they* think, Matt." After a moment of silence Charlie shrugged his shoulders and unlocked the handcuffs.

Matt felt the weight fall from his wrists and clutched Charlie's fingers in mute gratitude. The deputy helped the boy from the car, and in that moment of caring the will to live flooded back into Matt's being as quickly as it had left.

Chapter Six

The day after the funeral Charlie's shift rotated to days, and he arrived at the jail that morning, bubbling over with cheer and fresh resolutions. "Off your ass and on your feet," he bellowed as he unlocked the cell door. "Let's get with the program."

In the adjoining cell Crazy Jake jumped up and asked, "What program, Charlie?"

"Not you, Jake. Your regular job is waltzing with the mop. I'm talking to Matt."

"Yeah, but the kid can't talk yet, so I'm asking' for him. What program?"

Charlie entered the cell and plopped a bundle on Matt's chest as he lay on his cot staring up at the ceiling. "Calisthenics, my friend. This kind of living will make you flabby and give you too much time for thinking." Matt swung his feet to the floor and sat up, staring at the bundle that had rolled into his lap. "Gym clothes," Charlie explained. "It was Miss Mason's idea. I'll take care of the body, and she'll take care of the brain. You climb into those sweats, and I'll be right back."

Charlie returned to his desk, leaving the cell door open while he shuffled through a stack of papers on his desk. Matt seemed uncertain about what to do, but he realized that his legs and arms had begun to cramp in the confines of his tiny cell, almost matching the stiffness in his neck. He untied the string, peeled away the brown paper wrapping, and unwound a sweat suit that had been rolled around his canvas sneakers.

When Charlie returned, Matt was standing in the sweat suit

which bore his school colors and the emblem of a snarling bobcat. "Hit the deck, tiger. Sit-ups, push-ups, and deep knee bends—three reps of twenty. Then some jogging in place—eight minutes to start with—if you can handle that much."

Matt sneered at the thinly veiled challenge. He could breeze through such a program without breaking a sweat. He dropped to the floor and began snapping off push-ups effortlessly while Charlie counted, "One, two, three—all the way down, that one don't count—four, five, six . . ."

Matt was straining by the time he reached fifteen, and he was genuinely confused by his sudden and unexpected inability to perform the routine exercise. "Not so easy, is it, hotshot?" Charlie gloated as Matt set his lips in grim determination.

When Matt completed the prescribed number of push-ups, Charlie ordered him to roll over and start the sit-ups. By then Matt was beginning to perspire, and before getting halfway through the exercise, he wanted desperately to rest. Instead, Charlie stooped over to hold the boy's ankles to the floor. "This'll make it easier, candy-ass. Let's go! Eleven, twelve . . ."

The knee bends would be more tolerable, but by the time he got to them Matt was sweating profusely and gasping for breath. When it came to jogging in place, the cowboy's typical aversion to running asserted itself, and Matt's legs felt like lead stumps. Charlie began jogging alongside him, taunting and cajoling incessantly. "Get 'em up! Lift! Lift! C'mon, you pansy, you can do it. Watch me. I'm twice your age. Get 'em up! Get 'em up!" he puffed.

Suddenly it was over. "Time!" Charlie snapped, looking at his watch, trying to conceal his own panting. Matt put his hands on his hips and bent forward at the waist, sucking for air, waiting for the feeling to return to his trembling legs. Charlie controlled his own breathing and laughed derisively as he pushed on the boy's head, shoving him unceremoniously back onto the cot.

"If you ask me, we buried the wrong man," Charlie said with deliberate callousness, searching Matt's face for a reaction. When he was satisfied that the boy had finally accepted the reality of his father's death, Charlie wove unsteadily from the cell. "Just rattle your cage when you're ready for the second rep."

The deputy walked slowly around the inside perimeter of the room, trying to disguise his discomfort until the strength returned to his wobbly legs. He pretended to inspect the windows, the cracks in the walls, and the bulletin board laden with posters, clippings, and directives that had gone unnoticed for months. He finally reached his chair, flopped down with a suppressed groan, and lit a cigarette. He dragged deeply and leaned back, straining to lift his feet to the top of the desk. His brief reverie was interrupted by the cadence of soft grunts emanating from across the room. Charlie cocked his head to identify the sounds without looking. Then his face creased with a self-satisfied grin, recognizing that Matt had already resumed his calisthenics.

Miss Mason came by that afternoon to remind Matt about his schooling. She entered the cell apprehensively, trying to conceal her revulsion as she took in the open toilet, the tiny sink, and the rumpled cot. Crazy Jake reached through the bars to stroke her, and she leaped aside with an uncharacteristic shriek. Matt grinned and reached out to steady her, still unable to speak. He gently urged her to sit on his bunk, then backed away, reaching for his stool. There was a strange disorientation in her eyes as she mentally questioned the wisdom of coming to this place. Then she saw the blistered rope burn around Matt's neck, and her timidity vanished. "Matthew! What are you doing in this place? This is the height of absurdity!"

He shrugged his shoulders, mutely assuring her that it wasn't so bad, but she would not be mollified. She called imperiously for the sheriff and said angrily, "Mr. Walters, this young man has been my very best student for three years, and I can assure you he is no criminal. How *dare* you treat him this way!"

"Yes, ma'am," Lew Walters said softly, "but I'm afraid it's not up to me. Judge Turner—"

"Both of Judge Turner's children are students of mine," she interrupted. "I'll talk to *him* myself!" Miss Mason was again clearly in control. She turned to Matt and said sternly, "As for you, mister, I have written out your assignments, and I shall expect you to do your work!" She leaned over and stuffed the assignment sheet into one of Matt's unopened textbooks and strode from the cell, intimidating Crazy Jake with a shriveling glare. "I'll be back tomorrow," she announced to no one in particular, and slammed the front door behind her.

Matt grinned and shook his head. *Good old Miss Mason.*

At first Lew Walters strenuously objected to the favored treatment Matt was receiving. He reprimanded Charlie for taking the handcuffs off at the cemetery, and he scolded his deputy for always leaving Matt's cell door unlocked. "That's just sloppy police work," the sheriff insisted. "That kid is charged with arson, grand theft, and flight to avoid prosecution. It's not up to us to decide one way or the other. If he escapes, it'll be our ass!"

After a few days, however, the reprimands grew less intense, and the sheriff softened each blustering outburst by sending Charlie for a sackful of Matt's favorite hamburgers. On the ninth day of Matt's incarceration Lew Walters arrived for the afternoon shift in the middle of an unseasonably hot day and found Matt exercising strenuously outside his cell. He sidestepped the compacted bulk of the tall boy performing his deep knee bends, but when Matt launched vigorously into his running exercise, the office was filled with the loud sounds of grunting, puffing, and the slapping of rubber soles against the concrete floor. "Hold it! Hold it!" Sheriff Walters bellowed. "I can't hear myself think! Charlie, goddammit, that kid's got this place smelling like an old jockstrap." The sheriff pointed his finger at Matt and affected a menacing snarl. "As for you, don't forget you're a *prisoner.*"

Matt had learned how to deal with these periodic outbursts, so he lowered his head and started back to his cell. As he passed Charlie, however, he said in a raspy voice, "Hold the onions and pickles."

"I heard that, you smart-assed brat," the sheriff shouted, barely able to contain his own laughter. "I liked you a hell of a lot better when you couldn't talk. Maybe we ought to add a new exercise and have you try to hang yourself once a week."

There were no hamburgers that day, but Lew Walters felt good enough about Matt's rehabilitation that he ordered him to do his future jogging outdoors, on the pretext that it would keep from fogging up all the windows inside the tiny jailhouse. Charlie smiled delightedly, accepting the sheriff's mandate as a concession that his liberal treatment of the prisoner had been correct all along.

"I'm glad that makes you so happy," the sheriff said to his grinning deputy, "because you're gonna jog right alongside him."

The smile vanished from Charlie's face. "You're kidding!"

"The hell I am! If this kid decides to run right on out of the county, one of us has to be in good enough shape to catch him again."

In a final gesture of compromise Sheriff Walters agreed that Charlie could follow Matt in the patrol car, but if the car was not available, Charlie was to ride behind on one of the unclaimed bicycles.

By the end of June Matt had been a guest of the county for three weeks. Miss Mason had successfully tutored him through the final examinations in all his courses, and preparations were being made for his trial. Lew Walters and Charlie Sanner had appealed to Judge Turner for a court-appointed attorney, but they were advised that the constitutional privilege of right to counsel was not extended to juvenile offenders.

Miss Mason retained Will Pennington, a lawyer from Jackson, to represent Matt, but after the first interview he reported to her, "The boy admits burning down the cabin, and the cabin belonged to Frank Johnson. The horse also belongs to Johnson, and the boy freely admits that his intention was to take the horse with him. Frankly there is nothing any attorney can do to rebut the substantive charges."

Miss Mason was not satisfied. "Surely there is *something* you can do."

"It is entirely in Judge Turner's hands," Pennington explained sadly. "There are extenuating circumstances, of course. . . . Matt apparently *thought* the horse belonged to him. But there is also damaging testimony from the boy himself. For instance, Matt admits that he burned down the cabin only after he had learned that it belonged to Frank Johnson, and he did not want Mr. Johnson to take possession of the home he and his father had lived in." Pennington paced the room nervously, trying to control his frustration.

"This is absolutely ridiculous!" Miss Mason snapped. "Surely no jury will ever convict this boy of—"

"You don't understand," Pennington interrupted. "There will be no jury."

"Rubbish!" Miss Mason snapped. "*Every* citizen is entitled to a trial by jury."

"Not if he's a juvenile," Pennington said. "When a child under the age of eighteen commits a crime, he is *not* entitled to a lawyer, and he is *not* entitled to a trial by jury."

"I have never heard of such a thing," Miss Mason said incredulously.

"Look at it this way. Under the doctrine of parens patriae, which is binding throughout the United States, the state assumes the role of the child's parents, and it is strictly up to the judge to decide what's best for the child. Some courts have begun to permit lawyers to speak for the juvenile offenders, but many judges still see this as a kind of interference, and they resent it." Will Pennington continued to pace the room to allow time for the information to sink in before continuing. "Believe me, Miss Mason, Judge Turner is intimately aware of all the extenuating circumstances in this case, and my best advice to you is to allow him to make his own judgment without any hint of outside interference."

Chapter Seven

The full impact of the pending trial did not strike Matt until the night before the scheduled hearing. "What's going to happen to me, Charlie?" Matt rasped softly.

"There's nothing to worry about," Charlie said lightly. "Fat Frank's got his horse back, and most folks say that old shack you burned down was too ugly to keep anyway. Matter of fact, I wouldn't be surprised if they gave you a ribbon for beautifying the valley."

"Very funny."

"Eat you hamburger."

"I'm not hungry. I'm kind of scared. That lawyer from Jackson told me I was going to jail."

"That's *not* what he said, and you know it," the deputy scolded. "What he said was that the judge might send you to a training school for boys."

"Reform school," Matt corrected.

"Same thing. Reform school . . . training school—they're the same thing. Point is the judge has to send you someplace to live while you finish high school and maybe learn a trade."

"Why can't I just stay here?"

"Can't be done," Charlie said, trying to sound convincing. "This is no place for a kid to grow up. This is a jail, and a damned small one at that."

"I know, but things have sure gone well here. I could go to school . . . maybe even get a job . . . and live here nights." Matt began to get excited about the prospect as the scenario unfolded in his mind. "I could talk to Sheriff Walters. I don't think he'd care."

Charlie placed his own hamburger on the desk and looked sadly at Matt. "It's not the sheriff, Matt. There are rules about what happens to kids who have no parents. In your case it's even more complicated. You broke the law." Then Charlie reached out for Matt's shoulder and said, "If it's any comfort, I asked the judge if you could come and live with me . . . so did Miss Mason . . . but he said he couldn't let you live with anyone except licensed married foster parents, and there's no such thing in this entire basin."

"I wonder if the reform school is anything like the orphanage," Matt said, recalling the drugged children he and his father had seen several years earlier.

"I tell you, there's nothing to worry about," Charlie assured him confidently. "If the judge decides to send you to a training school, he'll probably send you out of the state." That was new information to Matt, so he looked up sharply. "That's right," Charlie continued, "if you'd have murdered someone, we would have kept you in Wyoming, but your case kind of falls between the cracks. The judge will probably send you to Colorado or Nebraska. Personally I'm hoping he sends you to Clearwater."

"What's Clearwater?"

"Clearwater's about the same as all the rest of them except they've got a real good school there for kids who want to study. I understand that some of them even go on to college from Clearwater. Besides, I've been hearing some real good things about the new head man there. They say he's really interested in the kids." Charlie did not have enough hard information to discuss the matter further, so he ended by saying, "Let's wait and see what the judge decides to do with you. Wherever he sends you, I'll find out all there is to know about the place so you won't be walking into any surprises when you get there."

Charlie Sanner and Will Pennington had tried to describe what the hearing would be like, but nothing they had said quite prepared Matt for what actually happened. Matt had expected a regular trial, but he was led past the large courtroom to the conference room adjoining Judge Turner's office. Charlie guided Matt toward one of the armchairs around the long conference table; then he moved to the back of the room. Matt expected witnesses—especially the Johnsons and perhaps the sheriff—to be present but he and Charlie were there alone.

After fifteen minutes of their waiting in silence the door at the front of the room opened, and Judge Turner appeared with two other men, whom Matt recognized as the assistant prosecutor and the welfare caseworker, both of whom had interviewed Matt during the past two weeks. The three seemed quite convivial, laughing about an eastern dude who had come that weekend to tempt the local trout with every device known to modern science only to abandon his expensive gimmicks in the marshland home of an enraged bull moose.

Their laughter did not set a tone appropriate to the adversary proceeding Matt had expected. Then the judge's first question indicated that the facts in the case had already been decided. "Why did you burn down Frank Johnson's cabin?" Judge Turner asked as soon as he took his seat behind the desk at the end of the long table.

Matt was surprised and wondered if the trial had already begun. He had expected a bailiff to intone something like "Hear ye, hear ye, the Criminal Court of the Fifth Judicial District is now in session. Please rise," but instead, the judge had sat down, opened his file, and asked the first question.

"Matthew?"

The boy started and suddenly realized that the judge had asked another question and was staring at him patiently. Matt started to rise; then he sat down and shifted nervously. "Please relax, Matthew," Judge Turner said gently. "Our purpose here today is to try to find out why you did what you did; then it is up to me to decide what future course of action will be in your best interest. Do you understand?" Matt nodded, but the uncertainty in his face moved the judge to continue. "You say you understand, but obviously something is bothering you. Tell me what you are thinking at this very moment."

Matt glanced around the room nervously, then asked, "Is this the trial? I mean, where's the jury, and witnesses, and stuff like that?"

"I'm sorry, Matthew," Judge Turner said, glancing with displeasure at the welfare caseworker, "I thought this had been explained to you earlier." Then he walked from behind his desk and took the seat next to Matt at the conference table. "Perhaps I had better explain it myself," he said indulgently. "Have you ever been in a courtroom before?"

Matt nodded his head. "Last year . . . Miss Mason took the class to see the first day of Turk Maddock's trial."

"Of course." Judge Turner nodded. "I remember . . . that case involved the theft of hides from the tanning company, right?"

Matt again nodded his head. "And there was a jury, and the room was filled with people."

"Okay," Judge Turner said pleasantly, "that explains your confusion. You see, your case is different." Then a momentary shadow passed over his face. "Don't get me wrong," he said, "the charges against you are just as serious, maybe more so, but you are a juvenile, and we don't try juveniles in the same way as we do adults. In the first place," the judge said, rising to return to his own desk, "we don't have a jury because the law says it is up to the judge to decide what is best for an orphaned child—irrespective of whether a crime has been committed." Judge Turner was again seated in his own chair and flipped open a thick folder before continuing. "In your case, there is no question but that you set fire to Frank Johnson's cabin and rode away on Frank Johnson's Appaloosa, right?"

Matt shook his head vigorously. "No, Juniper was *my* horse. My dad gave her to me for my birthday."

Judge Turner was trying to remain patient. "But your father did not fully reimburse Mr. Johnson for the purchase price, and title to the animal was never transferred."

The assistant district attorney, Jerry Samuelson, interjected ceremoniously, "Your Honor, you may recall that the state has recommended that the charge of grand larceny be dropped in this case because the defendant apparently lacked the intent to steal the horse since he had some reason to believe that the horse was his own."

"Indeed, I *do* recall such a recommendation, Mr. Samuelson," the judge said sarcastically, "especially since that recommendation was made only fifteen minutes ago." Judge Turner's anger continued to rise. "And what is the state's recommendation concerning the charge of arson?" he asked rhetorically. "Does the state condone the burning of homes by angry children, Mr. Samuelson? This isn't Omaha! Not yet at least . . . not if I have any say in it."

The judge's reference to the recent unchecked crime sprees by juvenile gangs in Omaha was not lost on Charlie Sanner, who had sat in considerable discomfort through the alarming transition in Judge Turner's attitude. Without intending to speak out, Charlie did the unpardonable. "Your Honor," he heard himself say as he pushed himself from the chair.

"Well," Judge Turner said, fuming, "another precinct heard from. What now?"

"I'm sorry, Judge. I know I'm speaking out of turn here." Suddenly Charlie was at a loss for words and wondered abstractedly why he was on his feet, making a fool of himself. "I'm sorry, Judge," he repeated, "it's just that you mentioned Omaha, and . . . well . . . it's just not that way with Matt here. He . . .he . . ." Charlie's embarrassment finally prevailed, and he dropped back into his chair, mumbling, "Sorry, Judge."

Judge Turner stared blankly at Charlie Sanner for several minutes while the chagrined deputy waited for the hammer to fall. But when he finally spoke, the judge's voice was calm. "I'm not sure I know what you intended, Charlie, but your intervention was quite timely." He looked at the two men on his left and said, "I apologize for getting carried away, but I cannot leave this matter without adding that it seems to me that the prosecuting attorney and the juvenile welfare caseworker could have made more of an effort to prepare this defendant for these proceedings, especially in view of the fact that he is not represented by counsel."

The judge rotated his swivel chair to stare out the window, and no one spoke. When he swung back to face the others, he said, "I think it might be best for me to talk privately with Matthew for a few minutes. Will you gentlemen excuse us, please?"

The three men arose as one and quickly vacated the room, happy to let the judge's foul mood spend itself in their absence.

Judge Turner walked around his desk and took the chair opposite Matt, facing him across the narrow conference table. He lit a cigarette to underscore the informality of the moment, and he said, "I'm really sorry about all this, son, but I'm afraid we haven't had much practice with this sort of case up here."

"I didn't steal Frank Johnson's horse," Matt insisted, "and that cabin was my *home*—mine and my father's—he built it himself. . . ."

"How can I make you understand, Matthew?" the judge asked sadly. "Those are not really the issues here . . . not anymore. No one wants to see you go to jail because of this—not even Frank Johnson." Matt looked up in surprise, and the judge added, "That's right. Frank and Martha came in to see me last week and said they didn't want to press charges, but I had to tell them it wasn't that simple."

"I'd be willing to get a job and pay Mr. Johnson for the damages," Matt said excitedly, beginning to raise his hopes.

"Dammit, boy, none of that matters anymore! Don't you see? The problem is that there's no one to take care of you now, so the state has to do it."

"Charlie said I could live with him. Even Miss Mason—"

"The welfare department rules are very explicit on that point," the judge said, shaking his head. "I cannot relinquish you to foster care unless the parents are licensed by the state. That means a married couple. The husband must earn a certain minimum salary. The wife must remain at home all day—and they must be able to provide a private room for you with at least one hundred and ten square feet of space. Hell, Charlie Sanner doesn't qualify in any one of those categories, besides, he lives in a boardinghouse."

Judge Turner rubbed his face and continued. "I've had the people down in Cheyenne looking for a foster home, but no one is willing to take in a kid who starts fires when he's angry. I even talked to the orphanage up in Harrison County, but it's filled up."

Judge Turner seemed so genuinely distraught that Matt experienced the incongruousness of feeling sorry for him. "You mean, you can't send me to jail because Frank has withdrawn the charges against me, and you can't send me home because my parents are dead?"

Judge Turner looked up and detected a trace of a smile, so he completed the cruel joke. "And I can't send you to a foster home because you committed the crime for which I can't send you to jail." The judge chuckled until the tragic irony struck home again. "Dammit, it all seems so logical until I try to explain it," he said angrily.

"Charlie figured you were going to send me out of state to Clearwater, but I hope you don't," Matt said. "They call it a *school*, but it's still a prison, and I don't think I could stand being locked away." Judge Turner seemed to be listening intently, so Matt continued with controlled enthusiasm. "I have worked for most of the ranchers in the basin, and they can tell you that I can break stock with the best of them. I *know* I can get one of those families to take me in."

Judge Turner continued to study the boy, listening to his plea. "It's hard to believe you're only fourteen years old," he said abstractly.

"Fifteen," Matt corrected. "I'll be fifteen next week."

"Fifteen," the judge conceded, "but you're built like a grown man. How tall are you?"

"Over six foot," Matt answered, stretching the truth a fraction.

"And you seem so mature. I tend to compare you to my own kids—you know Susan and Timothy—and they seem like babies compared to you."

Matt felt success within his grasp. "Susan is in my class, but I don't know many of the kids at school. Mostly I spent time with older people . . . or at home. You know, I used to take care of the house for my father. We took turns doing the cooking for both of us, and when he had a job that would keep him away, I used to live by myself a lot."

"You are truly an amazing young man," Judge Turner said as he walked to his desk and picked up the telephone. "Send Warren Stiles in," he directed, "and tell him to bring in a couple of Cokes." Neither of them spoke again until the juvenile welfare caseworker entered the room and placed the drinks on the table.

"Warren, I've explained to Matthew that I don't get many cases like his up here, so I have to depend on your experience. You've seen more of this up around Jackson, and Powell, and Cody, haven't you?"

"Yes, sir. More than ever in the past five or six years," he said. "Seems to run in cycles, you know. Sometimes when jobs are scarce, parents beat up on their kids and run them off or just won't take care of them. They blame this last cycle on the Korean thing, but I'm not sure that affected us too much out here."

"Well, I felt that you took great pains to educate me about all the alternatives at my disposal, Warren, but frankly I am still confused, and I find it difficult to explain the entire situation to Matthew. Perhaps you can help."

"If you had any living relatives, there wouldn't be a problem," Stiles said to Matt. "Mr. Johnson would drop the criminal charges, and Judge Turner would order the welfare department to put you on a bus and ship you back to your relatives. Your grandfather had two sisters, but they left these parts more than forty years ago. We were able to trace Hattie to Chicago right up to World War Two, but—"

"I think we are agreed that there are no living relatives, Warren. How about foster care?" the judge asked.

"We don't have many foster homes anymore. There are more kids than there are homes, by a long shot, so the foster parents can afford to be choosy." Stiles began counting on his fingers: "Babies, no problem; teenagers, very tough; handicapped kids or kids who broke the law, don't even ask—impossible," he said, shaking his head sadly.

"I've explained to Matthew about Deputy Sanner and Miss Mason, but he seems to think that there are ranching families who would be willing to take him in. This young man has a superb reputation as a cowhand in these parts," Judge Turner said. "Have you checked out the possibility of qualifying and licensing one of those families in the basin?"

Matt had remained silent, but when he shifted his gaze from

Judge Turner to Warren Stiles, he was nodding enthusiastically and smiling.

Stiles began shaking his head again. "That's exactly why we don't have as many foster homes as we used to," he said. "Ten, twelve years ago the Justice Department turned up a so-called boys' ranch that was taking in foster kids just for the cheap labor. They had about thirty boys out there, living in tents all year long. Finally, two of them froze to death, and the coroner brought in the FBI, because most of the kids were from out of state."

"I vaguely remember that case," Judge Turner said, "but that situation was corrected, wasn't it?"

"The legislature put a stop to it," Stiles confirmed. "But the state attorney general's office keeps close tabs on foster children who are sent to live on ranches. As a result, ranch families have to be nuts to take in a foster child. They'd be investigated if they so much as asked the kid to make his own bed in the morning."

Matt was disconcerted by the explanation, but he was comforted by the fact that he was participating in the decision-making process. He was sufficiently pleased to observe with a smile, "Shoot, I'd do a lot more than make my own bed if it would keep me out of reform school."

"Of course, the problem with that is we do not have a medium-security institution in Wyoming for juvenile offenders," Stiles offered in response to Matt's statement. "Willow Run was designed for incorrigible—"

"Warren," the judge interrupted, "why don't we give Matthew a chance to stretch his legs while you and I get some people on the telephone?"

Stiles realized he had said too much, so he nodded his head once and said, "Right, Judge. Sorry. I'll take Matt out to the deputy."

"Thank you. And ask Jerry to join us, too."

As soon as the three court officers had reconvened, Judge Turner announced, "Gentlemen, we're down to the nut cutting, and it doesn't get any easier. There are no relatives to take care of that boy, and foster homes are out. Where do we go from here? . . . Warren?"

"As I started to say in front of the boy, Judge, Willow Run was built for incorrigible offenders. It's on the same grounds as the adult penitentiary, and most of those kids just move from one building to the next after they reach eighteen. That's not the place for Matt."

"How about Clearwater?" Jerry Samuelson asked. "I thought that's what we had decided anyway."

"We did," Judge Turner agreed. "But that kid is so scared of reform school . . . and besides, I don't like the idea of sending our problems out of state." The judge thought for a moment longer and added, "On top of all that, as I understand it, Clearwater will not accept a juvenile unless he has been convicted of a crime, and Frank Johnson says that no crime was committed. In fact, he's willing to swear that the boy did him a favor by burning down that old shack."

"That's right," Stiles agreed, "but the simple fact is that we have no way of taking care of this boy . . . or any others like him . . . *unless he is convicted of a criminal act.*"

"You look mighty pleased with yourself," Charlie said. "What went on in there?"

"I think everything is going to be great, Charlie." Matt smiled. "How about a hamburger?"

"Where am I going to find you a hamburger at ten o'clock in the morning? Besides, Mr. Stiles said for us to stay close."

"Okay, let's find a candy machine," Matt said. As they walked to the basement of the courthouse, Matt shared his elation about the judge's attitude and concern. "I just asked him not to send me to reform school, and he's not going to."

"Did he actually say that?" Charlie asked dubiously.

"Not exactly, but he said I was practically like a grown man, and I told him how I used to take care of myself when my dad was out on a job."

"You better slow down, pardner. Don't get your hopes up too high."

"Shoot, Charlie, you worry more than Martha Johnson herself." Matt laughed and clapped Charlie on the shoulder. "Tell you what, weepy, I'll bet you a month's worth of hamburgers that the worst he'll do is find a family for me to live with. There's the Swensons, the Holdens . . . shoot! There are more than I can count. You saw all those people at the cemetery."

A half hour later Matt was again seated before Judge Turner. He had entered the conference room with an expectant smile, but the color drained from his face when he saw Judge Turner's grave expression.

Without preamble the judge announced his decision in a voice that seemed to quaver. "Matthew, I have considered all the options open to me in this case, and I regret to say that I must find you guilty of willful and malicious destruction of private property. You will be committed to the Boys' Industrial School at Clearwater for an indeterminate period not to exceed the attainment of your eighteenth birthday." The judge swallowed hard to control his voice; then he said, "I have directed Mr. Stiles to make the necessary arrangements," and he tapped his gavel with finality.

No one spoke. Matt sat and stared through the judge without seeing him or anything else. His face was white, his lips trembled, and his fists were clenched. Judge Turner walked to Matt's chair and squatted close to him. He placed his hand on Matt's arm and said in a trembling voice, "That was the most difficult thing I have ever done. I'm truly sorry." The judge left the building and went directly home to be with his own children.

PART 2: *Ralph, 1951–1963*

Chapter Eight: Ralph, 1951–1963

Drury is a small town up in the northeastern corner of the state. The old-timers still talk about the booming frontier days, but most of its 420 residents just sit around waiting to die or figuring ways to get out. Life there has always been harsh, and the personalities of its people reflect six generations of grim austerity.

Young Ralph Jorgenson was an exception. He was bright, sensitive, and happy, and by the time he was six years old he had become the town's favorite attraction. Children of all ages loved to roughhouse with him, and he always responded with a delighted smile, even when tears might have been more appropriate. Nor were the adults immune to his special qualities. He was too young to understand their jokes, but when they laughed at him, he smiled brightly and nodded vigorously, and that made them laugh all the more.

Ralph was a six-year-old mute.

He was the town dummy.

His mother, who had been forty-eight when Ralph was born, interpreted her son's affliction as God's punishment for her own mid-life promiscuity, so she ran her husband off and moved to an old farmhouse on the edge of town. She and Ralph subsisted on the monthly stipend the state provided her on the assumption that his inability to speak was attributable to mental retardation.

Ralph liked the people of Drury because he thought they liked him. He rode his bicycle into town every day, pedaling furiously down the quarter-mile dirt road, fearful of missing out on some happening there. He especially enjoyed being where people congregated: Kelsey's Texaco in the morning, Ruby's Café at noon, and Thorn's General Store when the other kids got out of school.

Sometimes he was intimidated by the rough humor of the older children, but he liked it when the grown-ups played a joke on him because it was usually followed by an offering of candy or gum. Once old man Harrington, to everyone's delight, had given him a plug of tobacco, but that had made him sick, so the boy put it out of his mind as some kind of mistake.

Ralph finally realized he was different one day when the older boys soaked a rag with gasoline from Kelsey's pump, stuck it in his back pocket, and set fire to it. The six-year-old boy ran in crazed circles, frantically slapping his rump, punching his face, and pulling his hair, his eyes bulging in terror and his mouth agape in silent screams while the men and boys laughed hysterically. When the burning rag was finally dislodged, he was unhurt, but Ralph had come to understand the cruelty of their laughter, so he stayed away from town as much as possible.

He remained at home for the next two years, tirelessly gathering and chopping the wood that was their only fuel for heating and cooking. As he approached his eighth birthday, he vaguely wondered when he would start school, but he dreaded the prospect and never asked. If the time ever came when they forced him to go back to town, however, it occurred to him that chopping all that wood had made him strong enough to protect himself.

He worked out a primitive system of communicating with his mother, but she discouraged it for fear that it might contradict the supposition that he was retarded and would result in the loss of her monthly stipends. Besides, like everyone else in the community, she assumed that a boy who could not speak had nothing worthwhile to communicate.

Ralph was eight when he met Connie Parsons. He was gathering wood on the edge of their property, and she was chasing after her puppy. Ralph scooped up the tiny dog, nuzzled its soft fur gently, then held it out to her with a tentative smile. No one had told the five-year-old girl about Ralph, so she was completely unafraid. They became friends, and other than his own mother, Connie was Ralph's only human contact. For three days he carried her on his shoulders through the high weeds and boosted her in and out of the trees whenever she asked. She was intrigued by his muteness and enjoyed the game of deciphering his signs as his fingers and hands moved patiently through the air.

One day Connie brought Ralph a chocolate cookie and climbed up on a tree stump to kiss him on the cheek. Suddenly the little girl stiffened, and Ralph spun around to see her father coming at him with an ax. The boy bolted toward the heavy timber near the creek and remained hidden until the sheriff's dogs treed him that night.

The entire community, including his own mother, was reviled by his grotesque indecency, and Ralph was too frightened and confused by their outrage to cry. He was taken to the old jail in handcuffs and leg irons, and there he remained while a doctor was called in from Sibley to examine Connie, and everyone talked about sending the boy to the state asylum.

Mildred Jorgenson was primarily concerned about the possibility of forfeiting her monthly checks, so she tearfully pleaded and promised to lock Ralph in the house if only they returned her son to her. When the county social worker pointed out, however, that Mildred would continue to receive the Social Security checks for her dependent son, she signed the commitment papers, and he was removed to the state asylum within the week.

The young social worker who came for him looked around the one-room jail and was immediately incensed. Ralph hung back a little, wondering why she was so angry. She sensed his concern and reached around his shoulder protectively before targeting the deputy. "This is disgusting." She seethed. "How could you treat a little boy this way?" Ralph followed her glare back into the tiny cell and didn't see anything particularly wrong, but what she saw reviled her: a filthy, foul-smelling mattress on the floor right next to a stark toilet, with no seat, stained inside and out with dried fecal matter.

"Ain't supposed to be a Hilton." The deputy shrugged.

"Hilton, my ass!"

The deputy peered at her, and his indifference turned to amusement. He took in her short blond hair, blue jeans, and saddle shoes, and he wondered whether there were breasts and hips beneath her baggy gray sweater. He was about to call her girlie and ask if she had learned anything in college besides cursing and dressing like a boy, but before he could frame the question, she and Ralph were through the door with a parting "Goddamn hick peckerwood sonva*bitch!*"

Chapter Nine

The asylum admissions officer tried repeatedly to elicit some kind of response from the eight-year-old—a nod, a gesture, anything that might help him to evaluate Ralph's level of awareness—but the boy was completely preoccupied with every detail of the trip: his first ride in a car, his first strawberry milk shake, and the genuine interest that Catherine displayed toward him once she had got over her anger with the deputy.

"Ralph, would you like to see your mother? Just nod, son." Dr. Foster waited for a response.

Someday I'm gonna drive a car, too. Even bigger than Mr. Kelsey's.

"How old are you, Ralph? Hold up your fingers."

She was a nice lady. She was the funnest lady I ever saw.

"Ralph, are you listening? Can you hear me, son? If you can understand me, just nod your head . . . Ralph?"

How come she talked to me that way? Like I was a baby? Like I didn't understand her? . . . Stromberry . . . That's what it was. . . . Stromberry milk shake.

Dr. Foster had hoped for something better. The boy had seemed alert to his surroundings when he entered the office, but now he was staring into space, seemingly beyond human contact. He motioned for the female orderly to come forward. "Hannah, this is Ralph. We'll have to put him on Ward C . . . at least for the time being." Then, as if to justify his decision, he added, "Besides, there *is* that police business."

Hannah's eyebrows raised in mild surprise, but she said nothing, aware that her job as an orderly was to care for the children, and not to question the medical staff. It was just that the boy looked so normal. So much like her own little grandson.

"You come," she said stiffly, in an accent that belied the fact that she had left Germany more than fifty years ago, "you come mit Hannah," and she gently took his hand and led him toward the door.

When they stepped from the old elevator on the fourth floor, Hannah was again in her own domain. A rosy flush crept back into her cheeks, and the stiffness left her legs and spine. She leaned over, looked Ralph in the eyes, and said with a bright smile, "You a nize boy, Walphie. We gonna ged you a nize bath, some nize pajamas, and you gonna feel good. Okay?"

Ralph looked at her quizzically, not certain that he understood her words, but quite certain that he liked her and that she could be trusted. Hannah's nonstop chattering lasted through the bath and selection of pajamas. She faltered only when it came time to spray the boy for lice, something she considered insulting and dehumanizing. When it was over, she held the boy at arm's length and praised him effusively. "Dot's a g-o-o-d boy, Walphie. Now we go meet the udder children, ja?"

Ralph had not forgotten his bitter experiences with the children of Drury, but his reluctance melted in the warmth of Hannah's presence. He smiled and nodded his consent, but Hannah was busy unlocking the door to Ward C and failed to see the spark of intelligence that the doctor had earlier tried to elicit.

Hannah drew the key from the lock and returned the key ring to her belt as she pushed in on the heavy door and shouted, "Hey, you lieblings, ve got a new boy here. Dis is Walphie. Everbody zay hello."

Ralph bent his head and stepped into the room under Hannah's outstretched arm. His expectant grin evaporated in the face of what he saw. There were nineteen children crowded into a ward that had been designed for twelve. Some of the boys were sitting in straight-backed chairs, staring vacuously into space, rocking their upper bodies with varying degrees of intensity; some lay quietly on their beds, staring at the ceiling; and some shuffled aimlessly around the room, arms dangling listlessly. Not one face had turned toward them, and there was no recognition or aware-ness of the newcomer's arrival.

Ralph pressed closer to Hannah in abject terror as he examined the boys of Ward C. Every bodily aperture seemed to excrete slimy wastes of yellow, green, and white: mucus, saliva, urine, and serous fluids from open sores. One boy sat on the floor smear-ing his face with fecal matter. Hannah bolted toward him, a damp cloth magically appearing in her hand. "No, no, Villy. Dot's b-a-d. Muzn't do dot, Villy," she said as she wiped his face and hands, and she concluded her mild scolding with a reassuring and hurried buss on the forehead.

One glance at the fear on Ralph's face confirmed her belief that the boy did not belong on Ward C. She hurried back to him, affecting a cheerful patter: "Ach, dese boys is a mezz! Hannah leaves for ten minutes, and she need six hands ven she comes back; hold still, Wudy, und I clean your noze; ach, you magin' me old before my time . . . poor Hannah . . . an old lady already at sixty-four." When she finally returned to Ralph, she smothered him against her bosom and kissed the top of his head. The cheer-fulness left her face, and she looked old as she whispered, "*You* know, my little *Knabe*. Dose shmart guys downshtairs . . . *dey* don't understand . . . but you know, don' you?" Then Hannah released him and held him at arm's length with a hopeful smile. "Hannah vill take care of you, Walphie, but virst you gotta cheer up. C'mon over here, and I show you your bet."

The resident physician attributed Ralph's extreme agitation to his change of environment, so he prescribed a mild sedative, which helped the boy through the rest of the day. That night, however, Ralph was plunged into new horrors. The semidarkness of the small ward was filled with the mindless shrieks and pathetic sobs of those who had never known any other way to express themselves. He tried to press his pillow into his face to blot out the world, but an ominous new sound soon insinuated itself into his consciousness—swish . . . swish . . . swish. The muffled sounds came closer. Then they stopped near his bed, and next to his head he could hear a labored breath: the liquid sound of air being sucked through respiratory passages filled with phlegm.

In a single motion Ralph flung the pillow aside, sat upright, and scrambled to the head of the bed, stopping only when his back thudded against the concrete wall. His eyes were wide in stark terror, and his mouth worked a silent scream, but the boy who had shuffled up to his bed seemed unconcerned. He simply stood there, pointing a finger, peering through half-closed lids, with a thick stream of viscous mucus bubbling from his nose, into his gaping mouth, over his crooked lower teeth and out onto his chin. Then he turned and padded slowly away, his loose cloth slippers swishing softly over the heavily waxed linoleum. His finger was still pointed forward, and his head was tilted to one side as if peering down the barrel of an imaginary pistol.

Hannah Green was a nobody. She had emigrated from Germany when she was fourteen and had worked as a maid for three years to repay her sponsors. When she was eighteen, she fulfilled a marriage contract that had been made for her five years earlier, and over the next decade she and Hermann Green had four sons, one of whom was later killed in the Pacific. Her husband had been a butcher, and she had helped him establish a successful neighborhood business in Brooklyn by working at his side and doing everything from delivering bundles of meat to spreading sawdust on the floor. They lost their shop during the Depression, but they were never without work. Eventually Hermann went to work for the A&P and moved west with his family. Hermann was crippled by a stroke in 1948, and Hannah took a night job so she could spend her days caring for her husband. When he finally died, in 1950, she went to work at the children's section of the state asylum, where she found comfort in helping those who had had it worse than she.

Hannah Green was a nobody. In the world of the state asylum she was uneducated, past her prime, one of many "foreigners" working for minimum wages, a kind of busybody, and a woman who had nothing to offer the children . . . except love. Above all, she had come to learn that her place was to care for the children, not to question the actions of her superiors.

But she knew they were mistaken about Ralph. True, he could not talk, but he was alert and aware of everything that was happening around him, and she had nursed too many brain-damaged and retarded children to place him in that category. She had already noted some changes in him: His revulsion had changed to sympathy; he was still a frightened child, but he had begun to care about the other boys, and when he thought no one was looking, he even tried to help them. None of the doctors saw the change because whenever they came on the ward, Ralph retreated into his shell and behaved like those around him. The doctors noted his anxiety, however, and their daily examinations were often followed by an increase in Ralph's medications. Hannah was not authorized to administer drugs, but she watched as the nurses popped more and larger pills into the boy's mouth, and she knew she would not have him much longer.

Ralph had not yet reached his ninth birthday.

She tried desperately to keep him alert by the sheer power of her will, even trying to feed his fears: "You better vatch out, Walphie, or someone's gonna come in here tonight und bite your neck." Soon, however, the night noises no longer bothered him, his fears dissolved, and the dark circles under his eyes disappeared. And while the medical staff congratulated itself on its success, Hannah began to despair. She arrived one morning, exploding through the door with her usual cheerful gusto, expecting to be rewarded by a single sign of recognition—a bright smile from Ralph. Instead, not a single face turned toward her. She walked slowly, fearfully, toward his bed and found him sitting on the floor, facing the blank concrete wall, slowly rocking his upper body.

Hannah Green's pathetic wail momentarily shook Ralph from his reverie, but they did not speak or touch. She turned and ran from the room, sobbing uncontrollably, and she never returned.

Chapter Ten

Ralph Jorgenson languished under heavy sedation on Ward C for three years before the state finally adopted an institutional reform. During that time the once-muscular boy had grown four inches and had gained more than sixty pounds—mostly fat—and had completely assumed the mannerisms of the profoundly retarded children with whom he had been incarcerated for so long. The state asylum was now known as the state hospital, and there had been a parade of orderlies, now known as child care workers, all of whom shared Hannah Green's basic quality of love and caring. Most of the other personnel had also been replaced, but Ralph had never noticed. His time was spent shuffling around the tiny ward or sitting, rocking and staring into space.

He was twelve years old when they unlocked the door to Ward C and wheeled him down the hall to physical therapy for the first time. He was tall for his age—five feet ten inches—but the boy who had once pedaled his bicycle furiously down the country roads had become so uncoordinated that he was now incapable of moving without stumbling, so obese that it was difficult for him to touch his knees.

The physical therapy intensified over the next six months, and the medications decreased. His neurological reflexes improved, and his coordination progressed, but there seemed to be no signs of intellectual awareness. Ralph performed the exercises by rote and did whatever he was told to do without expression or cognition. Some of the motherly child care workers fed him extra ice cream to counteract the stress of physical therapy, and he continued to gain weight.

Ralph was miraculously snatched from the precipice by the installation of a television set in the new children's lounge. At first the flashing lights and raucous canned laughter went unheeded, but a month later flickers of comprehension began to appear. The child care workers were the first to notice, and they shared anecdotes about their favorite "little boy" during the shift changes.

"I think Ralph likes Uncle Miltie. He looks at the screen and rocks only during the commercials."

"You should have seen him last Sunday . . . the Sullivan show . . . he rocked himself silly during the singing, then stopped cold for the elephants. I think he might have been smiling, too, but I'm not sure."

By the time he was thirteen years old the child care workers had concluded that he was clearly interested in certain programs, but more than that, he had taken it upon himself to change channels at the appropriate times. It was improbable, they reported, but Ralph seemed to have memorized the time slots and channels of his favorite programs.

Dr. Medjid was hopeful but dubious. He observed Ralph through the two-way mirror and speculated, "He changed the channel, all right, but that might be a manifestation of some kind of sequential conditioning. Nothing more. I would hesitate to attribute his actions to any conscious selectivity."

Vivian Kolchak knew better. Another of the long line of "nobodies" that had passed through the children's wards with no professional training and nothing to offer except love and practical experience, she was instinctively certain that there was a lively intelligence buried somewhere beneath the fog in Ralph's head. Sometimes it was only a feeling that his eyes were following her, and sometimes she thought she detected his disappointment when orange slices were substituted for ice cream on the evening snack tray.

There was only one way for Vivian Kolchak to find out. There were so many children and so few doctors that nobody had time to help her with Ralph, so she decided to test him herself. She knew there would be trouble if she were caught, so she would keep it simple, and no one would have to know, especially if she were mistaken. She knew that Ralph would be watching *Captain Kangaroo*, so she marched into the lounge and announced, "Let's see what the Mouseketeers are doing today," and flipped to Channel 7.

To her delight, he responded by reaching out and switching back with an indignant flourish.

Next, she asked, "How about *Edge of Night*, Ralph? You like that one."

The boy scowled and pointed to the clock.

The tests became more and more complex, but within two weeks Vivian was confident enough to stage a demonstration for one of the young interns, hoping he might be willing to approach Dr. Medjid on a professional level. The test was a success, and the following afternoon Dr. Medjid himself agreed to observe the proceedings from behind the two-way mirror. He was joined by three interns and two nurses. Then several of the on-duty child care workers ventured in, and they were finally joined by others who had come to work early to watch the test.

The demonstration was short but effective. Ralph was absorbed in *The Secret Storm* when Vivian asked if she could turn to *American Bandstand*. Ralph shook his head vigorously. "Why not?" she asked. "What's wrong with *American Bandstand*?"

Ralph threw his head back as though the question were too ridiculous for words. Then, with his head laid back as far as he could get it, he opened and closed his mouth rapidly, emitting short grunts and squeals, doing his best to imitate a singer.

Vivian laughed and slapped at him playfully. "Okay, so you don't like singing, but I do. You let me watch *American Bandstand*, and I'll bring you some strawberrry ice cream tonight. How's that?"

Ralph sat motionless for a moment, and Vivian's hopes began to fall.

Please, baby, don't fade out on me now.

Suddenly, however, the boy reached over and flipped to

Channel 9, *American Bandstand,* and the cheer that erupted from behind the two-way mirror startled them both.

In the next room Dr. Medjid smiled and said to the chief nurse, "I suppose we ought to find out how retarded that boy really is. Get me the name of someone at the School for the Deaf, someone who can teach sign language."

Superintendent Coltrain had long suspected that many children committed to the state hospital had been incorrectly diagnosed as retarded because of speech or hearing problems, so he responded immediately to Dr. Medjid's request for a conference.

"It won't be easy," he said after reviewing Ralph's file. "The boy cannot read or write, so finger spelling is out of the question. We usually start out with signing anyway, but in this case we will have no choice."

"What's the difference?" Medjid asked. "I have a vague idea, but—"

"Finger spelling means just what the term implies: using the hands and fingers to form letters and spell out words. But that's out." Dr. Coltrain shook his head slowly and continued. "Signing can involve pantomime, facial expressions, and the use of the hands and fingers to form symbols. That's the key word . . . symbols. There are about two thousand such symbols, but each one of them represents a *concept,* not just a word." Coltrain leaned forward on his elbows. "Can Ralph deal in concepts? He's been vegetating for four years now. Is he still capable?"

"That's what I want you to tell me."

Dr. Coltrain assigned his most experienced therapist to perform the initial assessment. Mrs. Harrison observed Ralph for fifteen hours over a five-day period, particularly noting his behavior patterns and the quality of his interaction with different staff members—especially the child care workers, the physical therapist, and the doctors.

She found him to be relaxed and outgoing with the older female workers on the ward. His facial expressions were animated and bright, and he used his entire body to express opinions about everything. In return, the women plied him with ice cream, cup-cakes, and anything else that might elicit a positive response. By the third day Mrs. Harrison had concluded that the boy was ma-nipulating them to get what he wanted with the least possible effort. For years they all had assumed that he was retarded and had treated him accordingly, but they had spoiled him rotten in the process, and he now knew how to take full advantage of them.

Ralph was more subdued with his physical therapist, showing only anger and resentment as he was made to exert himself without reward. Mrs. Harrison quickly learned to interpret his walking patterns: on the way to therapy, sluggish and meandering—in no hurry to get there; inside the gym, shuffling and uncoordinated—pleading for sympathy; and at the conclusion of therapy, quick and determined—eager to get out and return to his sympathetic benefactors on the ward.

The first time she observed Ralph's behavior in the presence of a doctor, she was shocked. She was certain he had had a relapse: stiff joints, violent rocking motions, and vacuous stares. As soon as the doctor left, however, the boy recovered immediately. Mrs. Harrison came to like the boy's spirit and looked forward to teach-ing him to express himself in more constructive ways.

Chapter Eleven

The big day started for Mrs. Harrison with a conference with Dr. Medjid. "It is important that we maintain realistic goals," she said. "After all, Ralph cannot read or write, and he has very few social skills. It could well be that he might not speak even if he could. If that's the case, it will be infinitely more difficult to persuade him to express himself with his hands."

"Believe me," he said, "my expectations are minimal. We know there is no brain damage, but the degree of retardation is questionable. The only certainty is that his environment over the past four years has not been exactly conducive to his positive development."

"The lack of physical activity has hampered his dexterity, and he has what we call starched fingers, all of which will impede his ability to become fluid in manual communications," she said. "Nonetheless, I have been watching him for the past week, and I think we can help."

Dr. Medjid left the conference room as soon as Ralph was led in. The boy was going through his hopelessly retarded routine and started rocking as soon as he sat down. Mrs. Harrison explained that her intention was to show him how to speak with his hands and began with "This is number one," holding up the index finger, "This is number two," holding up the first two fingers before progressing through five.

"Now you try it, Ralph."

Nothing.

Mrs. Harrison reached over, took his hand, and manipulated

his fingers without cooperation from him. She smiled to herself as he began to rock again.

Mrs. Harrison was undaunted. Having taught deaf, mute, and blind children to sign, she was certain that Ralph could learn enough of the elements of manual signing to relieve himself of the frustration of having thoughts and not being able to communicate them. Her immediate intention was to teach him to use only a few of the standard signs—perhaps twenty nouns and modifiers—just to determine whether or not he was capable of recalling and assimilating their meanings in proper context. This would depend ultimately on the boy's ability to master the signs and use them to express abstract meanings.

"Look at me, Ralph. This is how you say 'book.' " Mrs. Harrison held her hands together, as if in prayer; then she opened them, palms up. "See how easy it is? It's just like opening a book, isn't it? . . . Now let me see you do it."

Ralph was staring into space over her right shoulder, his hands again in his lap.

Mrs. Harrison's tone became firm, and she pulled at his arms until his hands came up to the table. "Put your palms together, Ralph. Just like this."

He began to rock instead.

"Let's try this one. This is the sign for 'man.' " She raised the back of her open hand to her forehead, then moved it down to the front of her chest, fingers spread and pointed outward. "Look again," she said before asking him to repeat it. By the end of the hour she had demonstrated "boy," "girl," "candy," "food," "chair," "clothes," and the personal pronouns, but Ralph had not responded.

At the close of the session Vivian came into the room to take the boy to therapy, and as soon as they left, Dr. Medjid stepped in, disappointment etched in his face.

"I was watching," he said, gesturing at the two-way mirror. "It didn't go very well, did it?"

"Quite the contrary," she said. "He tried to appear uninterested, but he eventually stopped rocking, didn't he?"

"Do you think there's a chance?" he said with renewed enthusiasm.

"Most definitely. In this environment—forgive me, Doctor—he has been conditioned not to respond. His only reward has come from behaving just the way people expect him to behave . . . retarded. And from the size of him I'd say that most of his rewards have been caloric."

"Strawberry ice cream." He chuckled.

"And all he needs to do to earn that reward is to brush his teeth, comb his hair, or do his exercises. Then everyone laughs and praises him and fills his face with sweets, just for doing little things that he mastered as an infant."

Dr. Medjid resented her criticism but recognized the basic truth and tried not to sound defensive. "If I'm not mistaken, it was you people who invented the token reward system."

"Yes, but the reward must be appropriate to the accomplishment. I've got my goodies," she said, shaking a bag of M&M's, "but I feel it is wrong to use them as a bribe. That's what he wanted, what he expected me to do because that's the way everyone has been treating him."

The second day went much like the first—Ralph pretending complete vacuity and Mrs. Harrison trying to be patient and firm.

When the third session ended in the same way, Mrs. Harrison pretended to be angry. "Now look, Ralph, I know you understand me . . . every word. And I know full well you are capable of remembering and repeating the signs I have shown you." Then she stood up and forced a flush to her face. "I also know that you would be willing to cooperate with me for a piece of candy." She opened the bag of M&M's and spilled them onto the table. "Well, I'm not going to play your game," she said. "Everyone else around here treats you like a baby and feeds you candy to keep you from misbehaving, but I have too much respect for you. You are smart enough to learn how to speak, and you'll get no candy from me, young man." Then she dismissed him abruptly, drawing the session to an early conclusion.

As she had expected, Ralph was no more cooperative the next day, so pretending to be completely defeated and frustrated, she sighed and pushed four M&M's across the table at him. "You win. Here's your candy. I give up."

When Mrs. Harrison stood and stepped around the table, Ralph held up both hands. "What? You want me to stop? This is how you say 'stop.' " She showed him the sign. "Are you trying to tell me to wait? This is the sign for 'wait.' " She demonstrated, then positioned his fingers appropriately.

"Which is it, Ralph? . . . 'Stop' or 'wait'?"

Ralph thought for a moment, then repeated the sign for "wait" and pointed to her chair.

Mrs. Harrison resumed her seat and watched Ralph's face as he examined the four M&M's. Finally, the boy pushed two of them back to her and popped the other two into his mouth with an impish grin. She could not contain her laughter. "Compromise? So you want to compromise, huh? Well, son, that's as good a way as any to begin."

Mrs. Harrison reported to Dr. Medjid the following week. Dr. Coltrain was there, too, but he had already heard her recommendations. "It was a most gratifying experience," she began. "Nothing as dramatic as the breakthrough that occurs when a deaf, mute, and blind child suddenly realizes that someone is trying to make rational contact, but there are many similarities: before the breakthrough, extreme hostility and resistance; and following the breakthrough, a sudden burst of positive behavioral changes, followed by an impatient anger to learn more quickly."

Dr. Medjid moved to the edge of his chair. "We've all noticed that in Ralph," he said. "He is much more aware of things, but he vacillates from happiness to anger so quickly the people on the ward can't keep up with him. I think Mrs. Kolchak would rather have him as he was."

"That's part of the problem," she said. "Ralph is basically a lazy boy. He thinks he has it made here. He's surrounded by people who mother him to death, and he's not at all certain he wants to change that."

"Then how do you explain the results you've had in such a short time?" Dr. Medjid knew the answer, but he wanted to hear it from Mrs. Harrison.

"That's simple," she said. "Ralph's progress was inordinately fast for two reasons: In the first place, he can see and hear; more important, however, he can also think. His ability to think—in an environment where no one believed he could—has put him in control of his own destiny."

"Like the one-eyed man in the land of the blind," Coltrain injected.

"Something like that," she said, wishing her superintendent would keep his platitudes to himself for the moment. "I know it sounds crazy, but Ralph is much too comfortable here. He does not remember much about life on the outside, and what he does remember is not too pleasant. Here he has any number of middle-aged women falling all over themselves to take the place of the real mother who wants nothing to do with him."

"And that's not all bad," Coltrain said, not wanting to offend Dr. Medjid.

"Surely that kind of love and attention helped him survive during his darkest period," she agreed, "but now he has outgrown that stage . . . or at least he is ready to, but your staff is not ready to let him go."

Dr. Medjid understood the problem. "What do you suggest? It would be difficult to transfer Ralph to another unit, and it would be impossible to get those women to change their ways . . . especially with so many other children who need just what they are capable of giving."

"My recommendation, and I have already discussed it with Dr. Coltrain, is that you transfer Ralph to the school for the deaf. If you want the boy to learn sign language, he will need to be in an environment that affords lots of practice; he won't get it here."

Dr. Medjid was plainly relieved. "I was hoping you'd suggest that," he said. "How soon can you take him?"

"He is thirteen years old. The next class matriculates in August, and I would suggest that he begin then," Mrs. Harrison said. "That will give us almost three months to process him, and in the meantime, we can start him on a reading and writing program."

Chapter Twelve

Ralph's final three months at the state hospital were the most productive of his life. He was learning to read and write, he willingly labored in physical therapy to improve his strength and coordination, and he came out of his shell completely. In spite of his progress, however, everyone spoke of the problems he would have in meeting new people and making friends with the other children. After all, it had been more than four years since he had had any contact with the ouside world, they said as they clucked their tongues, wagged their heads, and spoke of their concerns in his presence, still not accepting the fact that he could understand every word.

They would have been surprised to know that Ralph had comprehended their concerns, and they would have been shocked to know that he disagreed. He might have been locked away for four years, but more than three years of that time had been blotted from his mind by sedatives. He was aware of a slight remorse about leaving Vivian, and that doctor with the funny name, but he was looking forward to spending more time with Mrs. Harrison. She was the only one who treated him like a real person. Besides, he was eager to be with other kids again.

When he was finally moved to the School for the Deaf, he was not disappointed.

He was thirteen, and big for his age, but the other children in his class ranged from six to eight years of age. All of them, like Ralph, had come to the school lacking social skills and self-con-

fidence. He should have been self-conscious about his age and size, but he was not. He was kind, gentle, and protective, and the other children treated him like a beloved pet bear. He became their friend and caretaker and the favorite of the staff and faculty as well. By the time the older children returned to the school in September the adjustment had been completed, and Ralph adapted with even greater ease.

He could not have conjured a happier fantasy. By December he was living with eleven other boys and three supervisors who worked eight-hour shifts. As cottage leader he was responsible for selecting their Christmas tree, and he was accorded the honor of placing the angel at the top after the lights and ornaments had been hung.

The Christmas party was a particularly happy event. The parents of the other first-year boys were there, tearfully applauding the progress their sons had made since they had left home in August. Each of the boys introduced Ralph to his parents as a special friend, and the adults embraced him gratefully, treating him more like a staff member than a student.

When the boys and their families left for Christmas vacation, the empty cottage seemed drab and desolate, and Ralph dared think about his own mother again. A week earlier Mrs. Cutler, the daytime cottage counselor, had called Ralph into the living room and handed him the telephone. "It's your mother," she said with a smile. "You listen, and I'll get on the kitchen extension where I can see you. I'll tell her whatever you want to say."

Ralph looked quizzically into the mouthpiece and heard, "Mrs. Jorgenson? This is Mrs. Cutler, the cottage supervisor. Ralph is on the other line. Why don't you go ahead and talk, and I'll tell you what he is saying?"

The voice at the other end was hesitant and dubious. "What do you mean? My son can't say things . . . can he?"

"No, Mrs. Jorgenson. Ralph cannot speak, but he can understand you, and he can answer with his hands. I'll tell you what he says."

"I don't know what to say. I'm calling from the gas station . . . the social worker is right here . . . she told me I had to call you. I just don't know what to say . . . I mean, Ralph is a good boy and all, but he's not *right*. I don't know what to say."

Mrs. Cutler tried to hide her annoyance. "Mrs. Jorgenson, Ralph is fine. We're going to have a Christmas party for the parents next week, and your son wants you to be here."

"Oh, I don't know about that." Then she cupped her hand around the mouthpiece and lowered her voice, but her panic came through. "You don't understand . . . the police took Ralph away because of what he did to that little girl. People around here still talk about it. I pray every night. They took him to the asylum, and all . . . I just couldn't . . ."

"He's not at the state hospital, Mrs. Jorgenson. Ralph is in school now. Don't you remember? You signed the consent decree."

"I don't know about that. I just signed what welfare told me to. They said I'd still get my check every month, that's all I know. . . ." The voice was reduced to a whine. "I will, won't I? . . . The checks, I mean. That's all I got."

Mrs. Cutler could no longer contain her anger, and she realized it had been a mistake to have Ralph listen. "I don't know a damned thing about your checks, Mrs. Jorgenson, and I don't care. All we want is to invite you to a Christmas party that the boys are putting on for their parents." She spoke with brittle finality. "Will you come or not?"

Sensing that the conversation did not threaten her stipend, Mrs. Jorgenson raised her voice in indignation. "I haven't seen that boy since he did that terrible thing. He's just not right. I know it's not his fault, and I pray for him every night, but he's not right. He belongs where he is, and it won't do no good to pretend different."

Ralph put down the telephone and walked to his bedroom. There were tears in his eyes, but he was not sure why. He had forgotten the sound of her voice and rarely thought about her. Perhaps the tears had come with the flood of images he had long suppressed: how she used to cry when the people in town would laugh at them, how scared she was on dark nights when the other kids would sneak up to their "spook house" on a dare and break a window . . .

Suddenly a man's voice echoed through the empty cottage and interrupted his sad reverie. "Ralph? Where are you? It's Cator Pershing. Where you at?"

Images of the Christmas party evaporated along with the memories of his mother's voice. His friend had come for him.

Ralph brightened immediately. Cator Pershing had volunteered through the local Methodist church to be his neighborhood sponsor—a kind of Big Brother program, except Mr. Pershing was old enough to be his grandfather. His wife had died two years earlier, and his only daughter had moved to Sioux Falls. Cator had taken Ralph to his first movie in October, then every second Friday night thereafter, and he had promised to take him to a ball game in Omaha next spring.

Ralph lumbered into the hall and collided with the older man. "There you are, you big moose." He laughed. "I came to help move your stuff. Can't stay here by yourself over Christmas."

The two had become good friends. It was okay being with the younger boys, but Ralph felt a special warmth for this lonely old man. Cator Pershing had been an automobile mechanic for almost fifty years, and his Motor Inn Garage had become Ralph's favorite hangout. He spent all his free time at the garage, watching Pershing strip engines and handing him the tools like a surgeon's assistant. In the seventeen years that Pershing had served as a community sponsor at the school for the deaf, he had become proficient in finger spelling and signing, and he communicated fluently with the boys, but in all those years of volunteer work he had never become as emotionally attached to any of them as he had with Ralph. The others had been students with families of their own, and Pershing was never anything more to them than a temporary substitute, but Ralph was different. He, too, was alone.

They loaded Ralph's few possessions into the pickup for the short ride to Roosevelt Cottage, where the boy would be housed during the Christmas vacation, but Pershing was already having second thoughts about leaving. His luggage was on the front seat, and Ralph scowled in disapproval when he saw it.

"Sally'd have a duck fit if I missed another Christmas," he murmured apologetically. "Long trip, though. If this was a month from now, you could help me drive."

Ralph's eyebrows shot up.

"That's right. You can get a learner's permit when you're fourteen." His reluctance to leave Ralph continued to build as he coaxed the cold engine to life. "I don't like the sound of that tappet. Hear it? I'd sure hate to blow an engine between here and Sioux Falls."

Ralph listened to the purring of the perfectly tuned engine and heard nothing out of the ordinary, but he sensed the old man's indecision, and his blood began to beat in anticipation.

"Let's get us a sandwich and talk this thing out. Those grand-kids, God bless 'em, they wear me out. 'Specially at Christmas. . . . Yeah, maybe Easter would be better."

Suddenly it was settled. Ralph stayed with Cater, and the two weeks they spent together was the happiest time of Ralph's life. They exchanged gifts on Christmas morning—a new set of Big Ben coveralls for Ralph and Ralph's favorite baseball hat for Cator.

"Now we gotta talk."

Ralph looked at him quizzically. It seemed they had not stopped talking for a week.

"I mean, about your situation up there." He gestured generally toward the distant school. "I mean, about you being a special student and all. . . . You know what I mean, so why you lookin' at me that way?"

Ralph turned his palms up and curled the fingers of both hands inward, urging Pershing to continue.

"Well, you're in a school for deaf kids, but you're not deaf. They agreed to take you and teach you to read and write and talk with your hands. They had to prove you didn't belong up the road." He gestured more ominously toward the state hospital. "Now . . . you're doing real good in school, so don't get me wrong, but you're almost fourteen, and you're just starting. You're way behind the other boys, but if you decided to go on to college, my money would be on you making it."

Ralph smiled faintly at the compliment, wondering where Pershing was headed.

"The way I got it figured, though, by the time you got that degree, you'd be older'n me."

Ralph laughed silently and tattooed the tabletop with his fingertips in response to the joke.

Cator's expression became more serious. "Fact is, they're not gonna let you take up space up there forever. Come June, they're gonna move you out to make room for some little boy who really needs it. You're practically cured."

Suddenly Ralph understood the truth. He had known it from the beginning, but he had put it out of his mind. He had been accepted into the school for a year . . . just long enough to learn to communicate. But what would happen to him after that?

"I been thinking on this for some time now," Pershing said hesitantly. "I think you'd make a darned good mechanic, and I could sure use the help. If you'd be willing to try . . . maybe be my apprentice . . . you could live right here . . . and I bet we could get you enrolled up there as a day student." Cator sensed that the boy was struggling with some powerful emotions, so he continued talking. "I could sure use the company here, and you'd have a chance to stay in school."

Ralph's face was rigid, but tears welled up in his eyes. Crying was a new experience to him, so he did not know how to handle it until Cator stepped around the table and embraced his shoulders. Suddenly they were hugging each other and laughing through their tears.

Summer vacation arrived before they knew it. Thanks to the social workers, the school officials, and the local juvenile court judge, Ralph's custody was transferred from the state hospital to Cator Pershing. One month after the move, however, Ralph's mother was heard from again. Her welfare check had not arrived, and she was informed that since her son had been discharged from institutional care, the support money would now be provided to the individual who had been given custody. Mrs. Jorgenson was outraged and vowed to fight for her welfare money, even if it meant taking her son back. Cator Pershing had decided to place the money in a bank account for Ralph, and he was determined to fight the issue in court. The threats and verbal sparring stopped when the American Civil Liberties Union agreed to represent the aggrieved mother, and Cator committed most of his retirement savings to a legal defense.

Ralph remained insulated from the proceedings through it all. His waking hours were filled with school and work, and he was completely unaware that his life-style was being threatened. He noted the old man's escalating anxiety with increasing alarm, so the boy took on more of the work load as Cator's health seemed to fail.

The juvenile court and welfare officials colluded to delay the disposition hearing as long as possible, but a date was finally set for June 1, almost a year after Ralph had moved in with Cator Pershing. Two days before the hearing, however, the stress took its toll, and the old man fell victim to a stroke.

Ralph understood little of what had happened, but he blamed himself for his friend's death. He had returned from school that day just as the ambulance attendants were covering Cator's body, and a social worker found him sitting in the dark kitchen that night, just staring into space, slightly rocking his upper body in the straight-backed chair. She brought the boy directly to Dr. Medjid, at the state hospital, and there he received special care for the five days that were needed to prepare for his return home.

Mildred Jorgenson was filled with smug vindication when she learned of Cator Pershing's death and the imminent return of her son. It was God's way of making things right. The fifteen-year-old boy who stepped off the bus, however, bore no resemblance to the muscular eight-year-old she had last seen being hauled in chains to the local jail. All she saw was a waddling, shuffling mass of flesh standing next to the bus, looking lost, stupid, and confused. Her first instinct had been to turn and run, but it occurred to her that just as the Lord had provided her with victory, so was He now imposing His burden. Thus strengthened, she suppressed her shame and revulsion and stepped forward.

"You're Ralph?"

Just a nod.

"Follow me."

PART 3: *Tony, 1958–1963*

Chapter Thirteen: Tony, 1958–1963

Tony Washington did not have to open his eyes to know it was there. It was making no sound. Perhaps the rain splashing against the window and dripping on the floor was covering any noise it might be making. Taking care of that motherfucker was one of Tony's primary chores before he made his probable exit later that afternoon.

He could feel his little sister snuggling close with one small hand tucked under his ribs and her soft, warm breath tickling his back. She would be the one Tony would miss. But Booty was three, and it was time she learned to make it on her own. Tony and his little brothers babied her too much. It was her turn to grow up if she was going to survive. His throat was getting tight, and tears were squeezing through his closed eyelids. But the decision was made, and he was not about to start thinking and getting all confused again. There was too much to do, and it was getting late.

Tony quietly lifted his left arm and wiped his eyes with his closed fist before opening them to see that ugly old thing sniffing in the corner, not five feet from his nose. That was how he could tell when that old pisser came into the room—because it smelled like something dead. For two years Tony had tried to kill the rat, but only once had he come close. All he had learned from that experience was not to kick a cornered rat to death. The scars on his right leg began to itch just from his thinking about it. But this time the rat was going to be dead. It had to be dead because Tony would not leave knowing that filthy, snarling thing could again crawl up on their bed. Booty had to grow up and get wise—but not with the rat.

Tony inched his left hand under the pillow and felt the cold metal shaft of the slingshot he had swiped from Sears three days earlier. It was the super-heavy-duty type with thick yellow rubber and steel balls. For two days Tony had practiced firing while lying on his side. From the couch he could hit a matchbox ten feet away, but the matchbox did not move, and you could make all the noise you wanted while pulling and aiming. Hitting the thing was not the only problem. The rat was bigger than any cat in the neighborhood. The secret was loading and aiming the slingshot before the rat heard and dashed back through the hole behind the radiator.

As Tony wrapped the fingers of his left hand around the shaft, he realized there was another problem he had not thought of. That was the hand his old man had mangled two years before when Tony was eight. The crooked, bent fingers were stiff and weak—especially early in the morning. Under the pillow he slowly flexed his hand until the pain eased in the joints. It was now or never. With the left hand he inched the steel ball from his jeans pocket, all the while staring at the rat and praying it was preoccupied with the face of the doll it was chewing on. As he puled the slingshot out from under the pillow, the rubber caught on one of the loose mattress buttons, and made a muffled, snapping noise. The rat braced its front legs, took two jerky hops, and turned to stare at Tony. Its beady black eyes and body froze, but the nose and upper lip twitched up and down, exposing the yellow, protruding teeth. Tony stared back, hoping he could move slowly and evenly enough to avoid spooking it. After what felt like a whole day in school, the ball was in the leather sling. He was pulling back evenly when the rat turned again to run, but this time it was too late. The turning made it a bigger and better target. Tony released the leather pouch containing the small steel ball. There was a hollow thud as the projected missile entered the rat's body just behind the right front leg. The hairy scumbag seemed to stop in midair—and then it twisted its head around as if trying to bite at the hole that was just then beginning to ooze blood. After three swift complete rotations the rat dropped to the floor. Its snakelike black tail twitched and quivered as a greenish brown, runny ooze ran out of its butt. One of the front legs jerked, but the rat was dead.

"Holy shit, Tony, you killed the rat! You just up and killed the old rat!"

Tony had been hypnotized by his own concentration and was unaware that Booty and his two brothers were awake and taking in the whole gory scene. Tony had seen death before, but he had never witnessed such ugliness. He dropped the slingshot on the cracked linoleum floor and ran across the hall into the bathroom, where he vomited until his stomach ached.

Chapter Fourteen

Water streaked the walls and formed puddles on the cracked and splintered staircase. Tony supposed one of the toilets had backed up as he dodged and jumped, trying to avoid contact on his way to the front stoop. It wasn't necessary to push open the heavy door leading to the street. It lay on its side against the bank of rusted mailboxes.

There was a special place on the fifth step up from the sidewalk that had always been Tony's. From there one could see two blocks in each direction, or be on the street in one giant leap, or vault the short iron rail and be out of sight in a flash.

Tony could not remember when 16 Fourth Avenue had not been his home, his domain. But things had changed in the past five years. The buildings on both sides, 14 and 18, had been condemned. Most of his friends had left the neighborhood and moved into the new projects north of the boulevard. Murphy's Market, on the corner, was boarded up, and the pawnshop, across the street, just didn't open anymore. But the big white clock, with the pink neon light encircling and illuminating its face, was still in the shopwindow, behind the black metal gate.

It was now three minutes past nine. Tony figured he could sit there until nine-thirty before waking his mother and getting her ready for the long walk to the courthouse. This was his time. Perhaps it would be his last chance to look around and see things as they used to be, to remember the good old times, when he was a kid . . . when he was five.

*   *   *

Everything seemed to go back to that hot summer night five years earlier. The memory was so vivid that Tony imagined he could hear Rodney counting loudly to fifty before opening his eyes and seeking out the others. It was one of the few times Rodney and the other big boys had allowed little Tony to play. He remembered how excited he had been and how he giggled in his place. Timing. Tony knew it was only a matter of timing. If he jumped too fast, Rodney, closer to home base and a faster runner, would have time to turn and easily win the race to the lamppost. But if he waited until the last instant, he could jump out and streak past Rodney before there was time to react. Tony's legs flinched involuntarily as he relived his dash through the crowded street to the safety of home base a split second before the older boy.

Back then the street was always noisy and crowded. The memory was so vivid that Tony imagined he could hear the jazz music blaring through the open window of the Johnsons' first-floor front apartment. The mamas gathered on the steps, laughing with each other and yelling at their kids. The men stood in groups, prancing and jiving, speaking in shorthand, and ignoring the mamas and the kids.

Back then there were lots of people, and the people were happy. Maybe he had just been too young and stupid to see the problems, but now the street was all but abandoned, and the people who were left were mean and angry.

Tony wondered whether the whole thing might have started with his old man. David Washington had never been one to join the others on the street. He was one of the few men with a steady job. He would leave the apartment every afternoon at four, in his starched First National Bank security guard uniform. Mama would spend hours pressing those tan outfits just the way he liked them—trousers straight and stiff enough to stand on their own and two sharp creases down the front of every shirt.

He was not a tall man, but he was broad-shouldered and walked straight and proud. Whenever he stepped out onto that very porch, fat ol' Miz Johnson, practically filling the open window of her first-floor front, would give him a big OOWEEE and a couple of UMMM-UMS, and ol' Dad would walk down those steps as if he never heard a thing. The other men looked up to

Tony's father and treated him like a businessman, always greeting him politely instead of slapping hands or jiving.

When there was trouble, people came knocking at the Washingtons' door, and ol' Dad would send Tony and his brothers to their room. Booty wasn't born yet. Mama would pretend to be angry with him and ask how they would ever get their own house if they kept giving their money away to all the deadbeats and strangers. But you could tell she was proud to have people turn to the Washingtons for help.

Tony realized now that Rodney and the other big boys had allowed him to play with them because he was David Washington's son. And that's how people said it. "David" Washington. Not "Dave" or "Davie, baby." Always "David" Washington. At least that's how it had been until that night five years ago.

The anxiety associated with the memory was too much for Tony to control, so he jumped off the stoop and walked to Murphy's corner, where he had been hiding that night, ten thousand years ago.

Jesse James Willard had counted to fifty so fast that Tony had had barely enough time to duck out of sight. Jesse James opened his eyes and surveyed the street before warily moving in Tony's direction. Tony pressed himself against the wall of Murphy's store, aware that Jesse James was only a few steps away. Then he sidled through the open door and sprinted through the store to the back alley. There he flopped against the wall and smiled to himself. Safe at last.

The fading light of dusk had darkened the alley, but Tony failed to notice until the garbage can in back of the candy store fell over with a loud clatter. Suddenly the boy was alert to every movement, and when the compacted bulk of a man straightened in the shadows and staggered toward him, Tony pressed himself against the wall in terror.

The man passed under the light over Murphy's storeroom window, and Tony expelled his breath in relief. It was ol' Dad. Or was it? Tony peered through the darkness. It was ol' Dad all right, but something was wrong. The lunch pail hung limply from the end of his arm and flapped against his leg with every step, his shoulders were hunched, the starched uniform sagged, and he stumbled drunkenl as he walked.

David Washington passed Tony without seeing him. He turned the corner, walked up the street, and climbed the stairs leading to the apartment. The men he had passed stopped talking and began to gesture silently. The women were silent and stared after him. Where there had been laughter, there was mumbling, and even the children stopped playing. Rosa Lee sat motionless until her husband had pulled himself up the stoop. Then she stood and followed David through the door.

David Washington had lost his job. At first he had been accused of stealing trifles from the desks, but his supervisor later hinted that the bank president's son had a friend who needed a job. At first he was confused, but when the alcohol wore off, he became angry and resentful.

He answered the want ads, but every time he came close to landing a job he lost it. Rosa Lee blamed it on his drinking, but David was convinced that the false accusations were following him to every interview.

After three months the people from the furniture store came to pick up the bunk beds, the dinette set, and the new couch. Unable to deal with the shame of it, ol' Dad would stay out late and return drunk. The muffled arguments in the bedroom turned to screams, and Mama began to wear makeup to cover the bruised cheeks and black eyes.

Tony's father moved out two weeks before Christmas. Miss Engel, the social worker, arranged for emergency food and a small check to carry them over while their application for welfare was being processed.

By springtime his pretty mama was taking shots to relieve her pain and anxiety. Her addiction soon surpassed her ability to pay, so her supplier provided her with tight-fitting new clothes and began making appointments for her at the new Hilton, down by the river. Soon she developed into an adept free-lancer. If she got lucky, she would coax the john into her apartment, and while the trick was going down, Tony would sneak into the bedroom and take the money from his wallet.

By the time he was seven Tony Washington had become the

man of the house, and he had better things to do than go to school. The extra income had stopped three months before Booty was born, and after his little sister had arrived, the family's needs seemed greater than ever. Whenever money was scarce, Tony never hesitated to steal whatever they needed. He became a cold and calculating thief but retained enough of his boyish ways to charm himself out of trouble whenever caught.

As his criminal record grew, he saw less and less of Miss Engel, their social worker, and more of Mrs. Harris, his juvenile probation officer. Tony was proud of his accomplishment. How many other seven-year-olds had a JPO to run interference for him in court and to make excuses to the local merchants? He had learned to play on Mrs. Harris's sympathies and manipulate her responses with great success.

For her part, Wilma Harris was convinced that Tony was worth saving. Whenever he skipped school, she found him taking care of his brothers or changing Booty's diapers; if he was caught shoplifting, it invariably was food or toys for the other children. She had fought for him for more than four years, and she would continue to do so, but he was only a boy, and he was beginning to feel the pressure of trying to be a father as well.

Tony looked at the pawnshop clock and saw that it was time to wake his mama. He shook off the big black bug that had perched on his shoe, and he returned to the apartment. If he didn't hurry, they would be late for the hearing.

Chapter Fifteen

When they were a block from the courthouse, Rosa Lee stopped him. "I'm not going in there until you tell me what you've done this time."

Tony looked up at her and shrugged his shoulders. "It's the same as last week," he said. "The judge wants me to fink on Rudy and Frank, and he's goin' to send me away if I don't." He yanked on her hand and urged, "C'mon, Mama. We'll be late."

Her shrouded mind began to clear. "Rudy and Frank? Those men are bad, son. What are you going to tell the judge? They'll hurt you for sure."

"I tol' you, Mama, the judge said he'd send me up if I don't tell him." Tony looked at her sadly. Except for the puffy eyes, she was still pretty, but something was missing. Her skin was dull, her eyelids sagged, and the sparkle seemed to have gone out of her. She lived in a drugged fog and most of the time made no sense at all. "Don' worry, Mama, I won't say nothin'."

Rosa Lee was relieved. She was more frightened of threats from the street than of anything a judge might do. Besides, she had already seen too many judge-and-Tony shows to be worried about her son. "You can con that old honky, baby. I know you can."

"Maybe," he said dubiously. "But you gotta promise me you'll keep quiet, no matter what. If Frank and Rudy think we said something, they'll get us both."

* * *

The only empty chair in the waiting room was in the corner, behind a wilted rubber tree. Tony sat his mother down and found her a magazine to use as a fan. Then he walked across the hall to his JPO's office.

Wilma Harris met him at the door. "Is your mother here?" she asked.

"Yeah." He pointed toward the corner, where Rosa Lee was already asleep.

Wilma's face tightened. "Let's leave her be for now. Come on in." Wilma was angry. "You said you would come in last Wednesday to talk this thing over."

Tony swung his legs back and forth under the chair. "I guess I forgot," he mumbled without looking up.

She walked to the corner of her desk and crossed her arms over her chest. That was the signal that an angry lecture was coming. Tony didn't mind the lectures, but he liked her and was uncomfortable when she was angry. They had been together for four years, and he had confessed most of his sins during that time, but this case was different. He was holding out, and she knew it.

The determination in his face softened her anger. "You're not going to tell the judge about those two boys, are you?"

"How come you don' believe me?" he pleaded. "There was *no* two boys with me." How he wished they *had* been boys.

"It won't do you any good to continue with that story, Tony. The police grabbed you while the other two ran. Why must you continue this ludicrous charade?" Wilma's voice had risen in frustration.

"There was no two boys," he mumbled.

"I warn you, Tony. You're not going to walk clean this time. This judge means what he says, and no cute-little-Tony routine is going to save you. I've never lost a child to Clearwater," she said grimly, "but that's where you're going if you don't cooperate."

When he looked at her this time, the resolve in his face had hardened.

"That's it then. It's out of my hands," she said. "Go get your mother, and bring her into the courtroom."

Tony stood and walked to the door. He turned back to her

and wanted to tell her it was all right. He wanted to, but the words would not come, so he turned and left her office.

The bailiff did not need to tell Tony where to sit or where to deposit his mother. Judge Shapiro sat at the head of the table, Wilma Harris to his right, Tony and his mother next to her, and a man they called the guardian ad litem across from them. No matter who the judge was, he always started with the explanation that his guardian ad litem was an attorney appointed by the court to protect the legal interests of the juvenile. Tony was never clear about what his legal interests were, but if the dude wanted to protect them, it was okay with him.

Tony was always fascinated by the bigness of the wood table. Not only did its shiny bulk fill the room, but it was so tall that he could lean his chin on it without stooping. And the chairs were made so that little kids would fall through the gaps in back if they tried to lean against them. Tony was small for his age, but this courtroom made him feel dwarfed and lost. Maybe that's why he acted like a fool whenever he was there. Mrs. Harris called it "being cute," but Tony had learned long ago that when you are small and weak in a world where grown-ups called the shots, being cute was a good way to survive.

Even when he asked an honest question, grown-ups thought he was trying to be cute. During one of the previous hearings, when four of the Washington children were there, Booty fell through one of the chairs. Tony was upset enough to demand to know why everything was so big if the courtroom was supposed to be for kids. The judge laughed and called him "a cute character if there ever was one."

But today no one was laughing. Judge Shapiro did not wear a robe like the real judges Tony had seen on TV, and the thick gray hair framing the bald spot on top of his head stuck out in all directions. If he weren't so serious, he would have looked like Bozo the Clown. Judge Shapiro rapped his fancy hammer and said, "This is a continuation of last week's hearing. There will be no formal case presentation." The judge studied each person at the table over his funny little half glasses. When he looked at Tony, he said, "My question is the same as it was last week, young man.

Who was with you the night you broke into Patterson's Pharmacy?"

Tony stared at his own reflection in the polished table. His hands gripped the table leg he was straddling, but he did not move.

The judge changed tactics. "Rosa Lee, do you understand the seriousness of these charges?"

"Oh, yes, Judge, I understand how serious this is."

Tony was surprised she had heard the question. The last thing he needed was for his mama to start talking. He was relieved when the judge decided to make a speech.

"For everyone's sake, especially yours, Tony, let me summarize the situation. You were apprehended at the scene of a break-in at Patterson's Pharmacy. You were in the company of two older boys, who escaped. The MO of the Patterson break-in matches those of four other pharmacy burglaries."

Having recited the facts in the case, Judge Shapiro sounded solicitous. "It's those older boys that I want, not you, Tony. Those boys have already marketed the stolen drugs on the street. I'm sure of that. You are too young to have known what you were doing, but I will not have those other two running the streets. I want their names."

In the face of the boy's silence, the judge turned again to Rosa Lee. "Madam, this is your last opportunity to spare your son from the reformatory. If you have any influence over him at all, I urge you to talk some sense into his head."

"Please, baby, tell your mama who those boys were." There were tears in Rosa Lee's eyes as she pleaded with her son. She clutched at his arm and sobbed. "Please. They'll take you away. Who were they?"

Tony stared at her in shock. She had really forgotten! The reality of her disintegration came crashing down on Tony, and he jumped up, screaming, "*No!* Dammit, *no, no, no!*"

The quiet courtroom came to life. Wilma Harris reached to restrain the boy and made a plea of her own, Rosa Lee wailed hysterically and threw her arms around Tony's neck, and the guardian ad litem strained to be heard over the banging of Judge Shapiro's gavel.

When order was finally restored, Mama was humming quietly

to herself as she rocked in her chair; she did not hear the judge pass sentence on her son.

"Tony Washington, you are hereby committed to the Boys' Industrial School at Clearwater on an indeterminate sentence. The bailiff will transport you to the county detention home." The judge looked at Rosa Lee compassionately. "Mrs. Harris, I suggest that you escort Mrs. Washington home and check on the other children."

When Judge Shapiro stood and looked at Tony, the anger returned to his face. "I don't know how you could have done this to your own mother," he said. "You will be in the detention home for three days. If you change your mind, let me know."

PART 4:
Three for the System, August 1963

Chapter Sixteen: Matt

The days following the hearing passed slowly for Matt, and he lost track of time. Lew Walters decided that Matt might do anything to avoid being sent to reform school, so he ordered the cell to remain locked at all times, and he alerted his staff to guard against another suicide attempt.

Matt spent most of his time during the first few days pacing the confines of his tiny cell, reliving the anguish and frustration of being caged without reason or recourse. The deputies agreed to give him enough distance to work things out on his own, so no one spoke to him for three days.

On the morning of the fourth day Matt was awakened by the new night man as he pushed the breakfast tray through the slot at the bottom of the barred door. A long-forgotten image— only a fleeting picture— flashed through the boy's mind: He and his father were standing outside another cage, and Dan was tossing pieces of food through the wire. Matt struggled with the image, trying to call it back for a closer inspection, but it seemed beyond his control as the picture flashed across his mind repeatedly, like rapidly moving slides across a screen.

It was a silly game, but it was better than the boredom. It was like trying to remember the words to a tune that was haunting him; he couldn't get it out of his mind, yet he was unable to bring it into focus. Suddenly he saw six mangy mule deer inside the cage, and when he saw the young child wrapped around Dan's leg, Matt realized it was a scene from his own childhood. Enjoying a sense of real accomplishment about having solved the riddle, he jumped from his cot and dispatched the cold breakfast with new-found enthusiasm.

It occurred to Matt that it would be fun to share his pleasure with someone, but he suddenly realized that Charlie Sanner had not been around the jail since they had returned from the hearing. He shrugged away his curiosity and decided to return to the game of trying to relive his past, the ultimate challenge being his ability to recall minute details that might have escaped conscious recognition the first time around.

He thought about the spring roundups when his father had played center stage as the most accomplished broncobuster in the basin, and he smiled as he remembered Dan's pride when Matt became the youngest of the cowboys to tame the rank horses driven in from the winter range. Matt was only ten years old when he broke his first horse, and he had reveled in the good-natured teasing and backslapping of the older men. Dan had shared his pleasure but found it necessary to deflate his son's ego by welcoming him to the fraternity with the offer of his first—and last—plug of chewing tobacco.

Matt often daydreamed at the tiny window in his cell. One warm day in July he gazed off at the distant peaks and realized sadly that the gentian blossoms would soon be in full flower. A group of Northern Cheyenne had taught Oren how to grind the roots of the precious plant and administer the resulting mash for stomach ailments. Oren had converted the formula for use with his stock and passed on the ancient remedy to Dan, who subsequently shared it with Matt.

For as long as he could remember, Matt used to look forward to the mid-July trek with great anticipation. Unpredictable climatic conditions would dictate the precise time for harvesting the roots, so it was impossible to plan in advance for the exact moment. Matt would restrain his impatience until Dan's pronouncement that the time was right, triggering a flurry of activity that would end with their predawn departure into the mountains.

Their unchanging routine would see them resting the horses at the point on the face of the mountain where they could see the panorama of the basin below and the frightening shadows of Avalanche Pass to the north. The next leg of the long journey took them through the perpetually fog-shrouded pass and on toward the snow-covered peaks of Broken Man Mountain. On the way they fished for trout in the headwaters of Tensleep Creek and fried their catch among the iridescent fireweed that sprang from the carpet of moss along the banks.

Three hours away was the abandoned mine that usually served as their shelter for the evening. Unworked for more than fifty years, the mine was capped by a tower built from native lodgepole pine bleached white by the sun and snow. The dry mountain air had preserved the integrity of the timbers in the shaft, so whenever time permitted, Dan would lead Matt through the maze of tunnels, identifying specimens of rock in the outcroppings and occasionally scratching the surface for an elusive vein of gold. Matt, who hated confined places, never outgrew his dislike of the black caverns, but the pleasure of sharing his father's interest in mineralogy more than made up for his discomfort.

They would break camp before sunup and ride east, guiding themselves by the giant silhouette of Steamboat Tower, and the first rays of morning would find them on a level plateau surrounded by trees and covered with high grass through which the purple gentian erupted for a few short weeks in late July. The place had originally been named Oren Park, in honor of the boy who had been led there by his friends the Cheyenne fifty years earlier, but a later cartographer recorded it as *Autumn* Park, perhaps by error but perhaps in deference to the seasonal brilliance of the golden aspen trees that surrounded the area.

The routine that was started by Oren, then shared with Dan and later with Matt had survived long enough to become a ritual. They would invariably approach the park silently and stop on the fringe of the surrounding aspen grove, surveying the area upwind for grazing elk and deer and celebrating the miracle of the magnificent purple gentian. If the breeze was from the east, they were certain to find big game in the park, and they would sit astride their mounts for as long as it took for the animals to wander off, unmolested and unfrightened. Then Dan would extract two gunnysacks and toss the smaller one to his son. Matt would set about digging the tender roots of the younger plants, while Dan concentrated on the older gentian the more potent roots of which would provide stronger medicine for horses.

Matt was beginning to reconstruct the return trip when his wistful reverie was interrupted by the sound of his cell door's being unlocked, something that had not happened very often since the hearing. He turned questioningly and was pleased to see Charlie Sanner standing there—a worried expression on his face and the familiar sack of hamburgers in his hand.

"Where've you been all week?" Matt asked pleasantly.

"I've been gone more'n two weeks," Charlie said.

Matt shrugged his shoulders. "I guess I lost track of time."

Charlie was plainly concerned. "That's what they tell me," he said. "I understand you've been doing a lot of moping around. You feeling okay?"

Matt waved away Charlie's concern with one hand and reached for the hamburgers with the other, chuckling "I swear, you're getting more like old Martha every day."

"Maybe so, but you look like hell," Charlie scolded him. Relieved to discover that Matt was still in touch with reality, the deputy sat on one end of the cot and watched the boy open the sack of hamburgers at the other end. "How're you doing?" he asked softly.

"Great," Matt answered with exaggerated enthusiasm. "I have my own private bathroom," he said, gesturing over his shoulder toward the stark commode and sink behind him, "and my own bedroom." He thumped the cot loudly.

"And still a smart-ass," Charlie said with feigned disgust. He watched Matt devour the three hamburgers, then observed, "They tell me you've been kinda quiet, but there's nothing wrong with your appetite, is there?"

"Naw, I've just been spending a lot of time thinking. It's so boring in here . . . nothing to do . . . ever."

"What've you been thinking about?"

"Just stuff," Matt said with a shrug. "You know . . . when I was a kid and stuff like that."

"Your father?"

"Yeah, I think a lot about him, too. But it's like he's been gone a long time, you know? Sometimes it's like he never existed, and sometimes I get to laughing about things we did."

"Like what?" Charlie asked, trying to keep Matt talking.

"Well, this morning . . . no, yesterday . . . whenever . . . I was thinking about the time I broke my first horse out at the Callison place. It was like a regular rodeo. Everyone cheering and all. Then they started beating me all over with their hats and laughing, and I felt like hot stuff. Then my dad broke off a plug"— he laughed—"and I puked all the way to the outhouse and back."

Charlie joined in the laughter and added his own recollections of the roundups and brandings he had seen, with special emphasis on the fried chicken and potato salad, which had always been prepared in advance, and the Rocky Mountain oysters, which were always fried on the spot.

Matt's eyes glazed over in fond recollection of those warm and happy times, and he absentmindedly pulled out his father's watch and rolled it around the palm of his hand.

"What's that you got there?" Charlie asked.

"What, this?" Matt asked, holding up the watch. "It's my father's. You've seen it before."

"Yeah, I was going to ask you about that," Charlie said. "We ought to get it cleaned and oiled before you leave for Clearwater. You know, just in case."

Matt was reluctant. "I don't know," he said. "This is the only thing I have left of his." Then Matt balanced the gold plate that hung from the chain and read the inscription to himself: "To Daniel McFadden . . . A man I am proud to have as my son . . . Love, Pa."

"Oh, c'mon, nobody's gonna eat it. I'll have it back to you in a few days."

The following week, almost a month after the hearing, Warren Stiles arrived at the jail to inform Matt that he would be transported to Clearwater the following day. Matt did not react outwardly to the news because Charlie had been preparing him for this inevitable moment, but the boy awoke in the middle of the night bathed in perspiration and trembling with fear.

Chapter Seventeen

Charlie Sanner removed Matt's handcuffs as soon as the security lock had been set on the passenger side of the patrol car. "Might as well make yourself comfortable," he said. "It's a good four hours over to Clearwater."

Matt sat quietly and reviewed the busy morning with mixed feelings. Judge Turner had been the first of several visitors who had come to the jail to say their good-byes. He arrived before breakfast, looking haggard and drawn. He informed Matt that he had continued to search for an acceptable foster home, hoping to be able to modify his decision, but there were no openings for a teenage boy with Matt's record. The judge had hoped that the boy might be pleased to learn that he had not given up, but he came across as a man trying desperately to defend himself and expunge his guilt. The conversation further served to assure Matt that he himself was too odious a creature to be taken in by decent families.

Judge Turner realized that his visit had managed to depress the boy even more than he'd been so he left the cell, assuring Matt that he would be welcomed back to the basin as soon as he was released from Clearwater. Thinking back to the judge's offer, Matt smiled ruefully at the prospect of returning to that place, and his thoughts then turned to his final visitors, Frank and Martha Johnson.

Frank, too, had tried to soothe his guilt. "Goddammit, Lew, I didn't want it to turn out this way," he growled at the sheriff. "You know that."

"Sure, sure, Frank, your heart is as big as your gut," the sheriff said indifferently, ignoring the rancher while he completed the commitment papers and gathered Matt's personal belongings.

"I don't like your attitude, Lew," Johnson complained. "If you'd done your job that first night . . ."

"Matt? Are you awake?" Martha Johnson had walked to Matt's cell, and her voice startled the boy, who was lying on his cot, unemotionally absorbed in Frank Johnson's bleating protests.

The sad face of Martha Johnson appeared ready to dissolve into tears again, and Matt swung his feet to the floor and pushed himself to a sitting position. "Yes, I'm awake," he said listlessly.

"We heard you were leaving this morning."

Matt shrugged his shoulders in response.

"They say you'll be attending school where you're going. Regular classes and all."

"They're taking me to another jail, Mrs. Johnson," Matt said coldly.

The woman recognized the rebuke and responded in kind. "It's a place for older children," she said firmly. "They will take care of you until you are old enough to take care of yourself." Matt looked up at her without responding while she struggled to maintain her composure. "Anyway, that's not why we came." Now she was looking down, clasping her hands together. "I spoke to Frank about the money."

Matt had no idea what she was talking about, but his curiosity was piqued. "What money?" he asked.

"You told me about the money your father had in his wallet that night," she said.

Matt jumped to his feet and approached the bars. "The hundred and eighty dollars?"

She nodded once and added quickly, "They would have taken it away from you, and you never would have seen it again," obviously repeating her husband's words. "Frank told me he was keeping it for you. Anyway, I—we put it in your Christmas Club, and you can pick it up at the bank when you come back."

Matt was relieved to know he had been right all along, but he changed the subject. "What about my horse?"

"Frank said he would take care of your—the horse until you come back; then he will let you finish up the payments."

Matt's lethargy left him, and his alert eyes darted to Frank Johnson, who now stood quietly across the small room, listening to his wife. Frank nodded his head in confirmation. "It's a straight business deal," he said brusquely. "When they let you out, we'll figure up what you owe me, including the board. If you can pay it off, we'll see what we can do."

Martha turned and glared, forcing her husband into further concessions. "The horse will be here," he said petulantly. "And I won't charge you extra unless it costs me . . . for a veterinarian or whatever."

"And?" Martha prodded impatiently.

Frank shifted his weight and continued. "And if we breed her, I'll give you credit for half."

Matt suppressed a happy impulse to shout. Instead, he said warily, "I'll be away for three years."

"I know. I won't forget," Johnson assured him gruffly. "Besides, you spoiled that bonehead so bad she's no good for anything else anyway."

Matt smiled to himself as he thought about Johnson's discomfort. He and Charlie had been driving for two hours, and neither had said a word. Matt wanted to open a conversation, but he didn't know how to begin. Then he realized that Charlie was too serious for light banter, so he broke the long silence with a question: "What's it really like, Charlie? Mrs. Johnson said it would be like a regular school."

The grim-faced deputy glanced at Matt, then returned his eyes to the road while he formulated his answer. The question had been asked only as a way of breaking the ice, but Charlie's reluctance to respond began to concern the boy. "C'mon, Charlie, you told me you were going to find out all there was to know about Clearwater . . . so there wouldn't be any surprises. Remember?"

"I remember," Charlie said.

"Then how come you didn't do it?"

"I did that, and a lot more," he said, glancing again at Matt.

"I got the complete book about Clearwater, and I checked out every other place to hell and gone." Then Charlie grinned for the first time. "Believe me, I know more about Clearwater than any cockroach in the joint. I made two visits personally."

"Why didn't you tell me?"

"I didn't tell you because I wasn't sure you wanted to know."

"Well, I do want to know," Matt assured him firmly.

"I've been wanting to talk to you for a long time," Charlie said, "but you haven't been yourself since the hearing, and I didn't want you to feel worse. I knew the judge was still trying to find a foster home for you, and I kept hoping he would do it."

"Sounds like it's pretty bad," Matt murmured.

"It's bad enough, but you can take it. It sure as hell is better than a lot of other places."

Matt repeated his initial question: "What's it like, Charlie? You said you'd tell me the truth."

Charlie hesitated for a moment; then he said, "The bad part is that all those places are basically the same. You already found out you're too young to have any rights, and they won't let you forget that for a minute. All those systems are designed to make you forget you're a person and if you ever believe it, you're dead. You understand?"

Matt furrowed his brow and shook his head. "I don't think so . . . I'm not sure."

"There'll be a bunch of kids your age being admitted at the same time. You'll all be treated alike. First they'll shave your heads and spray for lice. Then they'll ream out your butts to find out how rotten your insides are. Then they'll give you some faded blue clothes so you look like everyone else. Everyone looks the same, and if you believe the crap they tell you, you'll all start acting the same."

"What should I do?"

"*Always remember who you are,*" Charlie said. "It's as simple as that. There's going to be some bad little dudes up there, and it's going to be easier to start acting like them instead of being yourself, but if you do that, you'll come out a lot worse off then you are right now."

"I don't think that's possible."

"Don't go feeling sorry for yourself, Matt. You just keep thinking about the good things you got waiting for you when you get out. You got friends. You can come and live with me and get a job. You got a horse. . . ."

"I wish I hadn't asked," Matt said.

"Listen, I've only told you the bad part," Charlie assured him. "In the first place, a lot of the boys are just like you. There *are* some bad asses, for sure, but most of the others are there because there's no place else for them to go. Some of them have been beat up by their parents . . . or abandoned. Some are there only because they refuse to go to school . . . or maybe they have no parents at all."

Charlie waited for the information to sink in, but the frown on Matt's face suggested considerable disbelief. "In the second place," Charlie continued, "the superintendent is a young guy, Gary Masters, who really cares about the kids. You stay straight with him, and he'll take care of you"

"Are you telling me the truth?" Matt asked thoughtfully.

"He's the best I've ever seen," Charlie asserted.

"No, I mean, about the other kids? If a kid is beaten up by his parents, are you saying they can send the *kid* to jail?"

"They *can*, and they *do*," Charlie said firmly. "All the time!"

"That's crazy! For playing hooky, too?"

"That's right."

"How can they do that? I mean, why?"

"Judge Turner said it to you a dozen times," Charlie said. "There's no place else to send these kids. If there's no parents or relatives or if the parents don't want the kid, the judge has no choice. They take a shot at the foster home routine. Then, when that doesn't work out, they have to send the kid to reform school."

Charlie continued to talk about the situation in Clearwater, but Matt was lost in his own thoughts. The terrain was beginning to flatten out, and Matt realized that he was entering a new world. He had never before traveled to a place where there were no mountains to be seen, and he felt exposed and vulnerable. The mountains had always provided him with boundaries and a sense of security, but now the land was flat and barren, and he was suddenly frightened.

"Break out the sandwiches," Charlie said, tossing a large brown bag into Matt's lap. "Ham and cheese. My landlady made 'em up special. Coffee's in the thermos on the back seat."

Matt followed instructions, trying to cope silently with the strange things he was feeling, but Charlie was determined not to give him any more time for thinking. "I spent a lot of time with this colored kid up there—John Culver's his name. A big kid—about your size—maybe a little older than you," Charlie said between bites of his ham sandwich. "Hell of a kid. Works in admissions, so I asked him to be on the lookout for you."

"He's my age and works in a reform school?" Matt asked.

"No, he works there, but he's an inmate," Charlie said. "Hell of a kid. You're gonna like him."

"What's he in for, tying his shoelaces wrong?" Matt asked sarcastically.

"I didn't ask," Charlie admitted, "but you're gonna like him. Smart as hell."

"I don't know any colored people," Matt said musingly.

"Sure you do! What about Ernie Pruitt at the gas station . . . and old what's his name . . . Campbell? He's got a kid your age, doesn't he?"

"Oh, right," Matt agreed. "I guess I never noticed."

"Well, anyway, John Culver's his name, and he's been there long enough to know his way around. He'll take care of you."

"Terrific," Matt said sarcastically, thinking how little comfort one loser was going to provide for another loser.

"We'll be coming up on it pretty soon," Charlie said. "Off to the right, up on a hill."

Matt looked out and saw that the flat terrain was broken by intermittent mounds rising above the plowed fields, and as they drove farther, the surface of the land swelled to undulating hills.

"There it is," Charlie announced, pointing off to the right.

On top of the tallest hill, about a mile away, Matt saw a large white building that looked to him like a square castle overlooking its domain. He opened his mouth to speak, but all that came out was a croaking sound. He shook his head and cleared his throat. "Is that it? Is that all of it?"

Charlie laughed and said, "No, from down here you can only see that administration building. The other buildings are behind it. Pretty soon we turn off the highway and get on the institution road. I'll drive clear around it and show you before we go in. We're a little early yet."

As they got closer, Matt could see that the brick building was three stories tall, painted white, and even though it was a simple oblong structure, there was a bigness about it that exuded authority. Charlie turned off the highway and followed the narrow blacktop road straight up the hill. Before long, Matt could make out a tall chain-link fence with a barbed-wire overhang that enclosed the administration building. It occurred to him that if the rest of the place was as creepy as that building, the authorities were going to need every bit of that fence to keep him there.

By the time they reached the top of the hill Matt could see the rest of the institution, and it was not as ominous as he had feared. Except for the tall wire fence surrounding the entire area and the bars on most of the buildings, it was a pleasant scene. The buildings faced a common square that looked like a manicured park with beautiful trees and colorful well-trimmed shrubs. The lawn was approximately two blocks long and a half block wide. Charlie pointed out the white two-story school building and gymnasium, the older red-brick admissions building and lockup units, and the three red-brick dormitories, known as cottages.

Charlie noted the tension building in Matt's face and hands, but he continued to rattle on, fearful of losing control of his own emotions. "That old barn isn't used much anymore," he said lightly. "I guess they gave up on that 'farming makes healthy boys' theory, especially since most of these kids come straight out of the city and don't know which end of the cow squirts milk."

"I don't want to go in there, Charlie," Matt whispered hoarsely.

The forced smile evaporated, and Charlie said softly, "I know, kid." Then he pulled off the road and stopped. "We don't have a choice, Matt. You know that."

"I can't help it," the boy said. "I'm really scared." There were no tears in Matt's eyes, but his compressed lips trembled, and his voice broke.

Charlie reached into his pocket and pulled out a small box. "You don't need to be scared, Matt. You're strong enough to make it." He opened the box and took out Daniel's gold watch. A second plate was now attached to the chain. "Your daddy was gonna give you this watch for your birthday. He asked the jeweler to make up another inscription before he died, and I had it attached to the chain." He held the watch out and said, "Take it. I want you to read what it says."

Matt took the watch in both hands and tilted the second plate toward the sun to read the inscription: "To Matt . . . my son, my best friend, and the McFadden with the best of all our pasts." He read it twice, and the fifteen-year-old boy became a man. Matt simply nodded his head and said, "Okay, Charlie."

Chapter Eighteen: Ralph

Soon after his return home Ralph despaired of his mother's capacity for love and understanding. Mildred Jorgenson had locked him away in her tiny apartment. She was willing to suffer her penance privately, but the loathsome perversion that was her son would never be seen on the streets of Drury if she could help it.

He kept away from her as much as he could, just to avoid the disgust and disapproval in her eyes. He would occasionally sneak out for long walks in the middle of the night, then sleep away most of the day.

It took fewer than three months for Mildred to decide that she had done enough penance, but then her God sent a timely message: The welfare checks began to arrive again. Nothing changed for Ralph, but the security of a place to live would spare him the shame of returning to the state hospital.

Soon after his sixteenth birthday, however, Ralph's case came up for periodic review, and the department of mental health finally concluded that he was neither brain-damaged nor retarded. Mildred was jolted by the prospect of again losing the welfare money, but her spirits soared when she learned that Cator Pershing had set aside almost $2,000 in a bank account for her son.

For the next three months Mildred Jorgenson was happier than she had ever been, and Ralph dared dream that his nightmare was over. His depression lifted, and he gladly respected her wish that he stay off the streets at night. But Mildred's forbearance eroded with the steady outflow of cash, and Ralph took to the streets again, a shuffling, stiff-jointed hulk on the darkened sidewalks and back roads of Drury.

Eleven months after Ralph had been returned to her, Mildred finally freed herself of the burden by disclosing to the sheriff that the fearsome "night prowler" was her own son, not the imaginings of some late-night drunks.

Ralph was returned to the state hospital over the strong protests of the staff. Batteries of psychological tests were performed, verified, reported, then repeated; all of them showed him to be educationally and socially disadvantaged but intellectually capable of leading a relatively normal life.

At first he was treated like an orderly, assigned to light work in the hospital and permitted to eat with the staff. He showed no emotion whatever unless his old friends from the School for the Deaf tried to visit him. Then his anger and shame were expressed in his adamant refusal to see them. Meanwhile, his free time was spent alone in his room . . . rocking.

After six months in the state hospital it was finally decided that it would be inappropriate to keep him there and impossible to send him home. The only alternative was the one chosen.

On his seventeenth birthday, Ralph was remanded to the Clearwater Boys' Industrial School—the state reformatory.

Chapter Nineteen: Tony

The Wagner County Detention Facility had become Tony Washington's second home over the past four years. In addition to the five times he had been sent there as a juvenile delinquent, he and his brothers had been taken in four times for custodial care following their mother's arrests for prostitution.

Detention had become a reprieve from the craziness in Tony's life. The food was good, the beds were clean, and the people were nice. It was a place he had come to know and trust. The other kids complained about having to make their beds and carry their food trays to the kitchen, but that was all they were asked to do, and for Tony, it was pure vacation.

When Judge Shapiro's bailiff delivered him to the front door, the old man thought he had stumbled into a family reunion. Three workers on break in the canteen next to the office rushed out to greet Tony, and he jumped into their arms with a wild whoop. As soon as the intake procedures had been completed, the bailiff left the building, shaking his head in disbelief, and Tony ran to the kitchen to hug Elsie, the cook. Elsie was fat, and ugly, and gruff. She came off as pure mean, but any kid who knew anything about detention loved Elsie and her big old cinnamon rolls.

Wilma Harris visited Tony every day, each time assuring him that Rosa Lee and the children would also come to say their good-byes. On the morning of the fourth day, however, the deputy arrived to take him to Clearwater, and Tony was relieved that his mother had not made it in to see him off. He knew how hard it would have been for all of them, especially Booty, who would

cry and cling to his neck. Booty was his. By the time she came
into the world the Washington family had become a nightmare.
Tony had had to feed and bathe her, change her diapers, and rock
her to sleep. She was pure, and clean, and untainted. He had
wanted to keep her that way, but it wasn't working.

Tony knelt on the front seat and waved to the staff as the
deputy took his place behind the wheel. "Buckle 'em up, Tony,"
the deputy said.

When the boy sat down and fastened the safety belt, the seat
seemed to swallow him. The only things he could see at his eye
level were the glove compartment in front, the door handle to his
right, and the deputy's elbow to the left. This suited him fine
while they were driving through the city because Tony could see
the tops of the tall buildings through the window. Then there
were fewer buildings and more telephone poles, but Tony was
still content. But soon, when the tops of huge trees supplanted
the buildings in Tony's line of sight, he became curious.

"This gonna be a long trip?" he asked the deputy.

"About four hours," he said. Then, with a friendly grin, he
asked, "Why? Do you have another appointment?"

"Uhh-uhh," Tony replied, "no other 'pointment, but I'd sure
like to see outside."

"What?"

"We still in the city?"

"Of course not."

"We in the country, right?"

The deputy looked at the boy without answering, wondering
what he was getting at.

"I never been in the country before. I'd sure like to look out
the window."

"Oh, damn, Tony, I'm sorry." The deputy laughed. "These
patrol cars weren't built for tiny desperadoes like you, were they?
Sure. Make yourself comfortable."

"If it would make you feel better, you could put those bracelets on me," Tony suggested, pointing to the handcuffs dangling
from the dashboard.

"I'll take my chances." The deputy laughed again.

Tony's face reflected his concern. "You'll use them later, won't you? The handcuffs, I mean . . . when we get to Clearwater. I wouldn't want to walk in naked."

"Yeah, we got your reputation to consider, don't we? Let me think on it." he said with appropriate gravity. "Meanwhile, why don't you climb up on the seat and take a look at the scenery?"

Tony released the safety belt and jumped to his knees. His city was disappearing on the horizon, and he was flooded with conflicting feelings. He was leaving everyone and everything he had ever known, but Frank and Rudy had made it too dangerous for him to remain. Satisfied that every mile was putting more distance between him and certain danger, Tony relaxed and tried to sort through the chain of events that had led him to this predicament.

He had underestimated Frank and Rudy. They were a couple of small-time local hoods who would get lost if they wandered three blocks from their own manhole covers. The two "boys" the judge and everyone else had been yapping about were thirty-five-year-old men who would kill their grandmothers for a sawbuck. Tony had been their passkey to the high-security drugstores. He could crawl through heat vents too small for others and provide access for the men without setting off burglar alarms.

On the Patterson's Pharmacy job Frank and Rudy had taken off as soon as they heard the sirens, but Tony knew he could not run as fast as they, so he hid himself in the bathroom and pried open a drainpipe to store the stolen bottles of drugs.

Two days before his trial he returned to Patterson's and retrieved the drugs. Fair was fair. Frank and Rudy had left him holding the bag, so he figured that he owned the bag. Tony sold the drugs to one of the local pushers and left the money with Rosa Lee.

Everything would have worked out perfectly except the drug dealer hit the streets without removing the pills from the Patterson bottles. Two of his buyers were Frank and Rudy. They had been outsmarted by a kid. They put the word out that Tony was dead.

Maybe the judge was right when he had said that Clearwater was no picnic, but then neither was 16 Fourth Avenue.

BOOK II:

The System

Chapter Twenty

The doors to the outside world slammed shut for Matt at the massive entrance to the old administration building of the Clearwater Boys' Industrial School. A guard had taken the commitment papers from Charlie Sanner, signed a receipt for the boy, and led Matt to the superintendent's office.

The thirty-five-year-old superintendent gave the impression of being older than he was. Gary Masters was about the same height as Charlie, a little over six feet tall and slender, but his hair was prematurely gray. His complexion was fair—almost too light for August. He looked to Matt like the sort of men in magazine ads—the kind of man who should be wearing a vested suit and running a large corporation. There was a gentleness about the man's features and general demeanor that was heightened by his casual clothes and friendly smile.

"You must be Matt," he said, extending his right hand.

"Yes," the boy said, shaking hands with some discomfort. The cowboys and ranchers from his part of the country were not "touchers" among strangers, and they shared their natural distrust of "glad-handers." There was something about the superintendent's appearance, however, that was reassuring. There were laughter lines in his face, but the deep furrows in his brow and the sadness in his eyes conveyed a sense of compassion.

"Where's Charlie?" Masters asked pleasantly.

"He left," Matt said, aware that Masters had already assessed the angry red scar around his neck.

"Sorry I missed him. He's quite a character. We could use a

lot more like him in this business." Still holding Matt's hand in his own, Masters put his left hand on the boy's shoulder. "Come on in. Charlie has told me a good deal about you."

Thirty years earlier the superintendent's office had been built to convey the impression of authority: dark mahogany paneling, molded plaster ceilings, and plush dark blue carpeting. The atmosphere had intimidated legions of already frightened children over the years, but the effects of the perennial cost-cutting initiatives were evident in the fact that the paneled walls were now marred and scratched, the ceilings were cracked, and there were worn paths in the carpet. The rusted air conditioner in the window jangled and popped loudly.

Matt surveyed the shoddy room and wondered if the rest of the place looked that bad. "Don't worry"—Masters laughed, correctly interpreting Matt's concerned expression,—"this is as bad as it gets around here."

Gary Masters motioned for Matt to sit in the worn chair across from his desk and said, "I understand you are a good student."

Matt shrugged. "Charlie said I might be able to finish high school in two years if I worked real hard."

"That's right, but don't consider that a promise," Masters said. "Frankly our high school is easier than most, but our expectations of you will depend on your ability, so you will have to work very hard if you want to finish in two years." Masters sat quietly and observed Matt's discomfort. "We will have a meeting of the entire incoming group in a few minutes," he said. "Do you have any more questions right now?" Matt shook his head vaguely, but the superintendent persisted, trying to encourage Matt to relax and speak out. "I'm certain Charlie must have filled you in about this place. Perhaps you would like to have something clarified before we meet with the other boys."

Matt recalled Charlie's parting comment: *They raise a lot of sheep around here. If I come back next spring and find any lambs that look like you, I'll nail your ass to the barn door.* Matt understood Charlie's need to exit with a laugh, but he had been embarrassed when Charlie said it in front of the guard, and he was embarrassed now, just thinking about it. In response to Masters's question, however, Matt simply shook his head and murmured, "No . . . no questions."

"Very good. Let's join the others then." Masters led Matt back through his outer office and down the short hall to an adjoining conference room. Five other boys were seated around an old conference table, and a guard in casual clothes stood in the corner closest to the door. Four of the boys looked up to inspect the newcomers, but Ralph sat quietly rocking back and forth on the hard wooden chair, staring vacantly into space.

Matt stared back at the boys and studied them curiously. The first one was a dark-haired youngster, about Matt's age, who sprawled on his chair indolently and smoked a cigarette, completely at ease in seemingly familiar surroundings. The smoke curled lazily from Alf Miranda's nostrils, and his bare arms revealed a tattoo of a cross emanating wavy lines. Tony, so small that his head barely cleared the top of the conference table, was seated next to Miranda. Matt dropped into the wooden chair that Masters had pulled out for him in passing, and the superintendent proceeded to the torn plastic chair at the head of the table.

"I won't bother to introduce you at this time, but there will be ample opportunity for you to get to know one another," he said, launching into his indoctrination speech. "You will spend the next three days in the admissions cottage, taking tests, getting your physical examinations, and having your hair cut. Our educational counselor will review your test scores and transcripts, and she will place you appropriately in our school. Study hard, and everybody will benefit."

Ralph started rocking again, and the vacant expression on his face caused Matt to wonder whether any amount of schooling would ever help him. Then Matt studied Tony and wondered why he was there. The ten-year-old youngster, who looked no more than six or seven, was resting his chin on the table and smiling broadly, his alert eyes darting quickly from Masters to the others in the room and back again. His face seemed so open and innocent that Matt found it difficult to accept his presence at the reformatory. When Masters mentioned school, the boy wiggled delightedly and bounced up and down in his chair, finally banging his chin on the table and recoiling with such painful animation that Matt was forced to smile.

"Are you all right, Tony?" Masters asked anxiously.

"Oh, sure," the boy answered, curling his legs under him and jumping to a kneeling position on his chair. "I never got to spend too much time in school, and I'm sure looking forward to it, Mr. Masters." The boy's articulateness and self-assurance belied his size and appearance, and Matt wondered if he might actually be a teenaged dwarf.

Masters accepted Tony's attempt to curry favor and knew instinctively that the boy was looking forward to school with about as much anticipation as a fish looks forward to a frying pan. Without responding further, the superintendent continued his memorized indoctrination speech. "Clothes will be issued, and if cared for properly, they will last, but if you require a new issue before the appropriate time, the cost will come out of your weekly allowance."

"Allowance?" Tony interrupted. "You mean, we gets new clothes *and* money?" Then his big eyes rolled toward the window, and he continued. "And we gets to live in a *cottage*, too?" Everything about the boy exuded so much genuine naïveté and sincerity that the sarcasm almost escaped detection, but Masters was wary and beginning to show his annoyance.

"Tony, I suggest that you sit still and listen. I'll give you a chance to ask questions when I am finished. Do you understand?"

"Yassah."

Masters's eyes flashed, but he decided to overlook the final insolence and complete his remarks. "You will receive—"

"How much?" Tony asked.

"How much *what*?"

"How much allowance do we get?"

Masters struggled for control, then resumed his recitation. "You will receive fifty cents a week in plastic money, to be spent in the canteen, which sells candy, comic books, shaving lotion, and cigarettes." Then he glared at Tony and said evenly, "Every boy starts here with a *clean slate* . . . so don't mess up."

Tony ignored the implied warning and nodded his head happily, then shook it gravely, indicating *yes*, he was happy to be starting with a clean slate and *no*, he had no questions to ask.

The superintendent looked at the older boys and said, "Don't fight. . . . Don't try to run away. . . . If anything goes wrong, tell your social worker or your cottage parent. As a last resort, come to me." Masters looked at each boy in turn and asked, "*Now* are there any questions?" There was no response, so he concluded. "Good. Cooperate, and you won't have any trouble."

Instead of dismissing the group at that time, Masters sat back and mused about Tony's ability to rattle him so adroitly. He was a bright and perceptive ten-year-old who looked like a baby and had the instincts of a riverboat gambler . . . but *damn* he was cute. Masters was about to chuckle over the way he had been manipulated by the little imp, but he controlled his impulse and shared his final thought with the boys. "I won't say, Welcome to Clearwater, gentlemen, but I will say this: Good luck, and don't forget how to smile."

The guard opened the door for the departing superintendent and said brusquely, "Keep your seats."

At that moment Matt and the other boys got a terrifying preview of what it would be like to be inmates at CBIS. Six young trusties marched into the room in lockstep. They were dressed in faded blue work pants, white T-shirts, and their heads were shaved. Tony expressed the feelings of the group when he shrieked, "My Gawd, what . . . is . . . this?" The unsmiling trusties positioned themselves behind each of the newcomers and awaited further orders.

Matt, Tony, and two of the other boys sat wide-eyed and nervous, staring with revulsion at the shaved heads. Ralph continued to rock in his chair, seemingly oblivious of everything else, and Miranda crushed his cigarette in the ashtray disdainfully, not sharing the others' fear. This was the third time around for him.

"Quiet!" the guard ordered in response to Tony's outburst.

"But what they gonna do to us?" Tony whined. "What happened to their *haids?*"

"Quiet!" the guard repeated. "Each of you has been assigned a guide to conduct you on a brief tour of the facility. You will report to the admissions cottage in forty-five minutes." The guard looked into the faces of each of the boys seated around the table and asked, "Understood?"

As his gaze fell on Tony, the youngster raised his hand and waved it frantically. "I—I understands, but how come they got no hair? I—I mean, if we gotta walk around out there, I'd sure druther go with one of these other guys with a *regular* haid."

"Dismissed!" the guard ordered, trying not to smile.

Tony's guide was a tall, thin young black teenager who mischievously decided to play upon the younger boy's nervousness. He reached out and clutched Tony's shoulder and rolled his eyeballs upward as he spun the youngster around. Tony looked up into the vacant white eyes and shrieked in terror, hiding his face in his hands, screaming, "Zombies! They's zombies!" Then Tony's guide hoisted him off the chair and walked stiff-legged from the room with the smaller boy kicking and howling under his arm.

The comedic spectacle had relieved the newcomers' tension, and Matt suspected that little Tony had enjoyed it as much as everyone else. Matt's guide was smiling pleasantly, but he seemed somber in contrast with the unrestrained hilarity of the others.

"Let's walk," he said. "You're too big to carry."

"I wouldn't try it," Matt warned.

"Don't worry, man. I know a bad dude when I see one." He chuckled sarcastically. Matt's guide was over six feet tall, almost an inch taller than he, and he was equally well muscled. "I met your man," he said as they walked from the conference room.

"What man?" Matt asked cautiously.

"That sheriff dude . . . from Wyoming."

"Oh yeah . . . Charlie. He told me about you . . . I don't remember your name."

"John."

"Right."

They exited onto the large second-story wooden porch in back of the administration building. Matt started down the stairs, but John reached out to stop him, and Matt flinched and jumped aside into a fighting stance. John instinctively assumed a defensive posture, then dropped his hands slowly. "Hey, baby, you're too goosey. I just want you to stop here so I can explain the campus."

"Okay," Matt relented, "just keep your hands off."

Instead of taking issue with Matt's contentiousness, the older boy simply nodded and said softly, "That's okay, man. I know the feeling." John then turned and pointed toward the largest of the buildings. "That big brick building on the right is the gymnasium and classroom building, and the smaller building next to it is the admissions cottage. Those three buildings down the end are the dormitory cottages. Let's go."

"Charlie said there were *six* cottages," Matt said.

"Each building has two cottages," John explained, ignoring Matt's challenging tone. "There's no connecting doors, but there's a glass cage in the middle so's one guard can watch the dorms on both sides."

As they walked toward the nearest building, Matt was impressed with the neat, clean, orderly appearance of the grounds. It reminded him of a college campus, but something seemed to be missing. It suddenly occurred to him that there were no people around. It was shortly after noon on a beautiful August day, but there were no people on the campus.

"On the left here is the dining hall and kitchen," John said. "The food stinks, but you'll get used to it. Out behind there is the stock barns and welding shops."

The door to the dining hall banged open at that moment, and a group of boys marched out in double file. They marched silently, and most walked with their shaved heads down and shoulders humped. "They're from the older boys' cottage," John volunteered. "How old are you?"

Matt stood there and stared while a chill traveled down his spine and through his legs. "Fifteen," he said, mesmerized by the silent procession. "Why are they walking like that?"

"Like what?" John asked.

"All scrunched over."

"Oh, that," John said with a shrug. "They just walk that way so's they can talk and joke around without getting caught." Then he stepped back and examined Matt more closely, returning to a matter of more immediate concern. "Fifteen?" he asked incredulously. "Boy, you *are* a big one. I doubt they'll put you in the fourteen to fifteen cottage. I bet you end up with me in the sixteen to eighteen cottage. That's the last one down," he said, pointing across the lawn. "But it don't matter. It's all part of the same dung heap."

The pair walked silently for a few moments before John resumed his own version of the orientation lecture. "If you're fifteen, you get Miss Pratt for a social worker. You ain't askin', but I'll tell you anyway. She's about as good as any of them, ugly as sin, and cold as hubcaps in winter. That's what they call *professional distance*," he explained with a chuckle, "and that means she *acts* like she don't give a shit about you, but only because she really doesn't."

Matt nodded his head and grinned ruefully.

"Just don't waste your time with her or the other kids in admissions. Miranda, that greasy kid with the tattoos, is a repeater, and that fat one . . . he's a dummy. The rest of them are new. Not one of them could find his ass in a telephone booth without a flashlight, so their advice ain't worth spit."

The colorful images sparked a spontaneous smile as Matt began to warm up to John, and the older boy was pleased. Just before they reached the admissions cottage, John stopped him again and said, "I want you to know something. Last week I read your file."

"So?"

"*So?*" John asked, pretending to be offended. "You act like that's no big deal. Don't you know those files are strictly confidential?"

"Then why did you read it?" Matt asked, unconcerned, "Or how?"

"Funny you should ask," John said with a smile. "I do it upside down."

"Upside down?" Matt asked incredulously, trying to picture John standing on his head, reading files.

"That's right. I've been working in the superintendent's office for three years, and I found out early on that the best way to read that stuff is upside down—standing across from the secretary while she's reading it. It took a lot of practice, but I can read faster upside down than most people can right side up."

"Good for you," Matt said sarcastically but with a touch of humor.

"Shit, I don't know why I'm wasting my time with a honky cowboy," John said with feigned disgust, "but I know all about you and why you're here, and the two of us are kind of in the same boat." The somber expression returned to John's face. "Anyway, since I know all about you, I'd be willing to tell you about me if you want."

"No, thanks," Matt said.

"Since you ask so nice, I'll tell you," John said, ignoring Matt's demurral. "I'm sixteen now, and I've been here since I was twelve. My mama left me, and the state figured I'd end up here sooner or later anyway, so they greased the skids and shipped me straight. It was all legal—just like yours." John was serious again. "I'm telling you this because most of the boys here are just like you and me. The rest of them are real sickies. Miss Pratt calls them sociopathic personalities or psychopaths. I don't know the difference, but they are pure mean. There's only ten or fifteen in each cottage, but they run this place. They're not the brightest or the toughest, but they are downright bad. If we fought them, we could win a battle or two, but they'd just keep coming back at us until we got our asses cut raw."

Matt was struck by the transition in John's language and bearing brought about by the intensity of the moment. "If—if there are only ten or fifteen in each cottage . . . that's only ten or fifteen out of fifty or sixty . . . what are you scared of? What about the staff people?"

"Look, man, I can't explain it all now," John said, surrendering some of his intensity to impatience. "The staff can't run this place without them, so they give them more privileges to keep them quiet and on the right side. I know it's hard for you to understand right now, but just remember to stay out of their way. We try to stick together, but you can't expect too much help if they come after you." John pushed the doorbell to the admissions cottage and started back toward the administration building.

"How do I know who they are?" Matt asked.

"It won't take long." John laughed. "In my cottage it's Shacky and his twelve friends. They're always together. Shacky has red, curly hair, pimples, and a bad limp. Stay out of his way."

Chapter Twenty-one

The plastic attachment on the business end of the barber's clippers looked like savage teeth without a mouth. Oscar Stone was cutting wide swaths from the front of Matt's head to the base of his neck. It suddenly occurred to Matt that the huge clippers were actually sheep shears, which seemed grotesquely appropriate to his new station in life. Matt watched the thick brown hair tumble into his lap. He told himself hair wasn't so important, yet he found it completely dehumanizing to have his head shaved.

The fat barber sneezed and coughed through the smoke curling up from the cigarette dangling from his lips. "You get your hair cut first thing so we can get the lice and crap out of your head before you spread it all over the hill," he explained in a high-pitched, effeminate voice. "After you leave here, you get showered and sprayed."

Matt's cheeks burned as his anger rose. "I don't have lice and never have," he snapped.

"Well, *screw you*, you little punk! I was just telling you because Masters says we have to try to *relate* to you pukes. Instead of *thanking* me for being nice to you, you get all pissed off . . . and move your head. . . ."

Suddenly the massive shears bit savagely into Matt's right earlobe and tore through the tender flesh.

"That's how it happens . . . you move your head, and my clippers slip. My, my, your ear seems to be bleeding," the barber said with affected concern. "Here, turn your head so it drips on the apron."

Matt's tears soon mixed with the blood that was dripping into the puffs of shorn brown hair. He stared transfixed at the mess gathering in his lap, determined to deny the sadist the pleasure of knowing how much it hurt. He sat there until the barber released the neck clip and shouted, "Next!" Then he cupped Matt's chin in the palm of his hand, forcing his head back, and hissed menacingly, "Let me tell you . . . if you ever sass me again, I'll cut off more than your ear."

Matt slapped the man's hand away and sprang from the chair. The barber fell back and pressed himself against the mirror. All of Matt's hate and frustration focused on the fat little man with the pencil mustache twitching on his bloated face. His sole purpose in life was suddenly reduced to hammering the man into submission. Matt cocked his arm, but before he could deliver the punch, an unseen force picked him up and spun him around, holding him at bay.

Matt was a snarling, thrashing maniac, but the arms that had lifted him away from the cringing barber remained locked around his body until his frenzy dissipated. Then he felt his feet touch the floor, and he was released. Matt turned slowly and looked into the blank face of Ralph, the stocky boy who had sat silently rocking himself throughout the indoctrination session in Masters's office.

Oscar Stone, the effeminate sadist with the polished nails and dirty fingers, shrieked impotently in the background, "You keep him away from me! If he lays one hand on me, I'll have him shipped to the penitentiary! I'm warning you!"

Ralph shifted his weight, turned, and shuffled toward the barber chair. As he did so, Matt caught sight of himself in the mirror, and he was frightened and fascinated by the wild creature staring back at him: bald head, blood-smeared face, and incandescent eyes that did not belong to him. Charlie's warning echoed through the confusion and anger: *Hate can destroy*. But hate could also be useful, and as Matt glared at the pathetic figure of Oscar Stone cowering against the wall, he understood how useful hate could be.

Matt turned and stalked into the adjoining room, where the other boys were waiting on a long bench. Tony Washington's incessant patter stopped in mid-sentence as the bloody, angry, bald-headed monster emerged from the cutting room. The boys had been stripped to their shorts immediately after they had assembled in the admissions cottage, so the blood from Matt's ear splattered onto his muscled chest and dripped down his stomach to be absorbed by his shorts.

It appeared to Tony that Matt had been split from his stomach to his neck, and the scrawny little boy jumped up, muttering, "Oh, Lawd!" . . . Now they got poor Ralph in there, too."

Matt sat down at the far end of the bench, and Tony willingly surrendered his place at the front of the line to squeeze in next to him. The boy nervously inspected the damage and was relieved that things looked worse than they actually were. His reassurance was complete when Ralph shuffled out bald but otherwise unscathed. When it was finally his turn, Tony sauntered into the gruesome little barbershop, announcing, "Just a trim, my man, and if ya overdoes it, there'll be no tip from me."

Tony's continuing banter carried easily into the outer room. "Where's that broad with the big tits?" he demanded. "I'd like her to do my nails."

Matt leaned over and shook his head, trying to suppress a smile in spite of his lingering rage. Tony was bright, cocky, and for the most part fearless. Matt felt immature and awkward compared to the skinny ten-year-old kid who saw each catastrophe as a joke and each adult as a conquest to be won over with humor and charm.

Soon after the six haircuts had been completed, the door was unlocked by Rich Anderson, the chief of the admissions cottage. He was in his early twenties, and in the few minutes he spent with the group before sending them for shots, physicals, and haircuts, he had impressed them as being a nice guy.

"Let's go to the showers, my bullet-headed beauties," he called out cheerfully. Then he saw Matt and rushed into the room for a closer inspection. He held the boy's head in both hands while he inspected the wound. "What the hell happened, McFadden?"

"He said the shears slipped."

Anderson's face turned crimson, and he stalked into Oscar Stone's room, slamming the door behind him. "Goddamn, you stinking faggot, what the hell happened?" Anderson shouted.

Oscar was not intimidated. He shouted back in his high voice, "You just watch your mouth, smart-ass. If you got any brains behind that big mouth, you'll keep an eye on that cow-eyed country boy. He's got a mean streak. You mark my words, that kid's gonna hurt somebody!"

The boys in the outer room could hear every word, so as the argument raged inside, Tony went into another routine. Playing on the barber's description of Matt, he threw his hands over his face in mock terror and pleaded, "Ya gotta he'p me, Ralphie, this mean mother's gonna kill us both!" There was no reaction from Ralph, but the others were smiling. "*Please*, don't try to hide your head up your ass, Ralphie. . . . The cowboy'll find you there." Matt laughed in spite of himself, but Ralph continued to stare vacantly at the wall.

Rich Anderson emerged still angry and led the boys to the three metal showers in another part of the basement, where they were scrubbed with stiff brown brushes and sprayed with DDT. Matt's ear was treated and bandaged, and the boys were issued blue denim shirts and pants, white terry-cloth slippers, and new underwear.

The boys had not been favorably impressed by the first floor of the admissions cottage, but after an entire afternoon in the damp, windowless basement it looked rather pleasant. Rich Anderson led them to a large room with soft leather chairs, a television set, and tables that were strewn with magazines and comic books. "You boys sit here and watch TV," he ordered. "McFadden, you come with me."

Anderson's office was a cubicle with four glass walls. From his desk Anderson could monitor most of the ground floor—from the TV room to the long bedroom corridor.

He sat on the edge of his desk, and Matt sat on one of the two chairs facing him. "Stone claims you threatened him," Anderson charged.

Matt did not respond.

"Look, Matt, I have a pretty good idea what must have gone on in there. It's happened before. But let me tell you this. If you ever lay a hand on him or any other staff member in this place, they'll ship you to the penitentiary for sure, and there's nothing any of us can do to help. Do you understand that?"

"Maybe that wouldn't be too bad," Matt said indifferently.

"If that's what you think, you don't know your ass from third base," Anderson said angrily, jumping up from the desk. He paced the floor for a moment. Then he returned to the chair next to Matt's. "I know you've probably heard some bad things about this place," he said evenly. "Unfortunately Oscar Stone represents the worst of what you've heard, and all we can do is apologize for his presence. This place used to be swamped with his kind, but Masters got rid of them."

"All except one," Matt contradicted.

"Stone's brother-in-law has been a state senator forever," Anderson explained. "Masters could blow this whole program if he fired him, but believe me, his time will come."

"Meanwhile?" Matt asked.

"Meanwhile, you let us take care of Oscar Stone, and you follow the rules. If it's any comfort, I know you don't belong here, but neither do sixty percent of the other boys in this place. The difference is that you're smart enough to make the best of things. When you leave, you can make a real life for yourself on the outside. I'd like to be your friend, but while you're here, it's basically up to you to make it on your own."

Anderson would be easy to like, but Matt realized that he would be released from the admissions cottage in a few days and would probably never see him again. Matt had lost his dad, and he was already beginning to miss Charlie Sanner. The last thing he needed was to get attached to someone else before splitting, so he simply thanked Rich Anderson and asked if he could return to the group.

When Matt entered the TV room, Ralph was staring at the wall, and Tony was jumping up and down on the couch next to him. "Me and Ralph's been talking about this place, and he's gonna lead a riot and take over. Ain't that right, Ralphie?"

Matt knew it was cruel, but he couldn't keep from smiling. Ralph folded his arms and started rocking back and forth.

"You'd better be careful," Matt said to Tony. "He doesn't talk, but if he understands what you're saying, you'll make him mad, and he'll tear you a new one."

"*Sheeet*," Tony said mockingly. "This fat honky couldn't catch me on a bet. And even if I let him, he's so slow I'd have his ass whipped before he realized he caught me."

Alf Miranda joined the group as their dinner was carried in on trays. Miranda, the only returnee among them, informed the others that they would be going to the dining room starting the next morning. Someone said the food tasted good, and Miranda added, "It don't taste bad now, but when you eat it all the time, it just stops tasting . . . except when someone on the work detail gets hacked at the kitchen supervisor and pees in the soup or the potatoes. *Then* ya can tell the difference," he assured them.

In the absence of any authorities in the room, Alf Miranda spent the next hour answering questions about the place. He enjoyed the attention and was quick to exaggerate conditions to make a point. Finally, Sandy asked him, "Where do we sleep? Upstairs?"

"You better *hope* not," Alf answered ominously. "The upstairs part of this building is *lockup*."

"Lockup? This whole place is locked up, ain't it?" Tony asked.

"Not like upstairs. There's thirty cells, 'bout as big as a closet, with a mattress on the floor, a sink, and a dry john."

"What's a dry john?" Sandy asked.

"That's just an open pipe, about like this," Alf explained, forming a circle with his hands indicating a diameter of about ten inches. "No water to flush with, and it stinks up the whole cell."

With that description out of the way, Alf further described lockup. "They paint all the windows black, so no light ever gets in, and the place is full of crazies like Ralph most of the time . . . especially when the moon comes out. Those people go wild, you know. They scream and hit their heads against the wall and yell and yell till ya think your ears will fall off." Alf shook his head slowly and gestured toward Ralph. "Never get put in lockup, 'cause you'll end up crazy, just like him."

Ralph continued to rock, staring straight ahead, but Matt saw a tear slide down his cheek. "Goddammit," he said to Miranda, "leave him alone. He can hear you. Tony's not old enough to know better, but you are."

"Man, you're as dumb as he is," Alf said with a sneer. "If you wasn't, you'da picked someone else to take up with. How's this dummy ever gonna help ya in here?"

Matt walked away from the group, wondering why he had spoken up for Ralph. Miranda was right: He'd tear himself apart trying to stick up for the losers in that place. He flopped into a chair in the corner and stared at the pages of an old magazine, trying to think through his dilemma. He wanted to pull into a shell and take care of only himself, but he couldn't stand to see others hurt, and his dad had always taught him to respect the feelings of others, no matter who they were. Charlie had warned him to mind his own business and keep a low profile, but Charlie had also said, *Always remember who you are.* Matt finally decided that he would have to be tough, but he couldn't stop being his father's son.

An hour later Rich Anderson announced it was time for bed, and he assigned Matt and Ralph to the same room. Matt stripped to his underwear and jumped into the top bunk, and Ralph fell onto the lower bunk with all his clothes on. Matt welcomed the darkness as a time for more thinking, but the busy day had taken its toll, and he was asleep in minutes.

Matt never heard the strange sound that awakened him, and he had no idea what time it was. He lay perfectly still, waiting to identify whatever had interrupted his sleep. Then he heard a choking sob from the bottom bunk, and he realized the mute boy was crying. Matt leaned over the edge of his bed and looked into the empty, pasty face.

"Hey, Ralph, you stick with me, and by God, we'll *both* make it." Matt was unconvinced, but it felt better to think he might be able to help someone else.

Ralph stopped crying in a few minutes, and the room was quiet.

Wide-awake now, Matt stared into the night through the

heavily wired window, and in spite of his bravado, he hoped it wasn't time for a full moon.

The second day was devoted to psychological testing and educational placements. On the basis of their school records Matt was placed in tenth grade, Tony in fourth, and Ralph in the vocational automotive program.

Matt spent an uneventful fifteen minutes with his social worker, Miss Pratt. He was, as John had predicted, placed in the sixteen to eighteen cottage, along with Ralph and Miranda. Tony was assigned to the ten to eleven cottage, and the others wound up with the fourteen- and fifteen-year-olds.

Tony continued to enjoy center stage wherever he went. He charmed his social worker with lies and his counselor with promises. Matt watched him operate with utmost admiration. It didn't seem possible that a ten-year-old kid could be so mature—or that the adults could be so dumb. Tony made them laugh at his dirty jokes and told them how great they were, and they patted his bald head and gave him anything he wanted.

The boys in the group were pensive and depressed that evening as they relived the trauma of their first two days in reform school and dealt with the fact that they would be separated the next day. Matt entered the TV room and headed immediately for his favorite place in the quiet corner. He was not surprised to see Ralph there waiting for him, but he was touched to see Tony sitting there, too, talking soothingly to the unresponsive mute the way a child talks to a doll. Tony was absorbed with tying a knot in Ralph's broken shoelace, so Matt's sudden appearance caught him off guard.

"Oh, yeah," Tony stuttered, "I . . . me and laughing boy was talking about breakin' outta this joint and jumpin' a freighter to Australia and workin' up a song-and-dance routine . . . but . . . he has a little trouble tying his shoes." Tony was still glib and cocky, but this time there was an air of grown-up seriousness about him.

"Why are you in here, Tony?" Matt asked as he sat down next to him.

"Purse snatchin', breakin' and enterin', assault with a deadly weapon, and three parole violations," Tony recited quickly. "And don't forget panderin'."

Matt laughed and said, "I'm serious. Anyway, what's 'pandering'?"

"Panderin's like white slavery, 'cept it's when you do it for a nigger woman."

"You mean a pimp?" Matt smiled. "You were a pimp, huh?"

"No, dummy," Tony said disgustedly. "A pimp drives a huge car and wears shiny clothes. I *pandered* . . . kinda learning the business."

"So you were an *apprentice* pimp," Matt exclaimed, going along with the joke. "How many women did you pimp for?"

"Just my mama."

The reality struck Matt like a kick in the stomach. "I'm sorry," he muttered. "I thought you were still joking."

"Nothing to be sorry about," Tony said brightly. "It sure beat changing diapers. I had two baby brothers and one sister, and Mama used to spend her time drunk or runnin' away from my old man. I got caught the first time trying to steal a case of food out the back door of the A&P storeroom, but I couldn't read the label on the box, and it turned out to be a case of shoe polish." Tony was again in his element, telling stories punctuated by obscenities, infectious giggles, and broad gestures.

"Anyway," he continued excitedly, "Daddy used to come home once or twice a week, and if there was no money around, he'd start breakin' things up, so Mama'd get all duded up and go out lookin' for these white outta-towners to bring home. As soon as the dude took off his pants, I'd grab his wallet . . . back pocket, pants, and all. Then we'd agree to give him back his pants if he'd just leave and forget about his cash. And most of the time that's the way it came down."

"You mean you stole their money?" Matt asked, fascinated and incredulous about a world he had never imagined.

"Naw," Tony assured him. "They *donated* it. It's like paying a toll on a bridge. Ya ever paid a toll on a bridge?"

Matt shook his head.

"It's like this," the small boy explained patiently. "If ya need to cross a river, and ya don't have time to take the ferry, ya pay a toll to cross the bridge. That's how it was with those white dudes: They got to slobbering all over Mama, and by the time they realized they was trying to do business in the black neighborhood, without pants, they didn't have time to wait for the ferry. They paid the toll and took the fastest way out."

Matt chuckled and shook his head. "I don't believe you."

"It's true," Tony assured him. "And if they tried to make a federal case outta it, I'd go runnin' down the hall screamin' some white dude was rapin' my mama, and these black guys would come bangin' into the hallway, growlin' and snortin', and the honky'd take off down the stairs three at a time, with his pants in his hand."

Tony explained that he would have to split the take with the men who'd come into the hall to help out, but none of the victims had ever gone to the police, and Tony learned at an early age that two wrongs can make a deal.

"What did your father say about all that?" Matt asked, now completely absorbed in the story.

"All he cared about was the money," Tony answered. "One time he came home and started beatin' up on Mama just to prove he was still in charge." The boy hesitated, almost caught off guard by the fact that he had launched into the one story he had never expected to tell. When he spoke again, there was pain in his voice. "Anyway, I jumped up on his back when he was hittin' Mama, and I popped him on top of the head. I didn't hurt him none, but he pulled me off and said he was gonna tear my fingers off and stick them up my ass one at a time."

Tony pensively rubbed his left hand and said softly, "He damned near got the job done, too."

Matt looked down into the small boy's lap, where the fist of the left hand was now completely covered by the right. Drawn by some inexplicable curiosity, Matt reached down and encircled the tiny wrist, gently tugging on Tony's arm without knowing what to expect. The fist that appeared was normal, and Matt expelled his breath audibly, but when Tony unclenched his hand, the tiny fingers that emerged were more like gnarled and stunted claws. Matt stared in cold horror, mumbling, "Oh, God, Tony, I'm sorry. I never noticed."

As usual, Tony was the first to recover. He pried Matt's fingers loose and withdrew his hand, saying, "It could be worse. At least they stopped growing. If ya gotta have ugly fingers, it's best to have them nice and teeny. Suppose I had to carry a mitt the size of Ralphie's," he said, playfully slapping Ralph's hand. "At least this way people don't notice right off . . . especially if they're busy lookin' at my mouth or pattin' me on the head."

"Does it hurt?" Matt asked, still shaken.

"Only when I play the violin." Tony laughed, finally breaking the tension. "What about you, superhonky?" he asked, curious about Matt's history.

Matt shook his head distractedly and said, "Me? No, I don't play the violin."

Chapter Twenty-two

John Culver arrived at midafternoon to escort Matt and Ralph to the sixteen to eighteen cottage, more familiarly known as BB Cottage, for "Big Boy." Matt walked down the sidewalk next to John, and Ralph stumbled along behind. "How come they call it the sixteen to eighteen cottage?" Matt asked. "Miranda said that Shacky and some of his buddies are nineteen and twenty."

"Miranda's just like any other returnee in the admissions cottage," John said disdainfully, "usually full of crap. In this case, though, he's right. I don't know what the answer is, except there's no place for them to go, and no one wants to brag about the fact that we have people in here from six to twenty."

They arrived at the last of the three red-brick buildings that formed the western perimeter of the quadrangle, and John banged on the heavy steel door. "It's three o'clock, so both cottage parents should be here," he said.

Carl Gregston, the three to eleven o'clock parent, opened the door. "Come in, boys. We've been expecting you." Gregston was average size, with brown hair and brown eyes. Matt guessed him to be thirty-five—eight years older than he actually was. Ned Williams, the morning parent, was in his late fifties, a retired army officer. His hair was white, and he seemed grumpy, but John had assured the boys that the tough-acting man would give them no trouble if they stayed out of his way and obeyed the rules.

The main room of the cottage, which reminded Matt of the large Grange Hall back home, was designed for fifty boys, but there would now be fifty-eight. "This is the rumpus room," John explained as he led them through the maze of overstuffed chairs, study tables, and magazine racks. There was a Ping-pong table to one side of the huge room, and a large television set was positioned against the long wall, with several rows of chairs arranged in a semicircular pattern in front of it.

The open bathroom area consisted of fifteen exposed toilet stools and fifteen sinks lined up against the north wall of the main room, separated from the recreation area by a short wall, less than four feet tall. Standing in the middle of the reading area, Matt could clearly see most of the stools across the room, and he dreaded the thought of having to sit there in the open, for all the world to see.

They walked past the bathroom area toward a large concrete room with a poured tile floor at the end of the row of toilets and sinks. "This is the shower room," John said. "This is the only place that can't be seen from the living area. When Shacky decides to beat your ass during the day, this is where it's done."

Then John led the two boys back toward the rows of shelves near the front door and said, "This is the storage area." He handed each boy a box with his name taped to it and instructed, "Put your clothes in here, and find an empty place on one of the shelves."

John helped Ralph stack his clothes neatly in the box; then he directed both of them to the sitting area at the far end of the room. John sat on the couch with Matt, and they watched Ralph shuffle across the room toward them. "Can he understand what I'm saying?" John asked softly, so as not to be overheard by the approaching boy.

Matt smiled and nodded, pleased by John's concern for Ralph's feelings.

"Listen up, Ralph," John said quietly when the boy finally reached them. The three huddled together, and John whispered as if calling plays in a sandlot football game. "This first week the two of you do what you're told to do . . by anyone who tells you. You got a lot of rules to learn, and if you screw up, they'll turn you inside out."

"I thought you said they were okay," Matt said, nodding toward the two men standing at the desk a few feet from the front door.

"I'm not talking about Gregston and Williams," John said. "Cottage parents aren't good or bad; they're just here. I'm talking about Shacky and his group. The only way one cottage parent can control fifty-eight boys is to let people like Shacky run the place and keep things quiet."

"What are they going to ask us to do?" Matt was clearly concerned. "I'm not going to let one of them touch me."

"Don't worry about that yet. They'll spend the first month or so bidding for you and trying to make up to you."

"What will they ask us to do?" Matt repeated.

"Gregston will call you over in a few minutes. He'll explain the house rules, and he'll give you each five red tokens. They're worth a dime apiece. You use them to buy stuff at the canteen."

Matt nodded impatiently, confirming that they had heard all that during their indoctrination.

"Okay," John continued, "after dinner Shacky or one of his buddies will probably start talking to you and offer to sell you protection. They'll ask you for forty cents a week, but they settle for thirty. My advice is to pay it."

Matt's face flushed. "Why should I pay them my thirty cents?" he asked angrily.

"Give it to them," John warned, "or you'll be guest of honor at your own blanket party."

"What the hell's a blanket party?"

"Here comes Gregston," John said as he rose from the chair. "If you sleep light, you might see one tonight. A skinny little fart by the name of Rick O'Malley decided not to pay."

Fifty-six boys marched into the rumpus room at precisely four-thirty, and Matt had no difficulty identifying the leader. If it was possible to strut with a limp like that, Shacky Wallis carried it off. His entire body looked as if it should fall over backward with every step. The sneer on his pockmarked face was a permanent fixture that served simultaneously to intimidate others and to conceal his own feelings. He sported a bulbous nose that would have done justice to a seventy-year-old alcoholic. In that group of shaved heads, however, Shacky's wild red hair conspicuously identified him as the privileged one.

Shacky walked straight at Matt, and the other boys maneu-

vered around the room and positioned themselves for an unob-
structed view of the meeting. Carl Gregston, the cottage parent
who had returned to his desk near the door, buried his face in the
afternoon newspaper.

Matt took a step back as Shacky got closer.

"Hey, man, I don't bite. I just want to welcome you to BB
Cottage." His voice was unctuous and unthreatening, but the
expectant giggles from some of the watching boys indicated the
ritual had just begun.

Shacky sneered and enjoyed Matt's discomfort. "What's the
matter, boy, can't you talk? Don't tell me *you're* the dummy?
Well, if *you're* the dummy, then that thing over there must be the
cowboy." He took two steps toward Ralph, bent over, and stared
up into the mute's downcast eyes, playing broadly to an appre-
ciative audience of laughing boys. "This thing looks more like a
cow than a *cowboy*," he said mockingly, and he again focused his
attention on Matt.

"I know you're alive 'cause I can hear your little heart going
clippity-clop." The horse laughter from the other boys drowned
out their wisecracks, and as they crowded in, Carl Gregston buried
his face deeper into the newspaper.

Several of the quiet boys looked at John for a signal, but he
warned them to back away with a slight shake of his head.

"Well, well, what have we here?" Shacky reached into Matt's
breast pocket and pulled out the gold watch, holding it up for all
to see. "My, my. Such a pretty watch," he crooned.

Matt stepped forward and reached for the watch, but Shacky
clamped his fingers around it. He smiled as Matt vainly tried to
pry it loose. Tension filled the room as Matt's challenge played
itself out. Suddenly Ralph moved in, grabbed Shacky's wrist with
one hand, and began to force his fingers open with the other.
Shacky's arm trembled with the strain of gripping the watch, but
Ralph's strength was too much for him. Several boys moved toward them, but Shacky motioned them back and allowed Ralph
to remove the watch.

Shacky glared at the mute, but his words were dircted toward
Matt. "Listen, cowboy . . . and listen good. I'm gonna let this
one go by . . . but only because I like you." Shacky stepped back

and looked into Matt's eyes. "Besides, it don't feel good picking on retardos like him . . . unless I'm forced to. From now on I'm holding you personally responsible for this walking bag of snot. You better make sure he learns the rules."

Matt's knees turned to jelly, and he flopped into the nearest chair, pale and trembling. Ralph set next to him on the floor, and John came up to them, grinning nervously. "That was close," he said.

"How do you mean?" Matt asked, feebly trying to affect indifference.

"Oh, I wasn't worried about *you*. I was worried about Shacky," John said, teasing him solemnly. "One more word out of him, and you'd've puked all over his good shirt."

Their joking continued until Carl Gregston walked up to them a few minutes later. "What's this I hear about a fancy gold watch?"

Matt reached into his pocket and pulled it out. "You mean, this one?"

"It's against the rules," Gregston said, reaching for it.

Matt pulled back instinctively. "Whose rules?" he said.

"Maybe you better tell him, John," Gregston said.

John shrugged. "He's right. We're not supposed to have valuables."

"It's for your own protection," Gregston said. "It'll be locked away in the property room, nice and safe. You'll get it back when you leave."

John stepped between them and faced Matt. He spoke softly. "Shacky's getting his rocks off over there. Don't play into his hand. If you don't give up the watch now, you'll never see it again after tonight anyway."

Matt looked around the room and located Shacky. He was sitting on Gregston's desk, smiling coldly. Matt's expression remained impassive, but when he turned back to Gregston, he was grinning. "Mr. Gregston," he said loudly enough for all to hear, "this was my father's watch, and it means a lot to me. Could I ask you to place it in safe keeping?"

The edge faded from Shacky's smile. He had demonstrated his power, but had he been outmaneuvered in the process?

They marched in double files to the dining room. Matt quickly fell into the routine of walking slouched over so that he could converse with John without being caught by the cottage parent. "Where's everyone else?" he muttered, wondering why the large quadrangle was devoid of other people.

"Only one cottage at a time allowed outside," John answered. "The next cottage will be along as soon as we hit the mess hall."

At the head of the serving line, John picked up a set of hard plastic eating utensils—a tray, a dish, and a cup—and one metal spoon; then he helped Ralph assemble a set of his own. "I think your friend is going to be a permanent fixture," he said.

Matt grinned at Ralph and nodded.

The food was served by a motley assortment of part-time workers from the surrounding area: stoic farmers, genial matrons, and one elderly woman with one long black hair curling from a wart on her chin.

Matt and Ralph followed John to a table for six and sat down. "You learn to do everything with a spoon," John said, holding up the only metal utensil on the tray, "from cutting meat to spreading butter . . . but nobody ever got stabbed with a spoon."

Beneath the heavy layer of brown gravy, Matt identified roast beef, mashed potatoes, and lima beans. The hot meal was too heavy for August, but Matt relished every mouthful. He was about to attack the apple cobbler when the boys from the six to ten cottage marched into the dining room. The six-year-olds were tiny wastrels in work clothes far too large for them, and their shaved heads made them look like little men from outer space.

The ten- and eleven-year-olds marched in behind the younger boys, and Tony Washington was at the front of the column. He spotted Matt and waved happily. Standing behind the six-year-old boys, he no longer seemed so small, but even in his own group of older boys, he had obviously already taken charge.

Tony carried his tray to the table and set it down.

"Better not, squirt," John warned. "You can sit any place you want, but you have to sit with your own cottage."

Tony curled his lip in mock contempt, then leaned toward Ralph with an impish smile. "You see that old broad with the big wart, Ralphie?" Ralph looked at Tony but sat there without signaling a response, trying to bite through a thick slice of roast beef that was dangling from his mouth. "I asked her how come she didn't pull the hair out of her wart. You know what she said?"

"What?" Matt asked, grinning expectantly.

"I'm not talking to you, superhonky, I'm talking to my man."

"He can't talk with his mouth full," Matt said. "What did she say?"

"She said if she pulled out the hair, her ass would fall off."

After supper Carl Gregston ordered them to reassemble for the return trip, so Matt and Ralph took their places near the end of the long line. By the time they came through the front door of their cottage the television was already blaring, and four boys were playing Ping-pong. Immediately to the right of the front door a dozen boys were sitting on the toilets, and Matt instinctively headed for the farthest corner of the room to escape the noxious odors. He was soon joined by a short, thin boy who introduced himself as Rick O'Malley, whom John had previsouly identified as being scheduled for the next blanket party.

"This is Ralph," Matt muttered.

"What's his problem?" O'Malley asked when Ralph failed to look up or acknowledge him.

John arrived in time to answer the question. "He can take only one Irishman at a time, and McFadden got here first."

"I'm Scotch and English," Matt contradicted.

"Same difference." John shrugged. "Besides, O'Malley's got other things to worry about. I told you . . . he decided to get tight with his cash and challenged the man."

"I've taken his shit long enough," the boy said, nodding toward the muscular redhead flamboyantly holding court near the cottage parent's desk. "If he comes near me, someone is gonna get hurt." O'Malley glanced around surreptitiously and slid a screwdriver from his sleeve. The tip had been honed to a glistening point.

Matt backed away in fear, and the humor left John's eyes. "What are you doing, man?" John snarled. "If they catch you with that thing, Masters'll send you to the gooney hatch for sure."

O'Malley pushed the pick back up into his shirt sleeve while

John continued to scold him. "I told you yesterday . . . take your party and forget it. If you pull that thing out, you're gonna end up on the bottom, and you won't be coming out of it in one piece."

Matt was thoroughly shaken and walked away, sensing that something terrible was about to happen and knowing he wanted to have no part in it. He found an empty chair, picked up a magazine, and flipped through the pages blindly. "*Cottage*"—the word tore through his mind. He had always envisioned a cottage as a small house in the mountains where families sat by the fireplace, loved each other, read good books . . . and slept *securely* under warm quilts.

"Let's hit it, boys . . . nine o'clock." The room was filled with groans and protests in response to Carl Gregston's order to prepare for bed. Matt was still lost in his thoughts and was only vaguely aware of the movement around him until Ralph gently touched his shoulder.

"Last call for the crapper," Gregston shouted as some of the boys headed for the latrine and others began to undress as they lined up along the far wall.

In a reversal of roles Matt followed Ralph toward the bathroom area, but the sight of so many boys using the facilities without a modicum of privacy repelled him. He turned away and joined the line in front of the storage area, where he stripped to his undershorts without understanding why, except that was what everyone else in the line was doing.

Carl Gregston rose from his desk and unlocked the door leading to the upstairs dormitory. The line began to move forward as the boys deposited their clothing on a laundry pile and proceeded through the door and up the narrow staircase.

The dormitory was an enormous room with a sea of beds so tightly arranged that there was barely enough room to walk between them. The overhead lights were dim, but Matt could see clearly across the tops of the pillows and blankets, and the neatly arranged mounds reminded him of a graveyard.

Matt was directed to his assigned bed in the middle of the dormitory, and Ralph was sent to the far corner.

"Stand next to your beds, and be quiet!" Matt had been so awed by the specter of the beds when he had reached the second floor that he had overlooked the glass booth when he passed it. Startled by the abrupt command, however, he snapped around and saw a withered little man, with a microphone in his right hand, glaring out at them from the glassed enclosure. The old man then turned his back and barked at an unseen youngster in the adjacent dormitory, "Now goddammit, you younger boys better settle down. If I have to call for help tonight, some of you will be back in lockup."

So complete was the feeling of isolation within the building that Matt had forgotten that his cottage was separated from the adjoining cottage by a single cement-block wall. It came back to him immediately when he realized that the one guard in the locked glass booth was monitoring both groups simultaneously. On the other side of the glass cage the younger boys scrambled toward their own beds and stood rigidly at exaggerated attention.

"That's better," said the mechanically amplified voice. "Now let's say our prayers." Matt reacted to the ludicrous incongruity with a grin, but instead of the pealing laughter he expected to hear, the room was filled with the rumbling of indecipherable murmurs ending with "Amen," whereupon every inmate jumped into bed.

The huge dormitory, with fifty-eight boys, was unnaturally quiet. Matt lay there for an hour before he realized the overhead lights would remain on all night. He tried several devices to put himself to sleep, but when all else failed, he conjured his favorite vision. It always started with the fireplace, and his dad was reading something aloud. Then the image progressed to their hot chocolate, their laughter, and the late-night snacks. By the time the coals in the fireplace had burned down, as usual he was asleep.

At first it was a squeaky sound, like skin rubbing across a wet windowpane. Then Matt's bed vibrated slightly, and suddenly he was fully awake. He leaned over the edge of his bed just as a body slid past . . . then another. They moved on their backs on white blankets, propelling themselves with their heels, grabbing the overhead bed bars for additional acceleration. On top, all was quiet, but the floor was alive with bodies slithering in every direction.

Matt shot a glance toward the glass cage, but the night watchman was completely oblivious. As he turned his attention from the guard, however, Matt caught sight of a movement across the room. Ralph was sitting up in his bed, rocking back and forth.

"You there, on the far wall, you lay down and get to sleep!" The voice booming from the glass cage was angry and loud, but none of the boys reacted, not even those who were really sleeping.

Ralph continued to rock as if nothing had happened.

"Dammit, boy, I said lay down, or I'll have security throw you into lockup."

"Hey, Pops, he don't unnerstan' ya . . . he's the new dummy." The voice came from nowhere, and the giggles came from everywhere. Someone got out of bed and walked over to Ralph, but Matt was too apprehensive even to sit up to see who it was. The boy talked to Ralph for a moment, and Ralph went back down.

"Culver, this ain't none of your affair. You just stay in bed. I can handle things without *your* help."

"Yeah, Pops, I know that," John said in a subtly mocking tone. "I was just tellin' him he better straighten up 'cause even though you're a wonderful man, you can be awful tough if ya have to be."

"Well, thank you, John," the mollified voice said, "but from now on I'll handle it. No one gets outta bed, you know that."

John returned to bed, and Matt rolled over on his stomach, ashamed of himself for having been too frightened to help Ralph. He peered down over the edge of his bed again to observe the action on the floor, but all movement had temporarily stopped, and he fell asleep wishing he had gone to the bathroom before coming into the dormitory.

He dreamed about rats. Thousands of rats crawling all around him. They crept closer and closer until they were nipping at his skin. One particularly large rat stood next to his head, glaring into his eyes while the others feasted on his flesh. Matt's sleeping body was frozen with fear and revulsion, and a voice cried out for mercy and moaned with pain.

Find a Safe Place

When the cries finally awakened him, he lay still, drenched with perspiration. His eyes were open, and he was perfectly quiet, but he could still hear the sobbing. The noise was close, but there was no movement, so it was impossible to tell who it was.

At precisely six o'clock the heavy steel dormitory door was unlocked and pushed open with a bang. Ned Williams, the morning parent, stepped into the room and stood there with his feet spread wide and his hands behind his back. The retired army officer looked and sounded like a tough platoon sergeant. "All right, young men, let's roll out of those bunks," he bellowed. "Get your showers, and draw fresh clothes. Let's go! Let's go! Move it!" he shouted impatiently while the boys stumbled out of bed, scurried toward him, and lined up in twos at the top of the stairs.

Williams's eyes swept the room as the boys hurried to comply with his orders. Through the confusion of moving bodies, he detected one boy who had not yet jumped from his bed. "Awright, awright! Move it!" he shouted as he threaded his way through traffic toward the bed.

Six beds beyond Matt's, Williams stooped over and snatched the covers away, revealing a small body curled up, trembling, and whining in agony. "What's the matter, O'Malley? You sick?"

The room was suddenly quiet, and no one moved as Rick whispered, "Yeah . . . I'm sick."

"Well, let's get you over to the doc and see what's wrong. Can you walk?"

Rick slid his feet to the edge of the bed in jerky motions and pushed his body upward with great difficulty, revealing a blood-stained mattress. He sat up and hunched over to catch his breath, sucking air in painful gasps. Williams reached over and tried to help him up, but the boy passed out and fell to the floor, bouncing off the adjoining bed and vomiting on his way down.

Ned Williams tried to catch him, but Rick's limp body slipped through his hands. The boy was unconscious before he hit the floor, but his tear-streaked face was twisted in pain, and his body jumped and jerked as if jolted by an electric prod.

Williams reached down and scooped up the small body, alarmed to see that the boy's blood had saturated the underside of the mattress and was dripping steadily into an expanding red pool on the floor. He rushed for the door with the convulsing body in his arms. "Shacky," he shouted, "you get the boys downstairs to the shower and get the clean clothes passed out. I'll run this kid to the infirmary."

Matt stepped forward tentatively, shaking his head in disbelief. John reached out and pulled him back into line, and Williams rushed past them without acknowledging Matt's attempt to get his attention.

"Doesn't he know? Doesn't he know?" Matt asked John, his dazed expression beginning to give way to anger.

"Keep your goddamn mouth shut," John muttered, jerking Matt's arm violently.

Suddenly Matt realized they *all* knew: Shacky was the person responsible for the attack on Rick, yet he had been placed in charge of the group while the cottage parent rushed the victim to the hospital. It was *Alice in Wonderland.* Everything was backward, and crazy, and wrong, and nothing was as it should have been.

Matt was completely absorbed in his own thoughts throughout breakfast as he struggled to reconstruct the missing details of his first blanket party. He cornered John as soon as they had returned to the cottage. "What the hell's going on?" he asked angrily. "Doesn't Williams know who beat up on O'Malley?"

John seemed amused by Matt's intensity. "Yeah, he probably knows," he answered with measured indifference.

"Then how come he let Shacky get away with it? And how come he put him in charge?"

John looked around before answering; then he explained in a deliberate tone. "He asked Shacky to take over because Shacky's the only cat in this cottage who *could* take over. With his troops he's the only one who can keep the lid on. Hell, if anyone else tried it, this place would be upside down. Shacky is *power*, and that's one thing no cottage parent has enough of—not with fifty-eight crazy, sick, and angry guys in the house." John paused for a moment to let the information sink in. "No one man can keep the lid on in here, so there's kind of an unwritten contract between Shacky and the man. No one talks about it, but every cottage needs someone like him to keep the peace. In return, he gets to pick off a few chits and mess around with the pretty boys whenever he wants to."

"And you go along with that?" Matt asked, trying to control his temper.

"Shit, man, I don't go along or not go along. That's just the way it is. That's how it is for you, for me, for the cottage parents, for Masters . . . and even for Shacky." Then John opened his eyes wide and waggled his head. "An' thass how it all come down," he mocked in his best Stepin Fetchit impersonation.

Matt had digested as much as he could. "You're a pretty smart toad when you try," he said with a reluctant grin, "but sometimes your English stinks."

"Tell ya what, honky. I'll keep yo' ass outta trouble, and you kin teach me good English . . . without the cowboy accent. An' Ra'ph here, he can imp'ovise as we go."

Ralph's smile seemed to indicate that he understood the difference between hostile ridicule and good-natured humor among friends.

"By the by," John said, switching to a bad British accent, "if we don't ablute ourselves, we'll be tardy for class." Then John turned serious again and put his hand on Matt's arm. "What I'm saying is, you can't beat Shacky unless you're willing to become another Shacky yourself."

The warning struck home, and Matt lost any doubt he might have had about John's brain power.

Chapter Twenty-three

Matt felt good being in school again. The teachers acted like teachers, the books had all the pages, and the place even smelled like a school—an island of sanity and reason in the middle of human degradation and suffering.

Four of Matt's six classes were with Miss Wilson, a sixty-three-year-old woman in orthopedic shoes who had been teaching at the industrial school for three years, following her forced retirement from the public school system. She had a reputation for being stern and academically demanding, but she was a feisty and skilled professional who could assess the differing scholastic backgrounds and abilities of her students, establish educational goals that were appropriate for each boy, then roll up her sleeves and speak the language they all understood.

"You're a damned bright boy, Matthew," Verna Wilson said as she examined his transcript and test scores. Then, with a mischievous twinkle, she nodded toward the scar around his neck and added, "Bright . . . but not *too* bright."

Matt self-consciously ran the tips of his fingers along the ring of scar tissue on his neck. He instinctively liked this solidly built matron who had freckles on her thick arms and wore strange-looking shoes, and he sensed that she would be a friend. Her manner was direct, and her robust voice contrasted sharply with his beloved Miss Mason, but Matt felt comfortable with her. She somehow reminded him of the sturdy old mountain ranchers, and when the corner of her mouth twitched, Matt knew he was in for more teasing.

"From the looks of that permanent necklace you're wearing, you've been known to do some stupid things, haven't you?" she asked with a grin.

"What, this?" Matt asked ingenuously. "This is like a tattoo. Something like the marks aborigines make on their bodies to identify their tribes. Everyone from the basin does it."

"Huh." She snorted. "How many live through it? Is that the mountaineers' answer to overpopulation? Haven't they ever heard of birth control?"

Matt would have been prepared to trade quips with her interminably, but her reference to sexual matters cut him short. "Guess not." He shrugged, trying not to blush.

Miss Wilson chuckled at his naïve discomfort and slapped him on the shoulder. "Okay, let's get on with it." She pushed a stack of books across her desk and said, "I'm what's called your core teacher . . . English, history, and sociology."

Suddenly her voice lost all traces of humor, and she said in a stiff monotone, "If you are serious about your education, I can move you through at a pace that will challenge you to the utmost. If you're not, you can sit back with thirty others in the classroom and swat flies."

"I'm serious," Matt said resolutely. "I want to go to college."

Her facial expression softened, and she said gently, "Good . . . what do you want to study in college?"

Matt shifted in his chair uncomfortably and rubbed his neck again. "Oh, I don't know," he mumbled. "I really haven't decided."

"Oh, come on," she said, trying to encourage him. "I'll bet you've given it a lot of thought, haven't you?"

"I used to," he said. "I mean, my dad and I used to talk about it a lot."

"Tell me about it," she persisted. "Maybe I can help."

"Naw, it sounds kind of dumb, now . . . I mean, with me in this place and all. . . . It just sounds dumb, that's all."

"I'll tell you what's *dumb*, kiddo. If I spend the next three years teaching you how to speak like Winston Churchill, only to find out that all along you wanted to be a telegraph operator. *That's* dumb!"

Matt laughed and slapped his leg, warming to the woman completely and finally decided he could trust her. "No, it's nothing like that," he said. "It's just that . . . like I said . . . my dad and I used to talk about it a lot. He was good at taking care of animals. He never had any training at it, but there were no veterinarians in the basin . . . just one regular doctor. So people used to bring their stock to us all the time."

Matt shifted in his chair again, finding it difficult to say the words and expose the private dream that had belonged only to him and his father. "He knew a lot of Indian remedies, and we were always grinding up roots and stuff for poultices and potions. He always said I was good with animals and should try to study about it in college."

"So that's it," Miss Wilson boomed. "You want to be a Cheyenne medicine man."

"No, no." He laughed with her. "A veterinarian. He wanted me to be a veterinarian."

"There!" she exclaimed. "That wasn't so hard, was it?" Matt shook his head, still grinning. "I know a little something about a vet's life," she said. "Lambing during spring blizzards . . . up to your armpits in a cow's uterus for a breech delivery . . . sloshing through muddy corrals. . . . Maybe you gave up too soon on being a telegraph operator."

In spite of her earthy façade, Miss Wilson was genuinely committed to providing her boys with a solid education. Her salty humor merely served as a defense against the academic failures that usually resulted within the confines of the reformatory. She recognized Matt's potential immediately, and she had not been so excited about a boy's intellect since her first encounter with John Culver, three years earlier. She had been frustrated by John's apparent indifference to classroom learning, and she blamed herself for losing him, but she was determined not to make the same mistake with Matt. She tailored a course of studies for him and called upon an old colleague at the University of Kansas, who had developed a system called In-Residence Independent Study, to help implement her program. The system utilized correspondence-course outlines, but instead of the student's mailing written lessons to be

graded by anonymous instructors, Miss Wilson provided tutorial
assistance and direction every step of the way.

After the first week Matt earned the privilege of completing
his lessons in the school library instead of the classroom, and Miss
Wilson scheduled more than an hour a day for personal interaction
on his work. Matt was excited and eager to learn, but the stimulation provided by his studies was neutralized by fatigue. He
fought going to sleep at night, trying to remain alert as Shacky's
gang slithered around the dormitory floor to assert their authority
over new victims. During the day he had to resort to taking catnaps
whenever possible. As a result, he found it increasingly difficult
to stay awake while studying by himself in the library.

During the second week of his advanced studies program Miss
Wilson searched him out in the library and found him dozing in
his chair. She shook him gently and said, "Matthew, my boy, I
believe you might learn more with your eyes open."

Matt woke with a start, and his embarrassment grew as he
realized that he had failed the only person he truly wished to
impress. "I'm sorry," he stammered, rubbing the sleep from his
eyes. "I just haven't been sleeping nights."

Her voice was gentle, and Matt realized he was in no big
trouble. "It has happened before," she said. "The first few weeks
are the roughest. Would you like to go to the nurse's office and
take a nap?"

"No . . . I'll be okay. I really am sorry I fell asleep."

She responded with the most beautiful smile he had ever seen.
"I have great hopes for you, Matt. Don't get discouraged." Miss
Wilson paused for a moment and looked as though she were debating with herself before continuing. "You know," she said
thoughtfully, "perhaps we can help each other."

He looked at her questioningly.

"You seem to be friendly with John Culver," she said. "John
is fully capable of joining you in this advanced studies program,
but he refuses to try it. I thought the two of you might work well
together. . . ."

"I don't know," Matt said musingly. "I want to go on to
college, but I don't think John does."

"He's capable," she said. "You both are."

"I'll talk to him," Matt promised reluctantly.

Tony Washington was busy holding court in another part of the campus. His first week in the institution had been even more eventful than Matt's. Shacky Wallis's counterpart in the ten to eleven group was a twelve-year-old tough named Billie Joe Winston who had been kept back to provide control in the cottage. Soon after Tony's arrival Billie Joe's boys set about to collect the thirty-cent protection money from each of the youngsters while the cottage parent sat at his desk cleaning a shotgun, ignoring the extortion taking place around him in soft whispers.

Suddenly Tony jumped up on one of the study tables and shouted, "Let's not waste so much time. Everybody line up on this table and get ready to pay Billie Joe his thirty cents."

The cottage parent jumped to his feet, sputtering as if he had not known what was going on in the room. "What are you talking about? . . . What's going on here?"

"We're just paying Billie Joe our protection money, Mr. Birch," Tony explained innocently, with his arms extended and palms up. "If we pay up, Billie Joe keeps his bad asses from beatin' up on our bodies . . . right?"

T. B. Birch stood there flushed and angry, struggling for something to say. Then he saw the incredulous look of surprise and confusion in Billie Joe's face, and he began to laugh, realizing that he could finally move Billie Joe into the next cottage now that he had found a suitable replacement.

The cottage coup had required little more than initiative, guts, and a gambler's instinct for timing, all of which had been keys to Tony's lifelong survival on the streets. None of those qualities, however, could cover up for long the fact that he could not read. Most of the other boys in the fourth grade were in the same predicament, but as their new leader Tony refused to let himself appear stupid in front of them. He was capable of memorizing an entire page if someone else read it aloud, but whenever Mrs. Goldberg pushed him into a corner to confirm her suspicions about him, he deliberately provoked her into sending him to the discipline room. There he would sit or squat on the concrete floor for the rest of the day with the others who could not tolerate the classroom regimen.

When the floor got too hard, a boy would request a brief respite in the bathroom, and for a restive boy like Tony those trips were frequent. One day he pushed open the door and almost hit Matt, who still refused to use the open toilets in the cottage. Tony greeted his friend enthusiastically, jumping straight up and wrapping both arms around Matt's neck, yelling, "Superhonky! How the hell ya been, baby?"

Before Matt could answer, Tony released his grip and dropped down, standing no taller than Matt's belt buckle and grinning from ear to ear. "How's ol' gabby Ralph?" he asked. "I sure do miss those long talks with Ralphie."

Tony's infectious humor never failed to affect Matt. Laughing freely, he said, "You little turd, you haven't changed a bit. . . . And Ralph's fine."

"You think he's ever gonna say something?" Tony asked more seriously.

"Ralph says things. He just doesn't use words. As a matter of fact, I think he's pretty smart," Matt answered.

"Well, tell him ol' Tony says hi, and if he ever do say something—with his mouth—I bet he say, 'You all better listen to Tony. He the smartest little fart in town!' "

"Right," Matt assured him. "I'll tell him hi from the smartest little fart in town."

Tony stuck out both hands, palms up, and Matt slapped down. Then they stepped around each other, and Tony yelled through the closing door, "Hey, big dude, let's meet in here once in a while . . . 'bout the same time."

As Labor Day approached, Matt noted a distinct touch of autumn in the air. He had decided against going out for the football team because of the foreign rituals consisting of cumbersome and extraneous equipment, strange rules, and outlandish drills. He was completely turned off by organized team sports, so he dedicated himself to the individual calisthenics and strenuous running demands of the physical education program.

He participated in the cross-court intramural basketball games because that was one of the few activities for which evening passes out of the cottages were provided. But the manner in which the game was played at the reform school intramural level bore little resemblance to the refined precision of the varsity teams that functioned under the watchful eyes of whistle-tooting, striped-shirted referees. A boy attempting to drive for the basket through a throng of intramural defenders was taking his life in his hands, so Matt learned to avoid the rabbit punches and eye gouging by popping the ball from the perimeter or by converting base-line passes to baskets by releasing the ball quickly—before his frustrated opponents could reach him to inflict bodily harm.

Because of his size and dedication to perfection, Matt quickly became the star of the intramural league, and he attracted the attention of the varsity basketball coach, Harrison T. Cole. From the very beginning Matt followed the routine of remaining on the court after the others had retreated to the shower room. Coach Cole interpreted this as further evidence of Matt's dedication to the sport, but it was nothing more than a wish to avoid the shower room until Shacky's buddies left.

One night Cole approached him and asked, "You like basketball, McFadden?"

"Yeah, I like it," Matt answered, somewhat embarrassed by the attention.

"How come you're not out for the varsity? We practice every afternoon."

"I don't know." Matt shrugged noncommitally. It was difficult for him to imagine that place encouraging team sports and competing with normal schools.

"What ya mean, you don't know? Do you want to play or don't you?"

"Well, I mostly play basketball so I can get out of the cottage three nights a week, but I'm also in Miss Wilson's special program, and I need the time to study," he explained. "I'd like to make good enough grades to get a scholarship to college."

Harrison Cole laughed. "You got a funny idea of how to get yourself a college scholarship. This ain't a prep school; they don't give academic scholarships to bald-headed kids graduating from this place."

Matt's face flushed with anger and embarrassment, and he brushed past the coach, saying, "Screw it then."

"Wait a minute, McFadden," Cole said, restraining the boy gently. "You're gonna need Miss Wilson's program to *keep* you in college, but if you want to get into the place with a free ticket, you gotta be a jock." The coach now had Matt's full attention. "It don't matter tiddly shit how smart you are—you can't start out from this place with only brains going for you. In the first place, people on the outside don't believe anyone in here could have brains, and good grades from Miss Wilson won't convince them otherwise."

Coach Cole grinned conspiratorially and spoke in a loud whisper as his open hands performed a quick ballet in the air. "You learn to put on some good moves out there in basketball or football, and you can take your pick of any college in six states. Suddenly every goddamn coach in the area will turn into a bleeding-heart knee-jerk liberal anxious to give a chance to a deprived kid. . . . You think it over. . . . Talk to Miss Wilson and see if she don't agree."

Coach Cole pressed his point as they walked to the locker room. "I hear you want to be a veterinarian. Well, let me tell you something. Maybe you can get into a school, and maybe you'll even graduate, but you'll never practice unless they give you a license. You're like a convicted felon, and they don't pass out vets' licenses to convicted felons. You're gonna need a special deal, and if you're the state jock, you'll be amazed how fast deals can be made."

Matt hadn't thought about it and knew none of the answers. He tried to untangle and assimilate the new information, and it suddenly occurred to him that getting out of reform school would be not the end of his nightmare but only the beginning. He shook his head and stared at the polished wood floor. When they reached the locker room, Matt mumbled, "I'll think about it."

Chapter Twenty-four

Barn detail wasn't bad. Jake Imbert, the detail supervisor, was a grouchy old man recruited on a part-time basis from one of the neighboring farms. He did most of the work himself and simply ordered the boys to stay out of his way. The livestock consisted of only two mules, seven sheep, four cows, and an old horse, but the brightly painted barn reflected the prevailing philosophy of city-dwelling legislators that the only thing needed to straighten out a bad boy was the wholesome life of a farm.

The barn was old but well kept, and there was little work for the boys to do, so they usually marched from their respective cottages into the barn and up the ladder to the loft to light up and relax. Jake counted the bodies as they entered the barn, and as soon as they were safely sequestered in the loft, he set about accomplishing what few tasks there were. If he had to leave the barn for any reason, he usually took away the ladder, supposedly removing the possibility of escape, but the gesture was purely symbolic since any one of the boys could have jumped down or utilized other convenient escape routes down the bales of hay or any one of the many posts and rails.

Walt Pate's crew cut identified him as one of Shacky's top lieutenants, so he was automatically accepted as the detail leader. Walt was almost eighteen years old, not as tall as Matt, but much more thickly built than he. Matt found him a likable and intelligent person in private, but in the company of Shacky's group, Walt followed along without saying much.

"This is a waste," Matt complained, sitting on a bale of hay and watching Jake Imbert rake up the manure downstairs. "Isn't there anything for us to do?"

"Not while the stock is in pasture," Walt explained. "Sometimes we repair stuff and paint, but usually we just sack out."

Matt could not understand why Walt Pate associated himself with Shacky's crowd of sadists. He seemed so much brighter than the others. Matt knew it would be dangerous to ask the question directly, but when four of the boys on their detail strolled over to join them, the question slipped out. "Why are you one of Shacky's goons?"

Walt's face turned red, and he looked more shocked than angry. "What the shit are you talking about?" he asked.

"Just what I said. Why are you one of Shacky's goons?" Then the image of Rick O'Malley's skinny little body sliding into the pool of vomit and blood on the floor came to his mind, and Matt restated the question. "Were you one of the heroes assigned to tear up tough old Rick O'Malley? I bet that was a real thrill."

"Let me explain it this way," Pate said, slowly rising to his feet. "You see that tree?"

Walt was pointing toward the open window of the loft, and Matt craned his neck to locate it. "Which one do you mean? The big one?"

Standing in back of Matt with a shovel in his hands, Walt swung with all his might. "I mean this one," he snarled just as the flat scoop struck Matt across the back of his head.

Matt heard the bong of the shovel hitting him before the lights went out. He had been knocked out twice before in his life and on both occasions had found the experience almost enjoyable until he came to. This time he welcomed the sleep that had been eluding him during his nightly vigils, and he ultimately resented the water in his face that was bringing him back to consciousness.

"Come on, McFadden. I didn't hit you that hard. Open your eyes, goddammit."

When Matt looked up at the white face of his thoroughly shaken assailant, he felt like the winner. Walt Pate was begging him to be all right, and Matt experienced a perverted sense of power. He pushed himself up on his elbows and looked around him, noting that the other boys were sitting at the far end of the loft, pretending not to have seen anything unusual. The thought struck Matt that they were giving a perfect imitation of cottage parents in time of trouble, and he chuckled in spite of the pain.

"You can't go around shooting your mouth off like that," Walt Pate said with a sense of relief, "especially in front of the other boys. I *had* to hit you. You forced me."

Walt helped Matt to a sitting position and propped him against a bale of hay. He reached for his pack of Camels, adroitly flipped a single cigarette to attention, and slid it from the pack with his lips. Walt tried to relax and act casual as he explained how people got hurt if they didn't cooperate and how the crack on the head was an act of mercy.

"I really did you a favor letting you have it clean and quick," he said earnestly. "I coulda put a gotcha on you, and you'da gone around knowing you had a blanket party coming but not knowing when or where. I've seen some guys go a month with a gotcha . . . just waiting and waiting . . . until they just fall to pieces. Then the cottage parent calls in the shrink, and the shrink says the kid is just polaroid."

Matt wondered why Walt was so nervous, but the lump on his head hurt too badly to dwell on it. Walt continued the one-sided conversation until it was time to return to the cottage; then he solicitously helped Matt to his feet and down the ladder, finally pairing off with him for the march back.

"You got Shacky all wrong, you know," Pate explained. "He likes you, and you couldn't have a better friend in this place. In fact, he told me to stick close and take good care of you."

Suddenly Matt understood Walt Pate's nervousness. Shacky had been patiently courting him for more than a month, and John had warned that Shacky might be moving in soon to demand some special favors. Shacky had entrusted Walt with the assignment of protecting Matt, but Matt had unwittingly placed Walt in the dilemma of having to save face or screwing up his assignment. His face hurt too much to smile, but Matt was smiling inside. "Don't worry, Walt, I won't tell Shacky about today . . . not right away at least."

The anxiety returned to Walt's voice as he muttered, "What do you mean, 'not right away'?"

"Just what I said . . . not now. . . . It's my own contribution to the gotcha system."

Walt Pate stared at Matt with new respect. When they reached the door of the cottage, Matt said, "By the way, it's not 'Polaroid.' The word is 'paranoid.' "

Chapter Twenty-five

Tony Washington rolled over and stared up into the dim light directly over his bed. It had been more than a month since he had usurped Billie Joe Winston, and Tony was not comfortable with the changes that had taken place since then. Billie Joe and all the eleven-year-old boys were moved out immediately, and the entire group of six- to eight-year-old boys was moved in to replace them. The official explanation was that there had been a sudden influx of older boys into the training school, and it was now necessary to combine two of the younger cottages into one. Tony understood, however, that the administration had accepted him as the future leader, and the older boys had been removed to smooth his transition to power.

The younger boys readily accepted Tony, and everything would have been fine except for the way they carried on at night. Some of the youngsters had been viciously abused by their parents, some had been abandoned, and some had been recently orphaned, but most of them still cried for their mothers every night.

Tony had tried to avoid thinking about his own mother and why she had run out on him, but the nightlong wailing of the other children made that impossible. In spite of himself, Tony's mind raced back to the grubby two-room apartment on the East Side, and he could smell the urine-stained mattress that he and his brothers and sister had slept on. He could hear the door slam as his daddy would charge in drunk and mean, beat everyone around, drag his mama into the bedroom, and later leave with whatever cash he could find. Tony's crippled hand would throb incessantly whenever he thought of the angry black giant.

Thinking about his mama just made things worse, so Tony rolled over again and stared down the long rows of beds, trying to force himself to sleep. Most of the crying had stopped, so he closed his eyes and hugged his own tearstained pillow.

The steel door banged open, and Stan Turpin shouted his morning greetings: "All right, let's get outta bed. You boys that wet your beds, strip 'em down and pile the sheets up next to the laundry door. Any more of this covering up is gonna get you in dutch. Come on, come on. Let's go!"

It was the same every morning. Everything was the same. The same speech, the same schedule, the same food, and the same teacher grousing at Tony over the same crap.

Tony hated school. He hated the fact that he couldn't read, and he hated pretending to listen to the teacher spouting the same dumb stuff. Who gave a shit if George Washington threw a silver dollar across the goddamn river and then chopped down the stupid cherry tree? His old man would have broken his goddamn fingers for a lot less.

When Tony assumed his rightful place at the head of the double line leading out of the dormitory, Stan Turpin handed him a typewritten note. Tony looked at it without comprehending the words and crumbled it in disgust. "What the hell am I supposed to do with this?" he demanded.

"Just take it to the superintendent's office," Turpin instructed.

"Masters wants to see me?"

"That's what it says, doesn't it? Right after breakfast."

Tony was tempted to ignore the summons, but he found Gary Masters waiting for him outside the dining room. "Mr. Turpin, I'm taking Tony Washington to the office," Masters said. "I'll try to have him back to the cottage before school starts."

Tony strutted three steps ahead of Masters as they walked toward the administration building. He noticed that most of the boys from his cottage were staring at them, so he kept his distance and appeared to ignore the superintendent's comments.

At first Masters tried to be friendly, but he soon realized that Tony had accepted the institutional code of behavior toward the staff and was performing for the other boys. "Go ahead and strut, Tony. You're putting on quite a show. Maybe if you turned around and took a swing at me, they could see how tough you really are."

Tony ducked his head and took a quick look at the "head screw." Masters's voice was sad, and Tony felt cheap, but he had to keep up the show until they were inside the building. Maybe the whole damned place was a show, Tony thought. At first he had to win over the staff with his charming and bright personality, even though he felt lonely and sick inside. Then he had to show the boys how tough and smart he was and how easy it was to manipulate the staff. He spent so much time acting funny or tough that it was getting hard to remember which was acting and which was real.

Tony flopped down into a chair in the far corner of Masters's office, the chair farthest from the desk. He didn't know why, he really wasn't angry, and he wished immediately that he hadn't done it.

"Come over here so I won't have to shout." Masters had his hand on the back of the chair he wanted Tony to sit in.

The boy got to his feet slowly and ambled forward with a bored, insolent look on his face. There were times lately that he had begun to wonder just how much control he had over himself. He remembered a movie he had seen about the mad scientist who had created a monster, and by the end of the movie the monster was in control of the scientist who had created him. Tony realized his own act was getting out of control.

Masters looked sad and tired. "Well, Tony," he said slowly, "you've changed, haven't you? And I understand you're making quite a name for yourself in the yard."

"What you mean?" the boy asked in a surly tone. Masters might be brain-smart, but he was one of those helper types, and with them you had to start off tough and let them break you down. As a clincher, you came on with the tears and the "You're the only one who cares" routine. Tony instinctively understood that helpers needed to know they were helping, and once you got them helping, they'd kiss your ass for the privilege of continuing. Helpers were about as street-wise as Barney Fyfe in Harlem.

But Masters refused to follow Tony's scenario. He sat up straight and glared. "I mean, at the age of ten you took over a cottage full of twelve-year-olds," he said sternly. "I mean that the people in the canteen say you have more money to spend than any tough-ass on campus. . . . I mean your teacher says you spend less than an hour a day in class and the rest of the time in the discipline room. . . . I mean your social worker thinks you're the most abused, fragile, sensitive child since Oliver Twist. . . . and I mean that you're sucking on this big stupid tit we call a correctional institution for all the sweet milk you can get." Masters's eyes narrowed to slits, and his lips were compressed. "Now do you know what I mean?"

Tony was not frightened by Masters's outburst, but he was plainly confused. He sat there with his mouth open, wondering what the man really wanted. His brain searched desperately for answers and loopholes, but he realized his old tricks wouldn't work. His only hope was to keep his mouth shut and wait to find out what was happening.

He thought fleetingly about playing it straight, but he wasn't sure what straight was anymore. He had to play the bad ass with his teacher to get out of class and avoid embarrassment. He had to be tough, self-assured, and glib in the cottage to keep his people under control and entertain the cottage parents. And with his social worker he had to be . . . *Ah, shit. Masters is different.* So what? Masters didn't have anything Tony wanted anyway. Masters was the man who said when you could go home, but Tony didn't have a home to go to.

"Now can we talk?" The superintendent's voice was calm and devoid of anger, but Tony was nervous and afraid.

"Whaddya want me to say? That I'm a bad boy? . . . A mean nigger like my ol' man?" Suddenly Tony was crying real tears and was forcing the words through wrenching sobs. "I gotta live in this place. I gotta make it the best I can. You pack up every day and go home, but I gotta stay an' watch the babies cry, and suck their thumbs, and pee their beds every night."

Gary Masters's shoulders slumped, and his own eyes misted in the face of the traumatic agony in the young boy's voice.

"There ain't been one boy raped in my cottage since I took over. How come you think that happened?" Tony asked angrily. "How you think we protect ourselves against the big studs? *You* run this place, so tell me," he demanded rhetorically. "An' you know I'm tellin' the truth 'cause the doc ain't sewed up one asshole in my cottage since I took over."

Masters sat there with a sad look, shaking his head slowly as he stared at the floor. He had seen the truth and didn't like it.

It was quiet, and Tony could smell the furniture polish. He looked around the room for the first time while he struggled to regain his composure.

Suddenly Masters sat up and took a deep breath. "All right, Tony, let's start from the beginning. For the past month real dollars have been coming into this place, and I want to know the source. I know you are involved, and I believe a staff member is also in on it."

Tony was taken off guard by the sudden disclosure of Masters's real agenda. He was also surprised by the fact that Masters apparently really wanted the truth after all. Tony decided he had said enough. If the head screw dug hard enough or had any brains, he could figure it out for himself, but Tony had said all he was going to.

Masters stood and walked to the window. He spoke with his back to the young boy. "I don't really give a damn about the dollars," he said. "The loudmouth toughs go around flashing green to show how big they are and talk about how they will use it after they run from here." Masters turned and looked at Tony. "But you and I know they're not the type to run. They haven't got the balls to make it on the outside. Out there they won't have kids to bully or push around, and they won't have stupid grown-ups to play games with."

Masters rubbed his eyes and continued. "I don't give a rap about the money. I'm concerned only with the airplane glue. In the past two weeks we've shipped two boys to the state hospital, and the doctors say they'll be basket cases the rest of their lives."

Masters walked back and placed his hands on the back of his chair, and the signs of anger returned to his face. "And by God, I'm going to find out where that shit is coming from!"

Tony began to put the pieces together: the shakedown last weekend . . . the whispers of the big boys . . . the loose brick in the barn. This was serious, and he knew some kind of deal would have to be made. "I didn't bring in no glue, and none of my boys been sniffin'."

"That's not good enough," Masters said. "I know for certain you have a money source, and I overheard two boys on detail in this building say you were selling. . . . They called it a fee-fee something or other."

Tony's mind skipped with excitement. The boy knew very little about the glue, and the man didn't know what a Fifi bag was. Tony had to pay $2 a week to the bosses of the other cottages to buy protection for his own boys, but the $2 was just what the man had said it was: show money—something to make the big boys feel bigger. The real protection came from the Fifi bags that Tony fabricated and sold, a few at a time, to each cottage. The big boys knew that if they messed around with the young ones, their supply of Fifi bags would be cut off.

Tony's mind raced through his options. He was walking on thin ice, but he had to preserve that precious source of protection. "Mr. Masters, can we make a deal?" Tony saw the anger returning, so he talked as fast as he knew how. "I ain't never had nothin' to do with no airplane glue, but I think I know how you can find out about it."

Masters sensed a breakthrough, and his shoulders relaxed imperceptibly but enough to signal progress to Tony. The boy spoke more slowly and thought things through as he went. He claimed to be able to find out who the suppliers were and where they were hiding the glue, but if he revealed their names, he said, the boys would be yanked out of school, thrown into lockup, and they would immediately blame Tony. If that happened, Tony would be dead.

"How 'bout if I tell you where the supply is hid, then I pass the word that your secretary say you have a good idea where the stuff is hid and you're gonna have a supershakedown? Then all you have to do is keep an eye on the place and grab them when they go an' dig the stuff out."

"I wasn't born yesterday, Tony. If you tell me the names, I have ways to cover for you."

"But I'm not *sure* about the names," he cried. "I just know where they have the stash."

Masters felt certain that Tony had the names, but he had enough sense to back off. "All right, what's the deal?" He was getting impatient, but he struggled to remain calm.

"If I tell you where the glue is hid and you catch them dudes, will you forget about the Fifi bags?"

Masters shot to his feet and knocked the chair over backward. He strode to the window with his hands locked behind his back, fighting for control. He turned and glared at Tony. "How can I possibly . . ." Then his eyes went blank, and he blurted in frustration, "What the hell is a Fifi bag anyway?"

Tony was tempted to exploit the superintendent's ignorance and curiosity for further bargaining leverage but decided against risking his gains by pushing too hard. "Well, you know, a Fifi bag is a small plastic bag that's filled with that Wildroot hair cream with a rubber band around the top."

The question had not yet been answered to Masters's satisfaction. "Okay," he said impatiently, "what's it used for?"

Now it was Tony's turn to be uncomfortable. It was one thing to dream up the idea, package it, and sell it to the older boys, but it was quite another to explain its usage in graphic detail to an adult. "Well . . . you see . . . you put your Fifi bag under the hot water about fifteen minutes before going up to the dormitory. Then you go to bed with it, and the big boys say it's the closest thing to real—"

"Enough!" Masters interrupted, realizing he was beginning to blush. Then he chuckled. "Okay, okay, I get the picture." He had been so caught up by the potential seriousness of Tony pushing something called fee-fee bags that his relief exploded into peals of laughter.

"Someone is furnishing you with the raw materials, and you know I can't let my staff get by with this kind of thing," Masters said after regaining his composure.

"What kinda deal is that?" Tony asked, wondering what was so funny. "I give you everything, and you take it all . . . is that the deal? Without the Fifi bags, the little kids got no protection."

Masters's expression was unyielding, so Tony thought for a moment and decided to risk his leverage. "They keeps their airplane glue behind a loose brick in the corner of the barn. You can see it from that window."

"And your Wildroot supplier?" Masters asked, fully aware that the perverted barber was the only likely candidate.

"I can't do that, Mr. Masters," Tony said softly, shaking his head. "You'll have to put me in lockup."

The full impact of Tony's plight finally began to dawn on Masters. He reached down and put his hand on the boy's shoulder. "If I put you in lockup, who would I get to pass the word about the glue? Anyway, I'd hate to think what would happen to this place if we lost our Fifi bag supplier. Go on, get off to school."

Tony jumped to his feet with a broad smile and wiped his eyes as he ran for the door. He didn't feel as though he had won, but he hadn't lost either.

Chapter Twenty-six

Gary Masters stood at the window of his darkening office and watched the sun setting beyond the rugged, gently rising prairies. In the last light of afternoon, the tall grasses and jutting rocks seemed to glow with new life, assuming muted shades of yellow and orange that contrasted vividly with the surrounding sea of burnt-autumn browns. He traced the slope of the hill downward to the point where the rough terrain blended with the flat green terraces of the reform school—the point where the tranquil scene was defaced by the chain-link fence, ten feet tall, with its barbed-wire overhang and gaping holes that offered the illusion of escape routes to the outside world.

Masters flopped into his chair with a sigh and crossed his feet on the low windowsill. The sight of the fence had shattered his euphoria. The unsightly monstrosity was a monument to the stupidity of the juvenile justice system. The boys went over it, under it, and through it at will, but when Masters proposed that it be torn down, newspapers, citizens' committees, and politicians had indignantly protested that his responsibility was to protect society. Even though the ugly, degrading barrier was useless and did nothing to stop the boys from running, the public felt safer thinking it did.

As if further to underscore the stark reality of the moment and the place, blocks of lights suddenly came on in clusters around the campus: the cottages, the gymnasium, the library, the mess hall—each activated remotely by unseen hands in the electrical plant. From his window it looked like a college campus coming alive, for he was too far away to see the bars, the heavy institutional screening, and the solid translucent glass blocks. And instead of groups of students talking, laughing, and strolling sociably through the grounds, the campus was deserted, except for an occasional "no more than one boy at a time" scurrying from one building to the next.

Masters reflected on the madness of it all. He had come to Clearwater, six months earlier, filled with idealistic dedication and dreams that were beginning to wane. As a private citizen he had been a respected and effective opponent of institutional custody of children, so the newly elected governor sought him out and persuaded him that the system could be changed only from the inside. Buried in the bureaucracy, Masters soon learned otherwise, especially answerable, as he was, to a director of institutions with completely antithetical concepts on care of prisoners. He was on a treadmill to nowhere, moving faster and faster, sapping his own strength and determination without approaching the goals he had set for his administration of the reform school.

In spite of his disappointments and frustrations, it was already too late for Masters to quit. He thought about the younger boys and how they stumbled over each other as they "marched" in formation. They huddled so closely that it was impossible for them to do anything but trip over themselves when they walked. Six-year-old prisoners! Baggy pants rolled up at the cuffs, oversize prison T-shirts hanging askew from their scrawny shoulders, and heads shaved clean. In spite of the cruelty of the system that Masters represented, they never passed him without waving. Perhaps it was a monument to the indestructibility of their spirits because whenever he got close enough, they reached out to touch him and smiled their gigantic smiles. It was always the same, and if there were no adults within reach, they held on to each other. Babies behind bars . . . simply because no one wanted them. It was too late for Masters because he had been exposed to their plight, and now it would be impossible for him to turn his back and forget.

He rose from his chair and walked toward the light switch. The old hardwood floors creaked, and his footsteps echoed through the spacious halls and empty stairwells of the administration building. Being alone there at night was an open invitation to the ghosts of children past, many of whom had taken up permanent residence in his own head. He reached the light switch just as the image of Tony Washington appeared, and he dropped his hand and returned to the window through the darkness. *I gotta live in this place. I gotta make it the best I can. You pack up every day and go home, but I gotta stay an' watch the babies cry, and suck their thumbs, and pee their beds every night.* Tony was right. Masters had thus far avoided exposing himself to that final abomination—the sights, sounds, and smells of the dormitory for six- to ten-year-olds at night, but he could do so no longer.

As if on cue, the upstairs cottage lights dimmed. Masters snapped the pencil he was holding and flung it across the room.

His master key admitted him through the front door, but before tiptoeing up the cement stairs, he removed his shoes to hold down the noise. He could hear the sobbing through the heavy steel door at the top of the staircase, and Masters struggled with an urge to turn and run. Instead, he gently slid the bolt and opened the door only far enough to squeeze into the room. In spite of the precautions, fifty-two tiny heads suddenly popped up and turned toward the intruder, who stood with his shoes in his hand and his heart in his mouth.

The angry voice of the night watchman startled him. "What the hell're you doing here?" the old man demanded. "How'd you get in?"

Masters had never seen the man before. He held up his free hand and tried to calm him. "Take it easy. I'm the superintendent. I'm sorry . . . I should have let you know," he stammered in a whisper through the small opening in the glass cage. "I . . . I just wanted to see how the boys—"

"I don't give a damn if you're the king of Roosia. The rule is no visitors in the dorms at night."

The huge room was completely still, and Masters didn't know whether he was pleased or displeased that the crying had stopped. "Listen," he whispered, suddenly angry, "I'll make a deal with you. You pass me that extra chair and shut your mouth, and I won't come in there and beat the shit out of you."

The old man frowned and reached for the chair. "I finally get these kids calmed down, and you come bustin' in here, and I gotta start all over again," he grumbled. Then he flipped on the microphone and announced, "All right, you little boys. The superintendent is here for a little visit. You all get back to sleep, you hear?" Then, in a tone that left no room for discussion, he snarled, "Get those heads down and go to sleep!"

Masters sat quietly on the wooden chair and examined the dormitory. Twelve dim bulbs were embedded in the concrete ceiling and bathed the cement floors and cinder-block walls in a grayish yellow light. The old-fashioned beds were constructed of steel, with rounded headboards and slats covered with institutional paint that was chipped and peeling. They had been provided to Clearwater after the board of supervisors of the state mental hospital had declared them unfit for their adult patients. The cold hostility of the large room immobilized Masters, and the odor of urine was pervasive.

When the sniffling started, Masters tried to tell himself that half the kids must be suffering from colds, but he knew they were crying. Most of the boys lay curled in fetal positions, and each was sucking his thumb. Several of them were holding hands across the spaces between their beds, and Masters stifled a sob when he realized that they were instinctively using every device of lost animals to achieve some modicum of security in an alien environment.

Gary Masters sat there unable to move, not knowing where to turn or what to do. Suddenly he heard the sound of bare feet padding across the concrete floor. One of the smallest six-year-olds, his thumb still in his mouth, walked up to him and crawled into his lap. There had been no hesitation and no request for permission. The boy simply curled up against Masters's chest and rested his shaved head under the man's chin. As Masters wrapped his arms around the child, other heads popped up again, turning first toward the superintendent, then toward the glass cage. The unspoken question hung heavily until it finally started: One at a time, some with blankets, some with pillows, they crawled out of their beds and stumbled toward him, settling themselves as close to the man as they could get.

They became a pyramid of sleeping children, attached to the nucleus by tiny hands clutching his trousers, his coat, his shoes, and one another. Masters sat there afraid to move, trying desperately to control the sobs coming from his gut. It was four in the morning before he dared move and began carrying the boys back to the empty beds.

So many more ghosts to assail him whenever he considered the possibility of leaving Clearwater.

Chapter Twenty-seven

John finally agreed to join Matt in Miss Wilson's advanced study program only because it represented an easy way out of the tedious hours of classroom routine.

Matt had delayed talking to John about Miss Wilson's suggestion, unconsciously adhering to the institutional code of looking after number one first, last, and always. He had selfishly feared that his friend's indifference toward education might mess up his own program and possibly turn off Miss Wilson's interest and dedication. Then one night Matt had dreamed about his grandfather Oren's sharing his food with the itinerant Indians who had come begging, and when he awoke, he thought about his father's gratuitously sharing ancient remedies for ailing stock belonging to other ranchers. Dan had never been selfishly motivated, and he had tried to instill the same kind of altruism in his son. Suddenly Matt was ashamed of holding out on his friend, but more important, he was alarmed at the way the institution was changing him.

When Matt finally asked John to join him in the program, John chuckled. "Hell, man, Miss Wilson talked to me two weeks ago . . . said you were going to get together with me right away. What took you so long?"

Matt was embarrassed. "She talked to you already? What did you say?"

"I said no," John said teasingly, "but the way you've been holding out, I got to thinking maybe it was a good deal after all."

"Then you'll do it?" Matt asked, feeling relieved.

"Why not?" John smiled, reaching out to gently touch the huge knot on the back of Matt's head. "The closer Shacky gets to your body, the more help you're going to need."

"That's as close as he's gonna get," Matt snarled.

"Oh, yeah? And what are you going to do when lover boy comes courting with all ten goons to back his play?"

"I'm working on an idea," Matt said.

John had been teasing, but not anymore. "What's your idea?" he asked seriously.

Even Ralph came alive and hit Matt on the shoulder and moved his hands as if to say, "Come on, tell us your plan."

"Not yet," Matt answered. "I need some more time to work out the details."

With John to keep him awake during the long periods of independent study, Matt rededicated himself to the academic program, and his enthusiasm was infectious. John responded competitively, and with Verna Wilson's tutelage and encouragement, the two boys progressed rapidly while their friendship grew.

John further surprised Matt in two ways: first, by joining him on the intramural basketball squad; secondly, by exhibiting great talent for the game. John had learned basketball in the schoolyard leagues of every one of the large cities his mother had taken him through, so he was immediately accepted as the team leader. He and Matt developed a crude variation of a double post offense and a zone defense, both of which were designed to showcase their respective talents with a minimum of energy. On defense, the smaller boys were assigned to chase after the ball while Matt and John stood like sentinels guarding the lanes. On offense, the two took turns shooting while one or the other broke for the rebound. Since they were six inches taller than anyone else in their league, they dominated the game while Tony Washington led the cheering and Ralph encouraged them silently from the sidelines.

Alone with John and Ralph in the locker room one evening, Matt told John about Harrison Cole's suggestion that they go out for the varsity basketball team, but John refused to consider giving up his work detail in the superintendent's office.

"Coach Cole says it's the only way we'll ever get a scholarship to college," Matt argued.

"College?" The word took on a comical scream as John jumped to his feet. "Who you jivin'?" John gibed, slipping easily back into his ghetto dialect. "Who's gonna give a scholarship to a black boy from prison? Man, your ass is pure stupid!"

"I'm not the stupid one," Matt snapped. "You're copping out, so why don't you take your poor mouth and cash it in for sympathy, then go spend it at the grocery store when you get out of this place? Some people call it welfare."

John grabbed Matt's shirt and cocked his fist. The two boys stared at each other, not knowing what to do next, but Ralph solved their problem by grabbing them by the hair and banging their heads together. They were soon laughing in relief, but Ralph was clearly disgusted with them.

Matt was not ready to give up. "I'm not joking, man. We're not going to make it on the outside unless we're good in sports. And Cole says nobody's gonna find out how good we are unless we compete with other schools and stomp their butts."

"Isn't that the shits?" John asked with a grin. "They lock us up in here because we're bad dudes, then they tell us we can't join the human race unless we get badder, and so they make us get out there and break up some small-town honkies."

Ralph appreciated the irony. He closed his eyes and smiled as his belly shook.

"Will you look at that . . . ol' Ralph is laughing!" John exclaimed. "Ol' ice is cracking up."

They finally agreed that they would work at it together . . . all three of them. John could excel at any sport, but Matt was still too clumsy for varsity basketball, and Ralph was altogether too fat and uncoordinated, so they agreed to work toward getting in shape for the next football season. John and Matt would continue with intramural basketball; then the three of them would work on the weights during the winter and go out for track in the spring. The following fall they would terrorize their high school football opponents. The three hopefuls sealed their pact with a handshake and left the locker room sharing an improbable dream that might hold the key to their future in the outside world.

* * *

That night Larry Belcher, a seventeen-year-old who had been admitted three weeks earlier, jumped up on his bed and screamed like a wild man. Then he ran across the tops of the other beds and tried to run his head through the steel mesh covering of a plate glass window. His first attempt stunned him, and he fell to the floor, where he sat with a blank stare and blood running down his face. Within seconds he was on the beds again, trying to batter his head through three other windows around the room until the night watchman showed up to carry him off to lockup. No one had gotten out of bed to help him, and Pops had never even left his glass cage.

Matt had been lying there fantasizing about the athletic conquests that would carry him to college, but after Larry's outburst and removal the reality of the place mocked his dream and brought tears to his eyes. He lay there for the remainder of the night without praying or hoping . . . just waiting for daylight.

Rick O'Malley returned to the cottage the following week. He stayed to himself and would have nothing to do with anyone else. Two days later they found him in the school bathroom, bleeding profusely from slashed wrists. Carl Gregston reported that he was alive when they got him to the hospital, but Matt never saw or heard about Rick again, and he never learned whether or not Rick had died. The incident served to remind Matt further of the chasm between the world in which he lived and the one to which he aspired.

Chapter Twenty-eight

John Culver had always been a professional survivor. He lived by two rules: Know as much as you can about what's going on around you, and don't get involved. He had worked in the superintendent's office for three years, so he had access to information that was useful in buying him immunity from the day-to-day entanglements of prison life. He might warn Shacky about an impending contraband shakedown, or he might alert the chief steward to a surprise kitchen inspection. In return, John was permitted to remain neutral in the constantly swirling power struggles of the cottage system.

Under the old superintendent the task had been simple and could have been performed with equal dispatch by any one of John's peers. Soon after Masters's arrival, however, John perceived a subtle change in the kinds of information that was becoming available to the office boys, and he realized that the new superintendent was not only aware of the intelligence network but was actually exploiting it for his own purposes. As a result, Masters was able to rid the cottages of drugs and weapons every few weeks, and his kitchen remained spotless. It was a brilliant way to compensate for the shortage of staff members ordinarily needed to conduct intensive inspections.

John was the only person to recognize the ploy, and he went along with it without saying a word, transmitting the information that he knew Masters wanted disseminated and withholding everything else. In return, Masters rewarded John with special tidbits of intelligence that kept the boy in favor among staff and inmates.

Without either of them having spoken about the arrangement, a mutual respect began to develop between them.

One day, in late September, John found a need to test his growing confidence in the superintendent. "Uh . . . Mr. Masters . . . excuse me," he stammered. "Bloody Bert needs to see you right away."

"That sounds like a knock-knock joke." Masters smiled. "Who is Bloody Bert?"

"It's no joke, Mr. Masters," John responded with overdone innocence. "That's Buckner . . . Bertolt Buckner's his whole name. He's the butcher. All the kids call him Bloody Bert. He told me to come up and get you. Something about the shipment of meat that just came in."

Masters felt some annoyance. "Tell him if he's got a problem to take it to his supervisor first. I don't have time to—"

"I think it's real important, Mr. Masters . . . I told him I'd try."

The uncharacteristic urgency in John's voice triggered an instinctive response. "All right. I'll get over there right away."

The foul odor of putrefied meat pervaded the room. Bertolt Buckner, oblivious of the superintendent's arrival, stood at the butcher block, hacking angrily at a side of beef, filling the garbage cans with huge chunks of meat. His face was screwed up in disgust, and he was covered with blood from his rubber gloves to his shoulders.

"What the hell is going on here?" Masters demanded, struggling to contain his nausea.

The butcher looked up, and the revulsion on his face was replaced by confusion and discomfort. "Vot you mean?" the German asked. "Nodding's goin' on."

"Nothing?" Masters shouted. "Do you call that nothing?" he demanded, pointing to the garbage cans filled with meat. "And what's that goddamned smell?"

"I chust do my chob, Mr. Masters. I tell Mr. Cotter . . . dat's all I can do."

"All right. All right. Can it!" Masters ordered angrily. "What's wrong with that meat?"

The butcher continued to struggle with his confusion and hesitantly lifted a large chunk of meat from the barrel as Masters advanced toward him. "Maggots," he explained. "Ve got maggots."

Masters's stomach churned violently when he got close enough to see the soft white grubs curling through the meat, and he suddenly needed fresh air. "You get the chief steward," he growled, "and report to my office immediately."

By the time Cotter Sherman was announced, Gary Masters's face had lost its green pallor. There were no amenities. "What happened to that shipment of meat?"

Sherman was not overly concerned. "That's the way we got it," he replied. "It's not the first time."

"What the hell does that mean?"

"Supplying meat to the state institutions is a big contract," Sherman explained calmly. "It's a political plum that's handed out by whichever party is in power. Three months ago the governor finally got around to rewarding one of his friends, and now one out of every three or four shipments of meat comes to us like the one you just saw."

Masters was completely incredulous, and he could not disguise his shock. "Do you mean to tell me this has happened before?" Sherman nodded without changing his expression. "Why wasn't I notified? How can that be? . . . The governor would never—"

"I'm sure the governor knows nothing about it," Sherman explained. "These things just happen. There was no need to bother you with it. I spoke to the institutional purchasing office, and apparently we're the only ones affected. They said to make the best of it."

Masters was outraged. "Damn you, Cotter, we've got three hundred and sixty boys in this stinkhole. How can we make the best of rotten meat?"

Sherman sat forward in his chair and spoke in conciliatory tones. "Try to understand, Gary. This could be political dynamite, and personally we like you too much to see you get yourself blown up by it. It's not all that bad, believe me. We cut away the bad meat and grind up the rest. Then we spice it up, add a little gravy, and no one can tell the difference." Masters stared in disbelief as the chief steward continued. "Believe me," he pleaded, "this thing will work out. As soon as the new supplier gets delivery on his refrigerated trucks, there won't be a problem. Meanwhile, there's not a damned thing anyone can do. We'll salvage enough meat to keep everybody fed . . . we won't make any unnecessary waves . . . and we'll keep the director of institutions off our backs."

Gary Masters was still livid when he got through to the director's office. "Goddammit, Hacker, we're existing on a starvation budget as it is. I don't fix the holes in the fucking fence so I can spend the money on food, and the crap your political cronies send us is crawling with worms."

George Hacker had been appointed director of institutions because he was a tough cop who had campaigned against the coddling of inmates. His strong objections to the appointment of Gary Masters had been overridden by the governor, and Hacker remained openly critical of Masters's administration of the Boys' Industrial School. He would not have intentionally supplied putrefied meat, nor would he be involved in political kickbacks, but he was not about to condone Masters's insolence either. "You're wasting my time, Masters, so I'm going to say this only once: You'll have another shipment of meat in two days. If that's not soon enough, why don't you favor me with your letter of resignation?"

"You want a letter, Hacker? I'll give you a letter. I'm going to start on it in about one minute from now, but it won't be my resignation, and it won't be to you. It's going to be a letter to the attorney general of the United States, and it's going to describe every piece of shit I see floating in this cesspool. And if that shipment of meat isn't here by Thursday, I'm going to hand-deliver that letter to Washington. If you won't listen to me, maybe you'll listen to the FBI."

Gary Masters wrote his letter, angrily exposing the indignities and injustices of the system, demanding a thorough investigation by the FBI. When the shipment of good meat arrived on schedule, however, he locked the letter in his desk, determined to continue the fight on his own for as long as he could.

As soon as the crisis had been resolved, Masters made another visit to the butcher shop. "Bertolt, I want to thank you personally for reporting that bad meat to me. It took a lot courage, and I really appreciate it."

Bloody Bert seemed confused and a little embarrassed. "Dank you, sir, but I chust tell Mr. Cotter. Dat's my chob."

Masters attributed the butcher's response to modesty, but as soon as he returned to his office and saw the pleased expression on John's face, he realized that Bloody Bert had not sent for him at all. It all had been John's idea from the beginning. As he walked past the boy, he clapped him on the shoulder and said simply, "Thanks, John. I owe you one."

The boy, who had been pleased that the superintendent had lived up to his high expectations, was equally restrained. "Yeah," he said. "Me, too."

Chapter Twenty-nine

The crisp air of autumn seemed to renew the boys' spirits and fill them with energy, so Gary Masters decided to try something new. He instituted a two-hour afternoon recreation schedule that freed them from all work details to play or socialize in the large communal yard however they pleased, while the cottage fathers sat together on a back porch and supervised from afar.

Yard time became a happy ritual for Matt, John, Ralph, and Tony. While the other inmates milled about aimlessly, each of the four regularly settled into the same self-assigned places: John on the cement block facing the chain-link fence; Ralph on the ground, with his back against the fence and his legs sprawled out in the dirt; Matt hunkered down, cowboy-style, next to John; and Tony kneeling or squatting in the middle of the circle.

Each had his own reason for finding comfort in the group, but the common denominator was trust. Tony could put on his act if he wanted to, but if he didn't, it was not necessary. And if he did, it was for fun, not for survival or control. Tony dubbed them the Fudge Ripples, and not feeling compelled to act out or manipulate, he could just relax and enjoy the comfort of their brotherhood.

For Ralph it was a place to lift his head and be human. In the cottage, on the square, or in the dining room, Ralph looked like a hunchbacked giant, head and eyes cast downward, encapsulated in his own quiet world. In automotive classes he read his manuals and did his work, but he slouched and shuffled about in such a way that his participation was plainly reluctant. Among the Fudge

Ripples, however, his head was up, and his expression animated and responsive. He listened intently and managed to communicate by gesturing and writing in the dirt. When he struggled with a thought too complicated to convey, however, he would scrunch up his face into an exaggerated look of frustration, and the group would laugh and poke at him good-naturedly. And then he would usually laugh at himself, unembarrassed by his handicap, unashamed at his attempt, and without regret for having made himself vulnerable. There was no ridicule in the reaction of his friends, only feelings of security, togetherness, and caring.

Matt found in the group an opportunity to rekindle the camaraderie he had enjoyed growing up with cowboys and ranchers. Although he would not have admitted it to himself, he also felt a certain superiority for the fact that he had been reared with love and a sense of heritage, while John had never experienced a real home, Tony was a product of the streets, and Ralph had been committed to institutional life as an infant by a selfish mother who had believed him to be hopelessly retarded. Matt's feeling of superiority, devoid of arrogance, gave rise to a certain security and fostered in him a sense of responsibility for the welfare of his friends. But if Matt was seen as the leader of the group, it was only because John Culver acquiesced to it.

An outsider might have perceived John as a reluctant participant. Togetherness, loyalty, and security were traps he had fallen into before, and he knew them to be human conditions that could feel the best and hurt the most. He knew that belonging to and caring about others in the cruel and unreal world of a reform school were completely insane. Before Matt's arrival and the accidental evolution of the Fudge Ripples, John had been completely independent—neither victim nor protector. He had turned his back on every wide-eyed, stupid greenhorn floating obliviously into the goons' traps, and he had resisted every attempt to be recruited into a leadership role with either the goons or the patsies.

In spite of his past insularity, John hungered for the warmth and companionship of the Fudge Ripples, but they also crowded his independence and dented his emotional armor. He was no longer living in his own world. Their problems became his problems, and their pain his pain. He knew that Matt was too inexperienced and unhardened to assume control in a crisis, but he sat back and permitted his friend to lead, all the time feeling impending responsibility approaching like an evil plague. He had succumbed to the opiate of friendship, and he knew it would be his undoing.

The four boys shared a common problem: They had been imprisoned simply because there had been no one on the outside to take care of them; that also meant they would have no homes to return to when they were ultimately released. As their friendship grew, they spent more and more of their yard time discussing their future together.

"In my neighborhood I could line us up a whole stable of cuties in two minutes," Tony offered confidently. "We would be living on Cadillac Street in no time flat."

Matt laughed delightedly. "I don't think my great-grandfather would have approved of me becoming a pimp." Tony's brow furrowed, and his expression indicated that he was offended by the older boy's disparagement of his own highest aspirations, so Matt stopped laughing and took another tack. "Sorry, but don't forget, the three of us will be out of here a lot sooner than you, and they won't let us take you out till we're old enough. How could we make it as pimps without you?"

"Besides," John added, "how long do you think these honkies would last in your old neighborhood?"

"Oh, yeah. I forgot about that," Tony said glumly. He was willing to forgive Matt's indiscretion, but he failed to see any humor in the situation.

Ralph tried to cheer Tony with a friendly nudge, but the tiny boy was thrown off balance and toppled toward John.

"I don't want him," John said, pushing him toward Matt.

"Me neither," said Matt as he completed the circle by roughly tossing the giggling boy toward Ralph.

Ralph caught him, stood up and tossed him high into the air like a bald giant juggling a rag doll. Then he caught the squealing boy and placed him gently back in his place, but Tony was laughing so hard by that time that he toppled over and rolled in the dirt, attempting to catch his breath and his balance.

Suddenly Matt was overwhelemed with sadness. Under all

that quick wit and crusty toughness, Tony was really a giggly little kid, rolling in the dirt on a beautiful autumn day. Only there, within the tight circle of the Fudge Ripples could Tony revert to normal behavior, and only there, in the confines of a juvenile prison, was the sight of a ten-year-old boy laughing out of control considered an oddity.

In the weeks that followed, the boys discussed every conceivable alternative living situation. Returning to a big city was favored by John, who wanted the creature comforts, and by Tony, who needed the action.

Matt was determined to return to high-country ranching, and Ralph's needs would be satisfied anywhere that could provide him employment in carpentry or automotive repair. Tony finally suggested the perfect compromise: "Let's find a place on the outskirts of Denver with a stable for Matt, a color TV for John, and I'll open a whorehouse over Ralphie's garage."

John's residual cynicism had thrust him into the role of the group's resident pragmatist. "Tell me this," he growled. "While I'm watching TV, and tweety bird is feathering his nest over gonzo's garage, and bowlegs is smooching with his horse, who's going to be taking care of *us*? I couldn't make a peanut butter sandwich. Can anyone cook?"

Ralph's face lit up, and both hands flew into the air as he smiled broadly and nodded enthusiastically. In precise pantomime he cracked an egg with both hands and carefully dropped it into an imaginary pan. Then he gently waggled the pan in his left hand and carefully flipped the egg with the unseen spatula in his right, concluding the operation with a self-satisfied smile.

"God help me," John muttered. "I'm beginning to understand him."

Chapter Thirty

Tony Washington had been on a personal high for more than a week. His plan for catching the glue pushers had come off perfectly, and he had escaped suspicion. In the classroom Mrs. Goldberg seemed to have struck an unspoken agreement with him that she would not call on him to read, and he would not give her cause to send him to the discipline room.

Tony stared intently at the large clock in front of the classroom, counting the seconds until the final bell. Two hours of free time! He hated school more than anything in the world, and when the bell finally rang, his entire personality changed. He jumped from his chair and headed straight for the door, snapping his fingers and shouting in a singsong voice, "How can dat final bell sound so good when dat first bell sound so baad?"

Suddenly she was there, standing between him and the door, hovering like one of those birds that eat dead things. "Tony, would you please remain for a few minutes?" The boy froze, too disappointed to move, while the rest of the class marched out. Mrs. Goldberg pointed to the chair next to her desk. "Just have a seat. I'll be right back."

Tony sat in the wooden chair, dangling his feet and morosely watching the clock eat into his yard time, wondering if the Ripples would worry about him. He should have known better than to be pleased with the way things were going. Every time he got things figured out, the damned grown-ups changed the rules, and they changed the rules whenever things seemed to be going good.

The vulture returned and perched on the edge of her desk,

but when she spoke, her voice was kind, not tough-sounding the way she usually spoke to him in front of the other boys. "I understand you had a talk with Mr. Masters."

"Yeah. A couple a weeks ago. He asked me to help him decide on which teachers to fire."

"Did he also tell you that I am tired of having you spend most of your time in the discipline room?"

Where was all this going? She knew damned well the head screw had come down on him for that. Why did she have to waste so much of his free time asking dumb questions?

"My purpose was not to get you into trouble, Tony. I spoke to Mr. Masters because I am tired of watching a bright young man wasting an opportunity to learn."

Tony stared at the floor as his feet swung back and forth under his chair. He didn't answer because she hadn't really asked a question, but the substance of her unspoken question filtered through his mind. Tony knew he was street-wise and school-dumb . . . that he was protecting the lives of six-year-olds in his cottage who could read far better than he. He had accepted the fact that he would never be able to read, but he didn't like the idea. Reading was magic—being able to make sense out of something printed on a page—but it was a trick he knew he would never master.

"You never act up during first hour, and I know why. That's when we study math," she continued, "and you have no trouble with math. But as soon as we start to read, you do something that forces me to send you to the discipline room.

"I know you think this arrangement is fine," she said. "I maintain class discipline, and you avoid the embarrassment of not knowing how to read. But every time I see you sitting on the floor of the discipline room, I see how wasteful this arrangement really is. . . . Tony, do you want to learn how to read?"

Tony was grateful for the opportunity to talk so he could take control of the tempo and end the meeting quickly. "Sure I want to read, but I'd like to fly, too, and I got as much of a chance of flying as I do reading. I just can't do it, so just forget about it."

"But you have taken tests . . ."

"Shit, I took eye tests, brain tests, and they even put me in a box with a picture machine. The readin' part of my brain don't work, that's all."

Suddenly she was smiling broadly, and Tony wondered why she was so happy. Maybe she figured if he really had a bad brain, it wasn't her fault that she couldn't teach him how to read.

"Do you really believe those tests prove you are incapable of learning how to read?" she asked pleasantly.

Of course that's what he believed! No one had ever talked to him about it, but what else could it be?

Mrs. Goldberg opened a large brown envelope and took out its contents. "I have the results of your tests right here. Every one of them says you are A okay. No brain problem, no seeing problem, and no hearing problem."

"Then how come I can't read?" he asked warily, trying to figure out why she was lying to him.

"My guess is that you got off to a very poor start, and when you finally realized how far behind you were, you just gave up. That's when you started skipping school and hating it so much." Mrs. Goldberg slapped the palms of her hands down on her desk and pushed herself up. "I'm glad we had this talk."

Tony sprang from his chair with a smile and a quick glance at the clock, pleased that he had lost only fifteen minutes of his free period.

"Just a minute," she said. "There's someone I want you to meet."

Tony flopped back into his chair and glared at her as she went to the door and motioned with her hand. "Tony Washington, I want you to meet Mrs. Penny Conlin."

Tony jumped from his chair again, but this time he gave no thought to leaving. The woman who walked toward him was the most beautiful creature he had ever seen. Her smiling lips glistened, her eyes twinkled, and her brown hair bounced pertly as she approached. All he could do was stare. He hadn't seen a foxy broad like that in his best days on the streets. *Put one like that in your stable, and you could sit back and watch the bread roll in. You wouldn't even have to peddle it. Just stick it out on the front porch, and get outta the way.*

"Hi, Tony."

She even sounded good. He could remember the big boys talking about this fox or that one, but up until now he could never comprehend their excitement.

"Mrs. Conlin lives in town, and she has volunteered to teach you how to read." By comparison, Mrs. Goldberg's voice sounded like fingernails scraping the blackboard. "From now on you will leave this room immediately after math period and spend the rest of the morning with Mrs. Conlin in the small office next to the gymnasium."

"How?" the dumbstruck boy managed to mutter.

"How what, Tony?"

"How she gonna teach me to read?" he asked without really caring. All that mattered was that the two of them would be crowded into that tiny room together every morning from now on. That second bell might not sound so bad after all.

Penny Conlin answered his question. "I don't know, Tony. We'll just have to work it out together. I do know we'll have to start from the very beginning. We will work hard, but we'll have some fun, too."

You sure got that right, lady, he thought, struggling to control his breathing. He knew she would not be able to teach him to read, but he was determined that it would take her as long as possible to find that out. He also knew it wasn't cool to stand there gaping, so he took the first step in the ritualistic courting dance by asking with feigned indifference, "Can I go now? My friends are waiting for me." The boy sauntered casually to the classroom door, but once out of sight, he sprinted down the hall to the yard.

It did not matter that the yard was crowded with boys, Tony knew exactly where his friends would be. He put his head down and scampered in and out of milling groups as he headed for the fence, eager to tell them about the beautiful new woman in his life.

"Grab him."

Tony had no idea who gave the order or who snatched him

up in mid-stride, but when he was set down again, he was set down in front of Shacky Wallis. Shacky was standing with his weight on his bad leg, and he tilted so precariously that it seemed the slightest shove would have sent him sprawling. His pockmarked face was framed in an enormous mane of flaming red hair, and his best smile looked more like a lascivious sneer.

"Some piece of snoose I saw you with, short stuff. You gonna share her with your friends, or is she partial to black meat?"

"She's no piece of snoose," Tony said angrily. "She's a lady."

"Oh, right." Shacky laughed. "And what would a *lady* want with you?"

"None of your goddamn business," Tony shouted. "You just stick with your boyfriends and leave her alone."

"Hey, hey," Shacky crooned. "Don't get so uptight. I'm just happy for you, that's all. Take it easy. I'm just trying to be friendly." Then Shacky's crooked grin evaporated, and his eyes turned cold. "If I wasn't, I'd squash your head," he said ominously. "Make no mistake about it."

"Yeah . . . well, okay," Tony said, trying not to tremble. "She's a friend of my mama's. She's a teacher or something. Anyway, she's interested in teaching some of the younger kids better, and she wants me to help her out."

"See how easy that was," Shacky said with a grin. "No need to be hostile."

"Well, I gotta go. See ya."

"Just one more minute," the older boy said as Walt Pate blocked Tony's escape. "I was wondering about the Lone Ranger," he said, nodding toward the fence.

"Matt? What about him?"

"I been real good to him. No protection money from him *or* his dummy friend. That could make me look bad. You know what I mean?"

"Yeah, I know."

"I just hope he *appreciates* it, that's all. He's been acting kind of snooty with me, and I was hoping he'd start getting more friendly."

Tony wished he could pulverize the pimply face and eradicate the hateful sneer forever. Instead, he mumbled, "I'll tell him."

Shacky placed his hands over Tony's ears and applied just enough pressure to the sides of his head to remind the boy that he could crush him at will. "Good. Good," Shacky said happily. "Any help would be appreciated. That's what friends are for. Right?"

The Fudge Ripples had not seen the encounter, but when Tony shuffled into their midst, he was plainly upset.

"What's wrong?" Matt asked as he came to his feet and approached the boy. "You're shaking all over."

"Nothin' . . . It's that shitheel . . . Shacky. I'm gonna get him." By the time Tony had finished describing the incident, along with his spontaneous embellishments, he was laughing again, but he had succeeded in transferring his anger and fear to Matt, who stood ashen, surveying the holes in the cyclone fence that might provide him an escape.

John touched his friend on the arm and said, "Forget it. It's already been tried. We'll figure a way to stop him."

The following day the three older boys found Tony waiting for them impatiently. "Where ya been?" he demanded petulantly. Then, without waiting for an answer, he said, "I got it."

"Got what?"

"You know that fenced-in pasture north of the barn?" Tony's crooked fingers were pointing in three directions, but he was too excited to notice that he had them exposed. He was also too excited to wait for an answer. "The field with all the poison ivy."

"Yeah, I know the one," John said with a smile. "What about it?"

"Well, our beloved principal, Harold Shmidt, is gonna ask Shacky to go out there tomorrow and pick the *weeds*, that's what. An' he's gonna invite Walt Pate, too."

Matt had to laugh in spite of himself. "Why would the principal do that?"

"He'll do it 'cause I got a blank pass, with his signature on it, that's gonna *say* he did it, that's why he'll do it."

The grin on John's face indicated that he already understood the plan, but Matt was still in the dark. "You're not making sense."

Tony picked up a stick and started scratching rectangles in

the dirt. "Look here, dummy. Sorry, Ralphie, I mean this dummy. This is the discipline room, see? And right across the hall is the principal's office, right? Well, when Shmidt wants to call someone in or to go do him an errand, he writes a note on this yellow paper and stamps his name on it. Then he leaves it in that wooden box on his desk, and the office boy picks it up and takes it to whoever it says to take it to."

"Okay, so what?"

Tony reached into the breast pocket of his denim jacket and carefully extracted a small piece of yellow paper stamped with the signature of the principal. "This is so what," Tony said triumphantly. "You write Shacky's name here, and down here you tell him some of the younger dopeheads been out in that field fooling with those plants with the white berries, and you want him to check into it."

"If we just send him out there to check on the plants with the berries, how are we going to get him to pick them?"

"Simple. Just tell him *not* to, ranger . . . just tell him not to."

In spite of the fact that Shacky's face and hands were so grossly bloated, he stared in fascination at himself in the full-length mirror in the nurse's office.

Walt Pate stood behind him, gingerly patting calamine lotion on his own blotchy skin. "I know who did this," he said, fuming. "You bet your ass I know who did this." Then he sidled up to Shacky in front of the mirror and stuck out his swollen tongue. "Look at that," he growled, patting some lotion on his lips. "I got it everywhere."

"You shouldn't have tried to eat the berries," Shacky offered indifferently. "Shmidt's note said not to."

"It was that goddamn cowboy. You just wait—"

Shacky pivoted around on his shriveled leg and lashed out at his chief lieutenant. "You stupid bastard. You don't know shit. It was that nigger . . . Culver. He's been in my hair for a long time, and he's gonna get his, but . . ." Shacky turned back to the mirror to examine his disfigured face again before resuming in a subdued tone. "But Matt's coming along fine. He's a smart boy. And I can tell he's beginning to like me . . . and respect me."

Find a Safe Place

Walt Pate whined in pain as he tried to apply the calamine to his face. "This stuff itches so bad it hurts. I mean, it really hurts."

"Pate, sometimes I wonder why I promoted you. You're the biggest fuckin' baby in the joint," Shacky said. Then he bent over and slapped at his crippled leg. "If you had one of these, you'd know what real pain is all about. This," he said, fingering the rash on his face, "this is humiliation, not pain. And you know what happens when the man gets humiliated and doesn't retaliate."

Shacky limped back and forth in the small office and spoke more to himself than to Walt Pate. "The stupid jerks in here don't understand the responsibility I have. When they screw with my image, they screw with the power that keeps this whole place going smooth, and when that happens, I have to muscle them back into line. Matt is probably the only one around here who's smart enough to know what I'm talkin' about. I can tell . . . and I think he really respects me."

Chapter Thirty-one

Matt had never fully acclimated himself to some of the offensive sights, sounds, and odors of the cottage. The concrete-block walls were painted institutional gray, and the concrete floors were covered with a shiny off-white enamel that was so hard it never wore out; it just chipped away. The routine punishment for a minor infraction of the rules was to have the boy scrape a ten-by-ten area of the floor and then repaint it. As a result, there was never a time when some part of the stark floor was not being chipped and repainted. The enameled floors were also waxed and buffed, upstairs and down, every day, and the hard, glaring surface reflected every light and sharpened every sound in the building.

In addition to the constant odors of prison paint and floor wax, the smell of mildew pervaded the walls and furniture as well as the boys' mattresses, sheets, and clothes. The steam from the shower room regularly coursed through the open latrine and into the recreation room, infiltrating every open pore in the building and quickly ripening into the noxious odor of mildew. As soon as the boys left for school every morning, the cottage father sprayed the rooms with fungicide, but it was a toss-up as to which smelled worse.

For Matt, the most unpleasant part of the day was returning to the cottage after school, when the combined odors and stuffiness assailed him. The rains of late autumn and the perpetually cloudy skies had robbed the grounds of whatever color had existed, and the foul drabness of the place had become intolerable.

For the first time Matt seriously began to consider the possibility of escaping. The ten-foot chain-link fence was riddled with gaping holes, but very few boys who tried it ever got far because the institution was so isolated, except for the city of Clearwater, where the shaved heads of the would-be escapees were spotted immediately.

The scuttlebutt was that Matt's cottage averaged three attempted runaways a month, but none of the inmates knew for certain because a boy might suddenly disappear for reasons ranging from release to lockup, and explanations were rarely offered. Runners usually headed straight for home and were quickly found and returned to lockup, but crack-ups and suicides just disappeared. No one talked about them or asked about them. They were just gone, and their beds were assigned to new boys immediately.

Matt disregarded the slim chances of success and began to talk openly about trying to escape. John listened patiently and laughed off some of Matt's more elaborate schemes. He was pleased to see his friend's enthusiasm returning, but he did not want it to get out of hand.

Matt questioned Miss Wilson about previous escapes, trying not to be too obvious about his intentions, but he was completely transparent. "Don't do anything stupid," she warned peremptorily. "If you go through the fence, you will be tracked down and caught."

Two days before Thanksgiving three twelve-year-old boys made their bid for freedom. Two of them were captured within hours, but the third made it all the way to his hometown, almost three hundred miles away. They found him on Thanksgiving morning, frozen to death in a culvert. John shared the information with Matt in the hope of discouraging him, and that, combined with the first heavy snowfall of the season, convinced Matt that all his planning had been futile.

Matt's depression deepened his feeling of hopelessness. Shacky was stepping up his pressure to have Matt join him by causing problems for Ralph and Tony. Most of it consisted of vicious pranks, but there were a few physical confrontations. In the days that followed, Matt avoided the Fudge Ripples, hoping to insulate them from further danger while he weighed the alternatives of escaping, fighting Shacky, or joining him.

Miss Wilson was quick to remind him that his studies were being neglected. She was concerned about the dark circles under his eyes, and it was clear that he was nervous and preoccupied. But she had made up her mind to find out what was bothering him. "You're not cutting it, Matthew. You might as well be back in the classroom, swatting flies with the rest of them."

"Yeah, maybe you're right. Things would be a lot easier."

"Easier? You're not spending any time at all on your studies. What could be easier than that?"

Matt shook his head. "You don't understand. It's not my studies. It's the other stuff—Shacky and the others—their gotchas and blanket parties."

"That boy is positively demented," she said angrily. "You're not afraid of him, are you?"

"No. Not exactly. At least not for myself. But he keeps picking on the others . . . Ralph and Tony especially. And he's going to get rougher and rougher on them unless . . ." Matt's voice trailed off.

"Unless what?" she persisted.

"Unless I join up with him."

Miss Wilson was not prepared for that possibility. "That's ludicrous!" she exclaimed.

"If I join up with Shacky, then I can protect Ralph and Tony. If I don't, they're going to get hurt."

"Ha!" she said derisively. "Who are you kidding? You couldn't protect anyone. Have you looked at yourself lately? You look as if you were on the verge of a complete breakdown . . . as if you'd shatter into a million pieces if someone poked you with a feather."

Matt shifted uncomfortably in his chair.

"If you ask me," she said, "you're just looking for an easy way out. If you want to join those thugs, then go ahead, but don't try to sound noble about it."

"You d-don't understand," he stammered.

"I think I do. Three months ago you came to me and said you wanted to go to college—maybe even become a veterinarian— because that's what your *father* wanted. Now you want to drop out because that's what *Shacky* wants." Miss Wilson searched his face for a reaction. "Look at me, boy." She touched her fingers to his chin and raised his head. "I know what everyone wants except you."

Tears began to form in Matt's eyes. "I want things to be like they used to be," he said softly. "No blanket parties, no knifings, not even college . . . just me and my dad."

Miss Wilson was suddenly struggling to hold back her own tears. "I know, son," she said tenderly. "Your dad's dead, but you can have the rest of the dream if you want it badly enough . . . if you're strong enough to fight for it. . . . Are you strong enough, Matt?"

Matt lowered his head and said softly, "I don't know anymore."

The following day Matt was transferred from the barn detail to the gymnasium. He recognized John's hand in the reassignment, and he felt a grudging admiration for his friend's influence. John had said that Matt needed some time to think in private, and the job of sweeping and dusting the highly polished hardwood bleachers was as close as he would come to privacy at Clearwater.

The balcony above the bleachers consisted of nine concrete steps that provided segregated seating for the townspeople when there was a basketball game with an outside school. The separation between the two areas was maintained by a chain-link fence. There were rarely any problems at the outset of a game, but the *"normal"* kids, parents, and cheerleaders spent so much time gawking at the boys in the bleachers, expecting them to behave like animals, that the inmates invariably accommodated them. By half time even the meekest of boys were growling, cursing, and fighting among themselves to impress the visitors.

Matt thought about the funny stories John had told about past home basketball games and smiled. He looked forward to seeing the spectacle for himself in just a few days.

At that moment Gary Masters came through the balcony door and walked directly toward him. "I understand that Shacky has made you an offer," Masters said.

Matt stared down at the broom and remained silent. He had not mentioned Shacky's offer to Miss Wilson, so it must have been John who had betrayed his confidence.

"I want you to know that I won't try to stop you. In fact, for my part, it might be very helpful."

Matt looked up sharply.

"That's right." Masters shrugged. "We're going to have to release Shacky one of these days, and if you are tough enough to take his place, you could keep those kids in line for me. I certainly can't do it by myself."

Masters had not smoked since coming to Clearwater, but he lit a cigarette before continuing. "You were sent to this place for the wrong reason . . . just like most of the others who are here. I just want to be certain that if you should decide to become another Shacky, you don't do *that* for the wrong reason, too. The fact is, you don't belong here at all. When you first came, you were outraged by the injustice of it all. Don't you remember?"

Matt had turned away and did not respond, but Masters perceived a slight tightening of the boy's shoulders that might have passed for a shrug. Perhaps he was listening after all.

"Let me put it this way," Masters continued. "There are only a few options available to boys like you: Either you release your pent-up rage, or you go crazy. Neither one of those will work for you because there is no acceptable way of releasing your rage in this place, and your head is on too straight for you to go crazy. So you take the third option, and we have seen it happen many times."

Masters exhaled the bitter-tasting smoke and crushed the cigarette on the floor. "You begin to believe you are really bad. That's what John refers to as the guilties, and it's not a bad name for it. Once you convince yourself that you *are* bad, then your confinement here is justified, and you get rid of the rage because you no longer have to deal with an injustice. The courts have labeled you a bad-ass, and now you can accept it, hook, line, and sinker."

Masters leaned forward, almost to the back of Matt's head, and spoke with a new urgency. "The next step is the killer, Matt, because that's when you team up with the losers—the real psychotics in this place. You join them because like most kids your age, you want to belong to something that fits. You want to belong, and you find yourself doing what the others around you expect you to do."

Suddenly things started to fall into place for Matt. That was precisely why the boys behaved as they did during the basketball games. The visitors expected them to be bad, so that was the way they acted.

Masters stepped down to Matt's level and looked down at the slumped boy. "I have seen the guilty syndrome destroy too many kids. Don't become one of them. You have too much going for you. You're the best . . . the best of all the McFaddens."

Matt stiffened, and his eyes filled with tears.

"It's against the rules to let boys have valuables, but I think you need to be reminded of who and what you are. *Keep* your outrage, Matt. You *should* be outraged. From what I've heard, I think you've got the guts to deal with it. I'm sure your father thought so, too."

The tears were falling from his cheeks as Matt reached for the old watch in Masters's outstretched hand. The inscription was still there: "To Matt . . . my son, my best friend, and the McFadden with the best of all our pasts."

The Lakeview High School pep band played a fight song next to the parked school bus near the Clearwater gymnasium. The mood was uncommonly festive as the townspeople and students filed into the gymnasium. Gary Masters and Rich Anderson were outside collecting tickets, greeting the visitors, and directing them into the building.

Masters saw Miss Wilson approaching and greeted her. "Well, Verna, with the sounds and smells inside that gym, we could be mistaken for any normal, red-blooded American high school getting ready for its first home game."

Miss Wilson was in no mood for pleasantries. "Yes, and if you peel one thin layer off that wholesome veneer, you can witness the destruction of one of the finest boys I have ever known."

The smile faded from Masters's face. "Dammit, Verna, your timing is lousy." He was tempted to dismiss her so that he might enjoy this rare moment of normal life, but he took her by the elbow and led her away from the crowd. "All right," he said impatiently, "what's your point?"

"My point is Matt McFadden," she said. "Shacky and his

goons are pushing him into a corner, and if that happens, this place, with all its sick systems, is going to destroy someone worth saving."

"I spoke to Matt the other day, and I know he's confused," Masters said, trying to remain patient.

"He *was* confused. But thanks to you and that stupid gold watch, I'm afraid he has decided to fight. You've got to do something, Gary."

Masters gestured toward a group of inmates marching to the gym. "Look at those boys," he said. "Every one of them needs special help. Are you saying that Matt is more worthy of our help than any of them?"

"I'm telling you that Matt is a bright boy from a normal home. He has the potential to be anything he wants to be, and I will not stand by and see him destroyed." She pounded a clenched fist into her open palm for emphasis as she spoke. "The fact that we cannot do much for those boys who come here wounded and torn is disgrace enough, but the callow destruction of Matt McFadden is a crime against everything we purport to stand for."

"What am I supposed to do?" he asked.

"You've got to get him out of this place before it is too late."

"Impossible! With his record, there's not another children's agency in the state that would take him. That's why he's here."

Miss Wilson's voice reflected her determination. "If he cannot leave through the front door," she said deliberately, "then I would not hesitate to help him leave through the fence."

Masters was shocked by her suggestion. "That's insane!"

"It can be done."

"Enough!" he exclaimed. "There are three hundred and sixty boys in this place, and more than half of them don't belong here. My job is to make their lives more tolerable, not to lead them over the fence in some . . . mass escape. You can't be serious!"

"Indeed I am," she said calmly. "I will do whatever is necessary to save that boy."

"I warn you, Verna, if Matt disappears, you will regret it."

The townspeople who had come to watch the game had filled the balcony, and the inmates were sitting in the folding bleachers on the floor of the gym. The teams were warming up on the court as BB Cottage marched in. Nothing that Matt had heard quite prepared him for the noisy crowd that was there.

"Where did they all come from?" he asked.

"We call them the Bennies," John answered.

"Bennies?"

"The people from town. When they come out here, most of them don't even watch the game. They just sit on those *benches* and watch us little criminals down here."

Matt smiled and nodded. "Bennies."

As they were filing up into the bleachers, Shacky reached out and stopped Ralph. "Not yet, dummy." Shacky pointed toward the players' bench and said, "Grab those wet towels, and take them to the locker room."

Ralph instinctively looked toward the cottage father, Carl Gregston, for confirmation, but Gregston looked away with a grin.

Shacky pointed Ralph in the right direction and nudged him forward. "Don't get lost, pushead."

The other boys sat down, and Matt watched Ralph shuffle away to gather up the towels. "He's scared," Matt said.

"How can you tell?" John asked.

"Look how he's walking."

Ralph's head was bowed, his shoulders were slumped, and his feet shuffled along the floor as he approached the metal door leading to the locker room. He had deposited the wet towels in the basket and turned to leave when Walter Pate, Shacky's lieutenant, stepped out and blocked his way.

"Those were bad-smelling towels, weren't they, Ralph?"

Ralph shrugged and tried to step around Pate, but two other boys suddenly appeared and pushed him back.

"We gotta do something about that, Ralphie, boy," Pate said. "We can't have you smelling so bad in front of all those Bennies out there. You'll give us all a bad name."

One of the boys had positioned himself on all fours behind Ralph, and when Pate pushed him again, Ralph fell over backward. As soon as he hit the floor, the three boys jumped on him, laughing and tearing his clothes off. They removed everything except his work boots and underpants and pushed him through the door.

There was a murmur of surprise from the crowd as soon as Ralph appeared. Then the teams stopped their warm-ups to gape. When Ralph began shuffling back toward Matt, the townspeople started to giggle, and soon the entire gymnasium was filled with laughter.

Matt buried his face in his hands, and Shacky slid down from a higher row to sit next to him. He smiled and put his arm around Matt's shoulder. "How about it, cowboy? Are you gonna cooperate? Or are you gonna hold out till one of your pets gets hurt?"

Matt jumped to his feet, sweeping Shacky's arm away. He glowered down without responding. Then he pushed himself through the crowd, removing his jacket as he went. Before he could reach Ralph, however, Tony jumped up on a bench and shouted to the younger boys, "Let's do it!" Tony tore off his shirt, and others followed suit. The idea caught on, and soon most of the boys were undressing.

The townspeople stopped laughing as the boys stripped and began throwing pieces of clothing at them. When that happened, the balcony emptied in record time.

Down on the floor, the cottage fathers were blowing whistles, frantically trying to restore order, but the boys were having too much fun to obey. Shacky and his lieutenants stood alone in the bleachers, seething with anger and glaring at Matt.

That night, after the group prayers had been mumbled, Matt crawled into bed, satisfied with the day's events. The fireplace crackled again, and his dad laughed about the burned popcorn. The dormitory still echoed with the usual sobs, giggles, and squeaks of blankets sliding across the floor. But Matt managed to block out all of it as he relaxed his muscles and dropped off to sleep.

Suddenly he couldn't breathe. His mouth was full and dry. At first he dreamed he was spinning through a black void. Then the Indians came out of nowhere to stake him to the ground on his stomach. He tried to scream, but the dry stuff in his mouth made that impossible.

Matt awoke from his nightmare on his stomach. His arms and legs had been spread and secured to the edges of the bed by heavy adhesive tape. His mouth had been stuffed with cloth and taped, and his pillow had been wadded up under his stomach. Panic gripped his chest as every muscle and nerve jerked involuntarily. The more he struggled, the more he felt that he would suffocate.

Matt wasn't sure if he had passed out or had simply blocked everything from his mind. Suddenly, however, he felt the tugging at his arms, and he knew someone was removing the tape. He tensed his muscles for a counterattack, but John's urgent whispers penetrated the darkness. "Keep still! . . . It's me."

John removed the tape from one side. Then he slid under the bed and came up on the side while Matt tore at the tape on his mouth with his free hand. "Take it easy. It was just a warning," John whispered, trying to calm his friend and avoid detection.

Matt succeeded in controlling his breathing just as John finished the task of freeing him. Then John tapped him on the shoulder and slithered away on his blanket without speaking. Matt lay there for two hours, and by dawn he knew what he would do. There would be a price to pay, but he was at the bottom, and the only way to go now was up or out.

The heavy steel door banged open, and Ned Williams assumed his position. "Let's hit it!" he barked. "Let's go! Let's go!"

Matt took his place in line and descended to the shower room with the others. If they knew what had happened, they didn't let on. He tossed his shorts onto the pile of laundry, picked up a towel, and proceeded to the shower.

"How're you feeling this morning, pardner?"

Matt turned slowly and looked into Shacky's ugly, leering face.

"I'm feeling fine, Shacky," Matt said, struggling for control. "I'm seeing things a lot clearer this morning."

"That's good, kid. Real good."

The line moved forward, and when Matt reached the entrance to the shower room, he turned and placed a hand on Shacky's shoulder. "I'm ready to talk. Let's meet back here as soon as we get dressed."

A self-satisfied grin spread across Shacky's pockmarked face, and he patted Matt's hand assuringly..

Matt stood under the pulsating spray only long enough to get wet. Then he stepped out, dried off, and picked up his clean clothes. John approached him with a question on his lips, but Matt warned him away without speaking. Ralph was aware of a change in Matt's attitude, and when he observed the unspoken exchange between Matt and John, he, too, turned away.

Matt dressed quickly and returned to pace the empty shower room, waiting for Shacky to arrive. The ugly redhead finally came limping through the door with a crooked smile on his face, still buttoning his shirt.

Shacky was strong and quick, and Matt's only hope was surprise. The assault had been planned for three hours, and every jab and kick was indelibly etched in Matt's mind. The intense fire in his eyes gave him away, however, and before he struck his first blow, Shacky's smile had vanished, and an expression of disbelief and alarm flashed across his face.

Matt swung both arms out and viciously slapped Shacky on the ears, puncturing both eardrums. Then he grabbed the wild red hair in both fists and pulled Shacky's head down into his upthrusting knee with all the strength he possessed. Pain shot through Matt's leg as Shacky's front teeth tore into his flesh, embedding themselves in muscle. Matt pulled up the mangled face to smash it again, but it was all over. Shacky's top front teeth were gone, and his lower teeth were hanging from his slack mouth. His bulbous nose was nothing more than a flat red blotch on his face, his unhinged jaw hung down at a crazy angle, and his eyes rolled back so that nothing except the whites was visible.

Matt was gasping for breath as he let the limp body slide to the wet cement floor. No more than fifteen seconds had elapsed. He assumed Shacky was alive, but he didn't care one way or the other.

Matt grabbed the kinky red hair once more, reached around the body from behind, and pulled it up to a semistanding position. Then he took a deep breath and dragged Shacky's body from the shower room, trailing blood across the bathroom floor, and into the living area.

The boys were lined up in twos near the front door, waiting to march to breakfast. Suddenly there was a loud gasp, and all heads turned simultaneously. Ned Williams, still at his desk, reading the morning paper, was the only one to move. He jumped up and knocked over his chair. It banged against the bare floor like a gunshot in an echo chamber. Then he raced across the room.

Matt tightened his grip on Shacky's neck and snarled, "You move any closer, and you can have this puke with a broken neck."

Williams slid to a stop and stared in disbelief and horror. "Now you just take it easy, boy. I don't know what's going on, but we can work it out for you." His plea was calm, but it had no effect on Matt. Williams inched forward, and Matt yanked up on Shacky's head, eliciting a loud moan from the boys as the increased pressure caused blood from Shacky's nose and mouth to spurt into the room.

"You're right about one thing, Wiliams. You sure as hell *don't* know what's going on," Matt growled. "What's my name?"

"What?"

"You heard me, asshole. What's my name?" Matt stared angrily at the cottage parent, who was racking his brain for a name that would not come. "How're you gonna work out my problem if you don't even know my name? You don't know who I am, or what I am, or if I hurt, or nothing! You just read your stinking paper and let Shacky and his rotten goons keep things quiet for you." Matt was struggling to breathe again, but he continued. "You turn the cottage over to Shacky after he just about kills Rick O'Malley, and when Belcher tells you they're after him, you tell him to grow up. Two nights later he bashes his head through half the windows in this stinkhole, and you say, 'I wonder what his problem was!' "

Williams moved his lips without speaking, seeming to conjure defenses for himself. "You're a *nothing!*" Matt screamed. "We could prop that newspaper up behind your desk, and you wouldn't be missed for a month. You didn't run this cottage . . . *he* did!" Matt pulled Shacky higher. "But he won't run it anymore."

"From now on, John Culver's in charge. He had nothing to

do with this—he tried to stop it—but he's got a crew of ten guys who can control this place. They'll be the watchdogs that will keep an eye on the punks twenty-four hours a day. At night we set up a schedule and watch to make sure they all stay in bed, and you better, by God, make sure it happens."

Matt stopped to adjust his grip on the limp body. He could see from the pathetically blank expression on Williams's face that the speech had been lost on him, but the boys had not missed a word. Most of them started drifting in John's direction and gathered around him like mindless cattle. Matt couldn't believe how incredibly easy it had been to influence these leaderless, insecure boys.

Suddenly Matt was tired. His legs and fists throbbed with pain. He released Shacky's body, leaned against the wall, and slid to the floor.

Williams sprinted to the telephone before running back to examine Shacky's prostrate body. John and Ralph went directly to Matt and helped him to his feet. They led him to the couch, and John whispered into his friend's ear, "Mr. McFadden, sir, you sure enough broke up the man's face."

Chapter Thirty-two

Lockup was about what he thought it would be. The walls and ceiling of the six- by eight-foot cell were solid steel, and the floor was concrete, but Matt was so exhausted that he welcomed the dark solitude. The cement floor was bare except for a thin, ragged mattress, stained and reeking with the urine of countless boys who had slept there in the past. A dry stool poked up out of the floor in the corner of the cell—nothing more than an open pipe, ten inches in diameter, unpainted, and speckled with chips of dried fecal matter. A bare cold-water sink protruded from the gray steel wall, and a heavy steel screen covered a small painted window above it. Matt could not see them, but he knew there were bars outside the window.

He lay on the concrete floor and reconstructed the events of the past hour. Two security guards had rushed in, conducted a brief conference with Ned Williams, then proceeded to carry out their assignments. One of them carried Shacky out the door, and the other led the boys to the dining hall. Ned Williams reserved the privilege of personally conducting Matt to lockup, and he took great pleasure in pushing the boy from behind every time his throbbing leg failed him.

When they reached the admissions cottage, which also served as the intake room for lockup, Williams forcefully propelled Matt through the door. Rich Anderson jumped up from his desk and caught him before he fell.

"What the hell happened?" Anderson demanded.

"He beat up on another boy. Maybe killed him, so just process him quick."

Rich examined Matt more closely and asked Williams, "Who did he beat up, and why?"

"Goddammit, what's the difference? Just get him upstairs."

Anderson frowned and looked at Williams. "Jesus Christ, you're nervous, Ned. What's going on?" Then he held Matt's face and asked, "How about it, Matt? Who was it?"

"Shacky Wallis," Matt said weakly. "He made a move on me last night."

Anderson was incredulous at first. "Shacky? . . . Shacky Wallis?" Then a broad grin spread over his face as he turned and taunted the cottage parent. "You mean that tough fag of yours finally got his ass whipped? A fifteen-year-old kid was the only one with balls enough to stand up to your top man?"

Williams kicked the desk and shouted angrily, "You may be Masters's top fish now, but when this is over, I'll have your ass nailed to the roof."

Suddenly the door flew open, and Oscar Stone, the barber, bounced into the room, screeching, "I told ya! I told ya that kid was dangerous, but you wouldn't believe me, would you?"

Rich Anderson grabbed Stone by the shirt, turned him around without responding, and unceremoniously pushed him out the door. Then he returned to Matt and said, "Okay, son, get your clothes off, and I'll take you upstairs."

Williams shook his finger in Matt's face and growled, "When I'm finished with you, you'll wish you never—"

"Never messed up your little tea party?" Anderson interrupted.

The glass shattered as Ned Williams slammed the door behind him, and Rich Anderson helped Matt toward the stairs. "I suppose it had to be done, Matt, but I'm afraid we've got our mammaries in the same wringer. Maybe it's time to find out whose hogs ate the cabbage."

Matt wasn't sure what Anderson's remark meant, and he was too tired to care. For now he felt safe and secure in his own little steel room.

                    *   *   *

When Matt opened his eyes, he saw Gary Masters framed in the entrance to the dark cell. He didn't know how long he had slept, but he felt rested. When he moved, however, an excruciating pain shot through his right leg, and he cried out in agony. His right leg had swollen to twice the size of his left, and there was a purple and black gash just above the spot that had once looked like a knee.

Masters's brow furrowed. "What did the doctor say about that leg?"

Matt shrugged. "Haven't seen a doctor."

Masters stepped through the door and squatted down to take a closer look. "You mean the doctor hasn't been here yet?"

Matt's mind was still foggy, and he chose not to pursue the subject. "How long have I slept?" he asked, wrinkling his nose at the tray of cold food on the floor beside his head.

"You've been in here eighteen hours," Masters said, squinting to examine Matt's wound. "It's three o'clock in the . . . Holy God!" he gasped. "I'm going for the doctor."

"Bring that light a little closer," the voice said.

Matt struggled to open his eyes and focus on the little man who was peering at his leg through a magnifying glass. "What's wrong?" he murmured. Suddenly he was conscious of the pain shooting up through his leg, all the way to the right side of his head. "My leg hurts," he said, half sobbing the words.

"Well, it ought to," the doctor said brusquely. "You've got at least two teeth buried in your right quadriceps muscle . . . along with enough infection to hobble a mule."

The doctor glared disapprovingly into Matt's eyes; then he turned his anger on the superintendent. "It's no wonder we have so many young animals on the streets," he said scoldingly. "This big punk beats up on a crippled kid, and you stand there feeling sorry for him and worrying about the condition of the same leg he used to pulverize that crippled boy's face!"

A bully! The doctor was accusing Matt of being a bully! He chuckled in spite of his pain as the voice of another boy in lockup shouted gleefully, "Hey, Doc, McFadden *had* to beat up on Shacky 'cause he's the only cripple in here. You wouldn't want him to go outside and beat up on a *regular* cripple, would you?" Matt passed out again as the taunting laughter echoed from every cell in lockup.

The fever broke the following day, and Matt woke up in a bright hospital room with heavy security screens on every window. He looked around warily without moving his head, sensitive to the pain in his leg and still feeling foggy. He felt better as soon as he cleared the cobwebs and focused on the slightly built bearded young man who was reading a magazine next to the window. He had consciously sublimated any human attachments beyond the circle of his three friends, but the sight of Rich Anderson's familiar face in those antiseptic surroundings filled him with warmth and gratitude.

"Rich?" His voice sounded like the crackling of thin parchment, so Matt cleared his throat, not wanting to sound sick. "Am I okay?" he asked in a much stronger voice.

"Well, welcome!" Rich exclaimed, genuinely pleased. "Yeah, you're okay. They've been sticking you with needles and draining off the infection, but you're in good shape." Anderson stood up and started for the door. "Let me go get the boss. He just stepped out for a cup of coffee."

Gary Masters must have been sitting in the hallway because he burst into the room before the pneumatic door had fully closed behind Rich Anderson. His clothes were wrinkled, he needed a shave, and his eyes seemed more tired than ever, but he was smiling broadly. He marched directly to the bed without saying a word and clenched Matt's hand.

Dr. Rodgers followed him into the room and edged Masters away from the bed to feel Matt's brow. Then he lifted the wet compress from Matt's leg, and the foul odor of the infection wafted through the room.

"Ugh!" Matt complained. "Is that me?"

"The worst is over," the doctor assured him brusquely. "We'll continue the compresses until the draining has stopped, but you'll have to use your *other* leg to kick people's brains out for a while."

Matt started to protest, but a curt gesture from Masters stopped him. Instead, he looked at the doctor and asked, "How come you brought me here?"

"Because I couldn't treat a hangnail in that filth," he snapped. "Which reminds me." He challenged Masters. "If you're so all-fired concerned about those boys, how can you condone that—that abominable filth in those steel cages?"

The superintendent smiled and answered in a low voice specifically intended to contrast with the doctor's bombastic tone. "We keep it that way so the people in the capital won't accuse us of mollycoddling young thugs who beat up on crippled kids."

Dr. Rodgers was clearly angry again. "I don't like your superiority, Masters. If those people from the state come around here asking me questions, you'll wish they hadn't." Gary Masters continued to smile, refusing to be drawn into another argument, so the doctor glared silently and walked from the room.

"Thanks a lot," Matt said sarcastically. "If you keep that up, the old bastard'll cut off *my* leg just to spite *you*."

"No"—Masters chuckled,—"he's a damned good doctor, but he's been on call for us for so many years he figures he knows all there is to know about running the training school. He's a pain in the butt, but he's a good doctor."

Matt looked into the sad gray eyes of the superintendent, and suddenly his mind was awash with doubts and questions. He realized that Masters and Anderson had spent the night at the hospital, and he wondered if that was normal. He wondered why Masters seemed so nervous beneath his calm exterior, and in the best tradition of inmates, he wondered fleetingly how he might best exploit the situation to his own advantage.

"What's next?" Matt asked, somehow harboring the ridiculous fantasy that Masters might tell him they were going to get him well and send him back home to live with Charlie Sanner, that Matt had already undergone sufficient punishment for a crime he didn't commit.

Instead, Masters's response indicated he was still thinking about the doctor's threat. "Oh, he's no problem. We're used to people telling us how to run the place," he said distractedly. Then his face brightened with another smile. "One time there was even a legislator who decided that the answer had to be *dogs*—a boy's best friend. No boy could go bad if he had his own puppy to play with, and love, and talk to." Masters began to laugh as he continued the story. "Every unwanted mutt in forty counties was brought here. The politicians loved it, the papers loved it, but the kids couldn't figure what the hell to do with four hundred and ten dogs. On top of that, there were new litters every day, and the whole place was covered with dog crap. Then the dogs began to run wild, and they'd attack the neighbors' sheep and cattle."

Masters shook his head and said, "The farmers raised hell, the old superintendent was run out of town, and the papers told how the unappreciative little delinquents at the training school were too far gone to be touched by any human emotions . . . including man's best friend."

Masters shook his head and flushed as he realized that it was no time for funny stories. "Shit," he exclaimed in frustration as he rose from his chair, "if I had my way, I'd burn that place to the ground."

"Whoa"—Rich Anderson laughed—"Ranger's in enough trouble. Don't give him any more ideas. Remember . . . this kid likes to play with matches."

"You're right." Masters chuckled. "I'm telling stories while Matt lies there wondering when the human race is going to grow up and when the superintendent will shut up and let him get some sleep." He reached over and gripped Matt's hand with a smile. "We'll be back for you as soon as the doc says you're ready."

Matt was disgusted with himself for having missed an opportunity to make some points. Masters and Anderson had been concerned about him, and they were obviously feeling some guilt, but now they were gone, and Matt was no better off than he had been. He got out of bed and hobbled painfully to the door, where he carefully surveyed his surroundings for some means of escape. To his surprise and chagrin, he found that the hallway was blocked by a metal door attended by a uniformed policeman. He returned to his bed more convinced than ever that to them he was a dangerous criminal and was doomed to be an outcast forever.

He resolved that he would never again depend on someone else to control his destiny. If he made it, it would be on his own; if he smiled, it would be for a reason; if he stole, he would cover his tracks; and if he hit, he would hit where it wouldn't show. If they ever let him out, he would grow long hair, but he would have known what it was like to be bald, and if he didn't screw them before they screwed him, he would someday be bald again.

Rich Anderson returned a week later to take Matt back to lockup. He was quiet and serious, and there was none of the good-natured kidding that had characterized their earlier conversations.

"What's wrong, Rich?"

Anderson slowed the car and looked at Matt. Then he took a deep breath and said, "We've got problems. Shacky got a call through from the hospital to George Hacker . . . the director of institutions . . . complaining about abusive treatment. I think Ned Williams called, too, maybe even Oscar Stone. One kid complaining about another usually wouldn't get the job done."

"What job?" Matt asked, sensing impending disaster.

"The dirctor sent one of his boobs down to investigate without telling Masters, and he met with a bunch of people out at the school and at the hospital."

"And?" Matt asked, almost afraid to hear the rest.

"And the first we heard about it was this morning. We got an institutional transfer for you."

"What's that?"

"The director of institutions is moving you to the state penitentiary. Masters raised hell, but it's completely out of his hands. They're sending a car on Monday."

"What's today?" Matt asked, struggling for the full meaning of Anderson's words.

"Friday," Rich answered.

"Three days," Matt mumbled, and the blood drained from his face as he realized what was about to happen to him. "Jesus Christ . . . can he do that?"

"There's more," Anderson said slowly. "They're moving John Culver, too."

Matt stared at Anderson with tears of self-pity and fear, not trusting his voice to ask why.

"Yesterday afternoon Walt Pate tried to muscle John, and they had it out. Then last night there was a riot in the dormitory, and Pops and Williams had John thrown into lockup. They set him up."

The corner was getting smaller and smaller, but they continued to stalk, to push, to crowd what little space he had left. "They're doing it again!" Matt cried. "At least the first time I had a trial!"

The choking sobs and tears came without warning, and it was a shock to realize he had any tears left. Anderson pulled the car over to the side of the road a few miles from the institution. Matt looked questioningly at his escort, struggling to bring his tears under control.

"It's out of our hands," Rich repeated painfully. "Hacker is not only the director of all adult and juvenile penal institutions, but the warden of the state penitentiary. The new governor brought him in as a 'law and order' man," Rich said bitterly. "George Hacker is a good director of institutions like Jack the Ripper was a good throat surgeon. He would have fired Masters months ago, but the press was against it. Hacker was waiting for a chance like this to show his muscle."

Matt heard and suddenly understood that he had unwittingly placed himself in the middle of a political football game—not as a player but as the football. He leaned against the door and studied the woods next to the highway. It was cold, there were patches of snow on the ground, and the light jacket he was wearing would provide little or no protection, but his choices were narrowing fast, and once they had him back in lockup, there would be no choices left. His hand inched toward the door handle.

"I won't try to stop you," Anderson said without looking at him. "But before you take off, have you thought about leaving John behind to face this thing by himself?"

He had forgotten about John—the guy who had had the system all figured out before Matt had interfered. If Matt had never come to the institution, John would still be snapping beaver in the superintendent's office and giving Shacky a hard time in his own subtle way. John would have put in his easy time and would have been out in two more years without any hassle. Matt's final alternative evaporated, and he blurted at Anderson, "You're a son of a bitch . . . just like the rest of them!"

Chapter Thirty-three

The sunlight was beginning to fade. Rich Anderson and Verna Wilson waited as Masters concluded a heated telephone conversation. He slammed the phone down and shook his head. "It's no use," he said ruefully, "they won't change their minds."

"But you're the superintendent," Miss Wilson argued. "How can they send those boys to the penitentiary over your objections?"

"Ned Williams knows the law, and he knows the political climate," Masters said. "The director of institutions has been waiting to put me in my place for a long time. The governor won't let him fire me, but this is as good a chance as any to stick it to me." Masters sat down and leaned forward with his elbows on the desk. "Let's face it," he said, "Matt and John are simply victims of a sick power play."

Verna Wilson opened her purse and took out a small notebook. "In spite of your previous warnings, I have proceeded to formulate a plan that will work."

Masters looked at her blankly.

"The escape," she reminded him. "I have contacted my niece, and Father Cassidy will—"

"*No!*" he shouted. "For the last time, Verna, I have sworn to *uphold* the law!"

"Just listen to yourself, Gary. You talk of sick power plays out of one side of your mouth, and out of the other you quote the law." She paused long enough for her indignation to subside; then she asked softly, "What about the laws of human dignity?"

Book II: The System

"You're expecting too much of me, Verna."

Her voice was firm. "You cannot send those boys to the penitentiary."

"And you propose that we let them escape?"

"Wrong," she said. "I propose that we *help* them escape."

Masters pushed back his chair and walked to the window. He watched the boys marching from the dining hall to their cottages. "You know how much I've thought about it, Verna. But I keep coming back to the same thing. It's against the law. It *is* against the law."

"Whose law?" she asked. "Man's law or God's law? You may be safe when you stand before a judge and say that you let those boys be destroyed because it was against *the law* to do anything else, but you had better hide your head when you say your prayers."

Masters listened intently and shook his head uncertainly. He eventually turned to Rich Anderson and said, "I haven't heard from you."

Anderson thought for a moment and said, "She's right, Gary."

Masters took a deep breath. "It would be risky for all of us."

"Not for the boys." Anderson laughed. "If they got caught, they'd just be sent to the penitentiary anyway."

"You're right," Masters said. "If we do it—I said *if* we do it—there must be an understanding that I will take sole responsibility. I want you two out of it. Is that agreed?"

"Nonsense," Miss Wilson said. "You can't possibly do it alone, and you would never convince the investigators otherwise. Besides, I have authored a foolproof plan."

Anderson added, "Don't even bother to ask. I'm in."

Masters laughed in spite of himself. "Dear God, what are we about to do?"

"Whatever it is, it had better be tonight," Miss Wilson said.

"If we can get them out of lockup around midnight, can you do the rest, Verna?"

She smiled confidently. "Without question."

Masters slapped both palms on the desk and gave the order. "Then it's settled. Now let's hear more about this wonderful plan."

*   *   *

| 235 |

The lights shining through the evening frost framing the window created a sparkling display, but it was wasted on Masters, who sat alone, staring through the glittering patterns into the night. The events of the past seventy-two hours had taken their toll, and he was again besieged by doubt. Had he made the right decision? Or had his judgment been clouded by fatigue and emotional shock?

How was it possible that he had just agreed to take part in a phony escape? There had to be a straightforward, lawful approach that would accomplish the same result. But no matter how many times he evaluated the possible options, he found himself up against the same rock wall. The director of institutions was in control, and Masters's appeals had fallen on deaf ears. Verna was right. There *is* a higher law, a humanistic code of ethics. And to avoid the real issue by taking refuge behind the letter of the law would have violated his every belief.

He slapped the armrest of his chair and stood, declaring aloud, "It's done. And by God, we're right!"

Matt lay on the thin mattress in his darkened cell, trying to blot out the maddening sounds of lockup: hysterical cries that turned into mocking laughter and then into piercing whistles or soft humming. Then he heard a different kind of noise, so he rose to his feet and limped to the door to investigate. It sounded like a muffled "Hey! . . . Hey!" but he couldn't be certain.

He peered through the slit in the steel door and repeated the sound. "Hey!" he whispered.

The voice that answered was vaguely familiar, but the words were slurred. "How ya feelin'?" it asked. "How was the hospital?"

Matt's pulse quickened. "Is that you? . . . John?"

"Who else would be talking to you around here?"

"Where are you?" Matt asked, excited and pleased to hear his friend again.

"I got the suite next door," John answered sarcastically. "A lot better view. How's the leg?"

"I'm okay," Matt said impatiently. "What happened last night?"

"I'll tell you what happened, *McFathead* . . . your plan stunk!"

Matt wanted to apologize and unburden his guilt, but he

turned away from the steel door and returned to his mattress without responding. He lay there for two hours, reliving every story he had heard about the terrors of the adult penitentiary, wondering if it could be as bad on young boys as it had been made out to be.

Matt did not intend to fall asleep, but the sound of people on the stairs awakened him. The footfalls were heavy and slow, so he assumed that they were older people and that one of them would be the night guard, a semiretired farmer whose name Matt could not remember. As soon as the second person spoke, Matt recognized Miss Wilson's voice. "They were my best students," she said, "and I simply had to say good-bye."

The man on the staircase mumbled a question, and Miss Wilson answered, "Yes, I promised my niece in St. Louis, and this will be my last chance to see her new baby before Christmas."

The two were now close enough for Matt to hear the man say, "That's quite a trip. You driving?"

"Oh, yes," she said. "In about an hour. I enjoy driving. Besides, I am taking a long weekend."

"Here we are," the old man said, stopping at the door to John's cell. "You sure you want to go inside?"

"Oh, I think so, Mr. Simpson. I don't think I'll be in any danger, do you?"

"Can't tell," he said, shaking his head. "I'll stay close, just in case."

"That certainly puts my mind at ease," Miss Wilson gushed with a sarcastic bite that completely escaped the old man.

Matt heard the heavy door to John's cell open, and the guard said, "Only five minutes . . . that's the rule."

"I'm sure that will be quite enough. Thank you, Mr. Simpson."

The door closed, and Mr. Simpson shuffled past Matt's cell to respond to the catcalls and jeers that his appearance in lockup usually evoked from the imprisoned boys. Five minutes later he shuffled past again to take Miss Wilson from John's cell and escort her to Matt's.

"How are you feeling, Matthew?" she asked, leading the boy to the far end of the small steel room. Before he could respond, however, she cut him off with a sharp gesture and proceeded in a calm whisper. "You have been talking about an escape. Do you still want to try?"

He frowned in the darkness. "What do you mean? . . . How?"

"There are risks, but it can be done if you are willing to try."

Matt was too excited to consider the potential danger to Miss Wilson, and thinking only about himself, he asked, "What happens if I get caught?"

"What's the worst thing they can do to you for trying to escape?" Miss Wilson asked in a challenging tone.

"Lockup?" Matt asked as a smile began to spread across his face. "Lockup . . . for two weeks," he asserted.

"And if you're a chronic case?" Miss Wilson asked. "What would they do to you then?"

"The penitentiary!" Matt laughed. "They'd send me to the damned penitentiary!" As long as Matt's new mailing address would soon be the state penitentiary anyway, he said, "I'm ready." Matt embraced the older woman spontaneously and repeated in her ear, "I'm ready. I'm ready."

"Shhh," she warned, pointing toward the door to indicate that Mr. Simpson might be able to hear him.

"What about John?" Matt asked, belatedly wondering whether his friend would also be a part of the escape attempt.

"John knows all the arrangements. He said he would go out if you did. The first quarter of a mile will be the most difficult," she warned. "It's cold out there, but the car will be warm, and there will be blankets, warm clothes, and something hot to drink."

As soon as Miss Wilson alluded to the cold weather, Matt realized that he had been standing there in nothing but his shorts, but before he had time to be embarrassed, Mr. Simpson unlocked the cell and beckoned to Miss Wilson.

Before turning away from Matt, Miss Wilson did a strange thing. She unscrewed the top of her huge old fountain pen and deliberately squirted ink on the sleeve of her jacket. As the black blotch spread across the tan fabric, she walked from the cell, complaining, "Mr. Simpson, look what I just did. Do you have anything that will remove an ink stain?"

"I'm sorry, ma'am," he apologized, peering at the glistening black spot. "Maybe I could have the missus—"

"No," she interrupted. "I'll take it to the cleaner's as soon as I get to St. Louis."

The door closed in Matt's face, and he gazed through the tiny opening as the two older people slowly descended the stairs, ignoring the shouting and taunting of the inmates at the far end of the hall. The full impact of Miss Wilson's participation finally struck Matt as he watched her leave. He realized that she herself would probably wind up in prison if she were caught, and he hoped he would see her again someday to thank her properly.

"Everything okay?"

"Yeah."

"Good. Let's get some sleep . . . three hours."

Matt paced his tiny cell like a caged animal, trying to recall every word, every intonation, and every gesture that had transpired between himself and Verna Wilson in those five minutes. John had said they had three hours to go, but how was it going to happen? Another piece of information he had was that the car would be a quarter mile away, and there would be warm clothes waiting for them. That meant they would be running a good distance on foot, and they would be doing so with no clothing except the shorts they were wearing. Matt pictured the well-traveled escape routes through the fences of the institution, and he eliminated most of them on the basis of the quarter of a mile distance from lockup to a place where a car could be parked.

Faced with the prospect of running a quarter of a mile on a cold night, Matt tested his bad leg and found it to be adequate. There was no pain, only a stiffness that he began to work out by deep knee bends and massage.

He was satisfied that he understood the plan well enough, but it suddenly occurred to him that he had no idea how they were going to get out of their cells and away from the admissions cottage. If Mr. Simpson was anything like the other nighttime guards, he would be asleep, so getting out of the cottage would be no problem, but who would unlock their cells?

Matt walked to the steel door and tested it gently, wondering whether it had been left unlocked, but it refused to budge. Would Miss Wilson return to unlock the door? That would be impossible. She would never be able to enter and leave quickly enough to avoid being seen. Besides, she was probably well on her way to St. Louis already. Then Matt recalled Rich Anderson's unusual behavior when he had returned him to the cell earlier in the afternoon—*We're trying to work something out*—and he concluded that Rich had to be in on it, too.

Matt flopped down on his mattress again and reconstructed the entire plan once more. He was working on conjecture and instinct, and he knew he would have to follow John's lead, but the information he had made him confident he would not have to be blindly dependent on someone else.

It sounded like a rifle shot in the hall, but it was only the sound of a key in the door of John's cell. Matt froze, and in an instant the noise was repeated in his own door. He walked slowly to the front of the cell and warily tested the heavy steel door. It swung open softly. He emerged just as John's door was pushed open. There was no one else in the hall.

John brushed past Matt and turned toward him at the head of the stairs. Matt hardly recognized his friend. The handsome black face had a broken nose that was reduced to two nostril holes embedded in swollen cheeks. An ugly red gash traversed his face from his left ear to the corner of his mouth, and his lower lip was twice as large on the left side as it was on the right. The eyes that twinkled with mischief and excitement beneath the swollen lids were clearly John's, and Matt reached out to touch the grotesquely misshapen face.

John flinched from Matt's touch and grabbed his outstretched arm. "Let's go," he whispered. "Quiet!"

They made their way down the stairs like cat burglars and stopped at the end of the lower hallway. John peeked around the opening to the office and saw Mr. Simpson fast asleep on the couch. He held one finger to his lips and tiptoed to the outside door, which had also been unlocked for them by their anonymous benefactor.

Suddenly they were outside, running barefoot toward the barn across the frozen ground. The first shock of the freezing air on their exposed skin had passed, but the rocks were cutting into their bare feet, and their lungs soon ached from the cold. When Matt's bad leg buckled momentarily, John fell back and pushed at him, yelling for him to keep running. "Wilford Road," John panted, "not far."

They went through the large hole in the fence almost without breaking stride, and thirty yards beyond the fence a waiting automobile came to life. The engine started, the headlights came on, and the back door flew open. The boys piled into the back seat on top of one another as Miss Wilson pulled the car onto Wilford Road and drove toward the highway.

"You!" Matt gasped. "I thought—"

The inside of the car was warm, and the blowers were functioning at peak capacity, but the boys were still frozen, unable to control their chattering teeth and shivering bodies, so Matt dived under the blankets and saved his questions.

At Miss Wilson's insistence, they remained under warm blankets and drank steaming coffee until feelings returned to their hands and feet. As their frozen bodies thawed, the numbness was replaced by pain in their torn feet, but suddenly one of the boys began to giggle, and almost immediately all three of them were laughing uncontrollably. Their response was partly due to the decompression that followed their successful escape, but they had also just driven past a large lighted billboard that proclaimed:

> *You are leaving Clearwater County*
> *We hope you enjoyed your visit*
> *If you MUST go, please hurry back.*

BOOK III:

A Safe Place

Chapter Thirty-four

Their sprint to freedom had lasted less than four minutes, but it took the boys almost an hour to thaw out, treat the cuts and bruises on their feet, and climb into the flannel shirts and denim jeans Miss Wilson had provided. There was little interaction after their initial outburst of laughter, except for passing out sandwiches and pouring hot coffee as they drove through the cold night. Matt remained mesmerized by his friend's swollen and disfigured face, intrigued by the grotesque distortions caused by eating, drinking, laughing, and talking.

"What's the matter, man?" John chided him. "You always told me to put on more weight. Now I add ten pounds to my head, and you act like you're gonna vomit every time you look at me." His lopsided smile confirmed the fact that he felt much better than he looked. "Tell ya what," he said, climbing over the seat. "I'll get up here with our driver, so's I can get some sleep without worrying about you puking all over me."

"Good idea," Miss Wilson said. "You're both to have a busy day tomorrow."

Matt was ready for a long sleep, but a more immediate concern had begun to gnaw at him. He leaned forward and rested against the back of the front seat. "What'll happen to you? If we're caught, I mean?"

"We'll talk about all that after you've had some sleep," she said. "But for right now I almost wish they *would* catch me. We'd have a trial that would make the front pages of every newspaper in the country . . . but they'd never let that happen." Then she glanced over her shoulder and said gently, "You'd better get some sleep."

Matt leaned forward and kissed the cheek of the most beautiful woman he knew. A thousand questions still raced through his mind, but he was suddenly too tired to think, or talk, or listen. Soon after they had crossed the state line, he curled up on the back seat and closed his eyes, knowing for the first time in months that he would sleep safely and for as long as he wanted.

The morning sun was slanting through the side window when Miss Wilson pulled off the highway and drove a short way up a dirt road. Matt came awake with a start, trying to remember where he was and what was going on. The soles of his feet hurt, and his neck was stiff. "What's wrong?" he muttered.

"We need some motion lotion," John answered.

Miss Wilson turned off the engine and handed John the key to the trunk. "First put on those wool hats," she said. "They probably haven't even found out you're gone yet, but those bald heads of yours are worse than red flags."

The two boys got out of the car, and John opened the trunk as Matt stretched his arms in the cold morning air. "How far'd we drive?" he asked.

"About three hundred miles," John answered, handing Matt one of the five-gallon gas cans.

"Hey, that doesn't look like St. Louis!" Matt exclaimed, peering toward the barely visible mountains in the west.

Miss Wilson looked at him quizzically, and John asked, "St. Louis? What're you talking about, man? That's in the opposite direction."

"I heard you tell Mr. Simpson you were going to spend the weekend at your niece's in St. Louis," Matt said to Miss Wilson with some concern. "And I guess I figured you wouldn't lie about that. I mean, it would be too easy for Masters to check out."

"Oh, yes. I can be quite devious when I need to be." Miss Wilson laughed, rubbing her hands vigorously against the cold.

John stopped pouring the gas into the tank and looked at her. "Have you ever done this before?" he asked.

Miss Wilson flopped both hands disdainfully. "We don't have

an underground railroad if that's what you mean. But don't worry, I know what I'm doing. . . . And I have had lots of help."

"Have there been others? . . . Rick O'Malley . . . Larry Belcher?" Matt asked.

"I am afraid both were committed to the state hospital," she answered. Then she gestured impatiently and said, "Hurry it up, John. It's getting cold. We'll talk about it in the car."

The two boys stared at each other curiously as their teacher returned to the car. John started to grin, and Matt quipped, "A regular Ma Barker. Hurry up! I can't wait to hear the rest of it."

By the time they returned to the warm car Miss Wilson had set out a breakfast consisting of hot coffee and doughnuts, and she was ready to talk. "You were right about St. Louis," she said to Matt. "When they piece together my visit to your cells, your escape, and my long weekend away from Clearwater, they will surely investigate. When I return to Clearwater on Tuesday, how-ever, I shall have signed receipts from gas stations in Omaha, Kansas City, and St. Charles, proving that I drove east, and I shall have a lodging receipt from the Lindberg Arms Hotel to account for two nights in St. Louis."

"What about your niece?" Matt asked. "They're gonna talk to her. What'll she say?"

Miss Wilson smiled mischievously. "My niece is a foster child whom I took into my home twelve years ago . . . right out of the girls' reformatory in Missouri. She was only sixteen then, but believe me, she knows the score."

"But they won't believe her," Matt protested.

"Do you remember when I accidentally spilled ink on my suit jacket last night? Well, Sharon has an exact duplicate of that suit—ink spot and all—and first thing this morning she will take it to her neighborhood cleaner. Monday night she will pick it up and mail it to me. It will have today's laundry mark on it, along with the indelible ink stain—proof positive that I was in St. Louis this weekend!"

"But how's that possible?" Matt asked, grinning with ad-miration. "You gonna fly out to all those other places?"

"As I said, this was a team effort. A lot of people are involved, and we all play our own small parts." Then she clapped her hands excitedly and said, "But you haven't heard the best part! By the time you set foot in another classroom you will have new names, new school records, and new birth certificates. You will be ready to start completely new lives."

John shook his head and smiled crookedly. "I can't believe this is really happening," he said. "This is the first time anybody's done somthing good for me."

Miss Wilson glanced at him quickly. "That's hardly true," she said in a mildly scolding tone. "All things considered, you really haven't turned out too badly. You have no right to be totally bitter. There have been many people who have cared about you over the years—social workers, probation officers, teachers—and maybe all the systems didn't work, but it wasn't because those people didn't care."

"They were just doing their job. This is different," he argued. "A bunch of people we don't even know got together, and now we got it made. We beat the system—all of us." John smiled at Matt and excitedly slapped him on top of the head. "She sure wired this scam, didn't she? If we ever decide to rob a bank, we better get her on our side."

Matt smiled in agreement and beat a tattoo on the backrest with his hands.

Miss Wilson regarded the two excited boys with sudden concern. "Perhaps I have given you the wrong impression," she said evenly. "This is not a game of cops and robbers. You obviously don't appreciate the soul-searching that has taken place in the confusion of the past three days. We had to argue with ourselves and each other for a long time before we did what we did. We all are law-abiding citizens—every last one of us. But we were finally forced to conclude that neither the letter nor the intent of the law would be served by sending you two to the adult penitentiary. We had to evaluate and balance some very basic principles and bottom-line standards of justice and human dignity before we arranged your escape."

She paused to give them time to digest her reprimand. "It is important that you understand. Do you? . . . John?"

"I'm not sure," he said. "All I know is we're out."

"That's not good enough, and you know it. . . . Matt? Can you explain it any better?"

Matt's silence reflected his confusion.

"You can rattle off the dates of the Boston Tea Party and the First Continental Congress," she said with annoyance, "but what kind of people were those colonists? Were they bad? Were they criminals?"

Matt's response was hesitant. "Well . . . the colonists were British subjects . . . living under British law. . . ."

"Go on," she said. "You're on the right track."

"But some of those laws were unfair, so the colonists decided to go to war."

"You have omitted the most important part," she said. "What did they do before firing the first shot?"

"Well, they debated the issues and tried to get the laws changed," he said, beginning to respond more confidently. "And it was only after parliament refused to listen to them that they broke the law. Even though most of them were English, they still broke the law. They had no choice. That was the only way they could survive."

"And there you have it," she said, finally satisfied. "We are a nation of laws—laws that have been in the making for more than a thousand years. We do not violate those laws frivolously, but the law is a living thing, and it changes to meet the special needs of contemporary society. Unfortunately those changes sometimes do not come quickly enough, and then—and only then—is it even remotely appropriate to take drastic measures."

Both boys nodded in response to her penetrating stare.

Miss Wilson brushed the crumbs from her ample lap and said, "We had better be on our way."

"How much farther?" Matt asked.

"Another four hours or so," she said, gesturing toward the west. "About halfway down the other side of those mountains."

John, a city boy to the core, was less than enthusiastic. "Only *halfway* down? Where we going? Butch Cassidy's hideout?"

Matt smiled with anticipation, and Miss Wilson chuckled. "No . . . someplace a lot safer." She looked smugly at the two boys and kept them in suspense while she started the engine and drove to the highway. "My brother, Earl, and I own a ranch over on the western slope," she continued, pointing to the eastern face of the blue Colorado Rockies on the horizon. "He's old, bigoted, mean, and stingy. When his wife was alive, he worked it very well, but now he lives like a hermit, and our cattle roam all over the county."

The cautious tone of John's question betrayed his fear. "So what does that have to do with us?"

"You boys will live in the bunkhouse, work for wages, and next fall you'll enroll in the local high school," she said.

"What kind of work?"

Miss Wilson looked at John uncertainly. "Why, you will work the ranch. Whatever needs to be done: bring in the cattle, mend fences—"

"Just like that?" John interrupted. "Bring in the cattle? That'll be great," he said sarcastically. "It'll be just like the old days. The guys on my block in Brooklyn used to say, 'Let's cop a ride on the trolley and sneak in the Paramount,' and I'd say, 'Can't. I gotta bring in the cattle.' "

"You'll learn." She laughed.

Matt was enthusiastic enough for both of them. "How big a crew does your brother have?" he asked excitedly.

"Do you mean ranch hands?" she asked.

Matt nodded and smiled expectantly.

"Enough," she said.

His enthusiasm flagged slightly. "How many?"

Miss Wilson smiled sweetly and said, "You"—then, nodding toward John—"and you."

"Just us?" It was Matt's turn to be wary. "How many cattle?"

"God only knows. Two . . . maybe three hundred."

Matt was plainly concerned. "Any saddle stock?"

"Look, the horses are rangy, and the cattle are almost wild," she said impatiently. "It won't be easy for you, but it will be a sight better than the penitentiary."

The boys recognized the rebuke in her voice, so they rode in silence as the mountains in the distance loomed closer. "Does he know about us?" John finally asked. "Your brother, I mean."

"He knows all he needs to know," she answered, her cheerfulness restored. "You two have just been released from St. Thomas Orphanage, in Morganville, Missouri. Father Cassidy runs the place. He's an old friend of Gary Masters, and he already—"

"Mr. Masters?" Matt exclaimed. "You mean he's in on this, too?"

"Never mind about that," she said. "I've written out everything you need to remember and slipped it into your geography book." Her tone indicated that they were asking too many questions, so both boys sat quietly, gazing out at the high plains, trying to assimilate the new information that was flooding their minds.

Soon after the highway had narrowed from four lanes to two, they began to climb, and Miss Wilson negotiated the curves leading over the mountain. "The ranch is twenty-two miles from the nearest town," she said, resuming the conversation after a long silence. "Next fall you will be bussed to the consolidated school in Pinetop—about fourteen miles." She thought for a moment and said with a smile, "That was my first teaching position . . . more than forty years ago. The old building is still standing, too."

When she spoke of her brother, the smile disappeared. "I have to warn you, you won't like Earl, and he won't like you. Don't ever assume that you will get anything from him except a place to sleep and barely livable wages."

"Sounds like I know him from somewhere," John wisecracked. "How come he's willing to take us?"

"The neighboring ranchers dragged him into court because he refused to fence his cattle," she explained. "Now he has until June to round up the cattle and mend the fences. We could lose a great deal if he doesn't, but I don't think he really cares."

John looked worried.

"What's wrong?" she asked.

"Well, you see, I was born in Brooklyn, and we moved to Cleveland when I was nine. Then Detroit, and Chicago, and Omaha—places like that—and we never learned much about wild cows and that stuff. What happens if I can't do the work? I mean, I *hate* cows and horses!"

Matt reached back and slapped him on the head. "Don't worry

about that." He laughed. "I'll make it every bit as easy for you on the ranch as you made it for me in the joint."

"I'm not shittin' you, man," John said morosely. "I hustled a free mule ride at the Prospect Park Zoo when I was a kid, and I got seasick."

They drove over the Continental Divide and wended their way down the western slope as Miss Wilson filled them in on other details. In September they would enroll as high school juniors, and they were to continue their independent studies until that time. She would return about once a month and spend two days tutoring them. If she decided to retire in August, she would move back to the ranch and make certain their education justified the grades that would appear on their falsified transcripts. Finally, they were to select new surnames before she started back to Clearwater on Monday, so that Father Cassidy could begin preparing the birth certificates and school records.

Miss Wilson pulled off the highway onto a narrow dirt road. They drove out of the heavy timber, and soon there was nothing to see except sagebrush, greasewood, and alkaline foothills. There were no telephone poles or utility lines, and before long even the dirt road had narrowed to a pair of deep ruts in the grass. She slowly maneuvered the car around the chuckholes, and the smile on her face conveyed the message that they were almost home. The two boys exchanged apprehensive glances.

"Holy God," John moaned as they suddenly came upon a dilapidated two-story frame house that had weathered gray. The house stood at the bottom of a gully, between two scruffy hills that seemed to prop up the old building. A rambling wooden porch hung from the front and trembled in the wind like the tongue of a panting animal, and the appended garage leaned into the side of the house to keep it from toppling farther into the ravine. John collapsed further into the back seat with an anguished groan, but Miss Wilson was undaunted.

"The bunkhouse is on up the ravine," she said enthusiastically. "You can't see it from here. Chances are it is in better condition than the house, but I wouldn't bet on it."

John groaned again, and Matt smiled as he tried to imagine

what was going on in the city boy's mind. The house looked pretty bad, but it was much like many of the places Matt and his dad had worked in Wyoming.

The car bumped to a stop, and Miss Wilson looked into the faces of each boy. "Don't forget what I told you," she admonished. "Earl Wilson is a bitter old man, but he will be fair about the work he will demand from you. That means I expect you to do what you are told." Her statement might have been taken as a threat, but Matt accepted it as a simple declaration of how things were going to be. The boys nodded silently, and she smiled.

"Let's get on with it then," she said cheerfully. She pulled up on the door handle, opened the door a few inches, then slammed it shut without moving. The boys had very little time to wonder about her strange behavior, because the sound of the door closing immediately evoked the attack of a massive dog that charged, howling, from the garage. To John, it looked part German shepherd, part bear, and all teeth.

The frenzied animal threw itself against Miss Wilson's window, spraying saliva. John slid to the opposite side of the back seat, wailing pathetically, and Matt instinctively locked his door. Suddenly the snarling beast disappeared from Miss Wilson's side of the car and reappeared snapping and clawing against the back window on the opposite side. Matt was so startled that he tried to climb over Miss Wilson, and John howled, "He's got us surrounded!"

Miss Wilson reacted to the confusion by alternately sounding the horn, protecting herself from Matt's flailing elbows, and pleading with the boys to calm down. "It's all right," she shouted. "The dog won't hurt you. Settle down."

Earl Wilson suddenly appeared on the front porch. He stared dispassionately at the attacking dog and the rocking automobile before snarling, "Bones!" The dog stopped barking and loped up to the porch to sit behind its master.

The man looked to be in his seventies, with short-cropped hair, a straight, slender body, a tanned weather-beaten face. His eyes were bluer than his sister's, set deeply in his dark, wrinkled skin. He was wearing bib overalls.

He was a scrub brush rancher, no more and no less. Matt

was on solid ground. He knew the type. It was not a matter of such a man being good or bad, mean or nice. He was a product of the land he wrestled with, a process that made men quiet. Such men stuck it out through the storms, and drought, and disease, and there just wasn't much left to say. Earl Wilson was a man who obviously demanded little from his environment, but he would control the isolated world he lived in.

"You gonna sit there all day, Verna?"

Miss Wilson stepped from the car, climbed the steps, and lightly kissed her older brother on the cheek. "Earl, I never thought it would be possible, but this place looks worse than it did last summer."

The corner of his mouth twitched a fraction of an inch as the boys stared from the safety of the car. If that was a smile, it would probably be the last they would see from him for a long time.

"A ranch ain't for lookin'. It's for workin'."

Miss Wilson snorted once and turned toward the car. "Come up here, boys. I want you to meet my brother."

Matt and John advanced tentatively, never taking their eyes from the dog at the heel behind its master. The hair on Bones's neck bristled, and he bared his teeth as they reached the first step, so they simultaneously retreated and waved nervously.

Earl slapped his thigh impatiently, and the dog cowered.

"Come on up," Miss Wilson said. "The dog won't bother you."

Each boy stuck out his right hand, and Mr. Wilson returned a strong grip and a single pump. His face was devoid of expression, and it was obvious that he was not about to waste his energy greeting the new ranch hands.

"Dammit, Earl, if you don't make a soul feel welcome." She chided him. "Come on, boys, let's see if this old skinflint has anything to eat."

They started toward the front door, but John froze as the dog snarled at him. "What's wrong with that dog?" John asked, his eyes popping from his swollen cheeks.

"Bones ain't never seen a nigger before," Earl said indifferently.

Miss Wilson kicked angrily at the dog and glared at her brother.

"I don't ever want to hear that word again," she demanded in measured tones.

Her brother returned her anger and said evenly, "I ain't no do-gooder. You need a place, and I need some hands. If they don't like it, let 'm leave the way they come."

They glared at each other without moving until John broke the stalemate by clearing his throat and offering a compromise. "I don't mind. If he keeps that dog off my body, he can call me anything he wants."

Miss Wilson tried to suppress a chuckle, and Earl peered at John as if seeing him in a new light. The skin around his eyes wrinkled. Then he grunted and walked into the house, followed closely by two nervous teenagers whose eyes never left the snarling dog as they backed across the front porch into the safety of the house.

The boys found their own way to the bunkhouse while Miss Wilson drove to town for supplies. It was a low building, forty feet long and twelve feet wide. The paint was peeling from the wood siding, but the door fitted tightly, all the windows were in place, and the roof was sound. The interior consisted of a single all-purpose room with rough planks for flooring, a scorched stone fireplace, and a large wood stove close to the short counter that served as the kitchen area.

It was like a dream revisited for Matt because the room reminded him of the house in which he had been reared. He entered the room smiling and walked about reverently, but John hung back at the front door, wrinkling his nose in revulsion. Matt was ecstatic about the prospect of living in the old bunkhouse, but when he forced himself to view it through his friend's eyes, he saw the dirty, unpainted cupboards, the filthy little windows, the exposed roof rafters that were weatherproof but only partially insulated. The piled-up furniture in the corner included broken bunk beds, torn and moldy mattresses, a three-legged kitchen table with a chipped enamel top, and a number of wooden chairs in varying stages of disrepair.

Matt decided that the best way to deal with John's despondency was to show enough enthusiasm for both of them. He flew around the room, blandishing the good features and shrugging off the bad. Then he forced open two of the windows to air out the place and proceeded to act out the placement of imaginary furnishings. "We'll each have a favorite chair in front of the fireplace—right here—and we'll have our reading tables right here. Can't you see it?"

The blank look in John's face indicated he couldn't, but Matt was not discouraged. "This is the kitchen area. You can't beat these old wood stoves for cooking and heating. And we'll cover up the ceiling with—"

"Oh, God, Matt, what's that?" John had taken one step into the room and was pointing at something on the kitchen counter. "What *is* that thing?" he wailed in a tone of burlesque despair.

"That's a"—Matt's brow furrowed, and his voice dropped as he recognized the implications of the question—"kerosene lantern."

"Does that mean what I think it means?" John asked, coming into the room to search for electrical outlets that were not there. Matt knew his timing was bad, but he began to laugh, and John responded with an exaggerated indignation that was not entirely ungenuine. "Tell me you see a light bulb, or a toaster, or a radio, or *anything* that comes to life when you flip the little switch."

Matt's laughter brought a little grin to John's face. "It's not so bad," Matt said. "I grew up without electricity *or* indoor plumbing, and—"

"*Indoor Plumbing*? Don't tell me." John walked to the back window and looked out. "Yep, there it . . . by God . . . is."

Matt followed his friend and peered over his shoulder at the stark little outhouse twenty steps from the back door.

John's behavior had been mostly for comedic effect, but as the funny look on his face turned to real concern, Matt realized that his friend was every bit as frightened about the prospect of living in that place as Matt himself had been the first day at Clearwater.

"You know, Matt," John said seriously, "I've seen poor people in my life, but that old man is *poo-oor.*"

"He's not poor," Matt said firmly, with a trace of indignation in his voice. "This is how he wants to live. I grew up in a place just like this. It's not as bad as you think."

It was John's turn to look at Matt as though seeing his friend for the first time. "This really *is* your turf, isn't it?" Matt nodded his head without speaking, and John said, "I sure hope you can teach me better'n I taught you."

John took a deep breath, shrugged at the inevitability of it all, and looked out the window, cheerfully uttering a prayer. "Are you there, God? I'm just checking in. I don't have much to say just yet. I can see you've never been to this place before, so I just wanted you to know where I am." Then he unclasped his hands and cupped an ear, pretending to be listening to something beyond the window. Finally, he stepped back shaking his head. "It's a long story, God, and you wouldn't believe me if I told you."

As if guided by an unconscious recollection of his father's preparing their cabin on that day of the spring blizzard, almost twelve years earlier, Matt directed John to gather firewood while he completely emptied the room of everything he could move.

He set a fire in the stove and warmed enough water to begin the process of scrubbing the place clean. Miss Wilson returned at some point and pitched in without being asked. In the late afternoon she put a smoked ham in the oven, and Matt helped John set a roaring blaze in the large fireplace. Gradually the look and feel of an abandoned house surrendered to the odors, the dancing shadows, and the warmth of home.

While there was still enough light to see, Miss Wilson led the boys to the main house on a raiding party for furniture, and since Earl used only one room in the old place, there was plenty to choose from. They dragged out two stuffed chairs and side tables and placed them in front of the fireplace, right where Matt had envisioned them earlier. They selected two mattresses and agreed to set them on the floor until there was time to repair the broken bed frames. Finally, they concluded their day's work by rescuing an old oak table and three dusty dining-room chairs from the garage. They had spent the day in such a panic that old Earl merely shook his head in disgust, and Bones decided to ignore them completely.

John led the final procession back to the bunkhouse just as darkness was falling. He pushed open the door with his foot, giggling about the dog's sudden indifference, and the atmosphere of the room engulfed him. He stopped and stared at the fire, sucked in the good clean smell of the place, flavored by the baking ham and smoldering wood, and he said simply, "Wow!"

Matt came around the table to join him, and John placed a hand on his friend's shoulder as they peered into the room, illuminated by the golden tones of the afternoon sun, the kerosene lamp, and the dancing fire. John said softly, "You were right, Matt. This is good."

Miss Wilson was moved, but she had other things on her mind. "Come on, you two. We're not finished yet. We still have to unload the car."

They carried the oak table and chairs into the kitchen area, and after returning to the car, she loaded their outstretched arms with the remaining boxes and bags she had brought from town. It was her turn to be excited as she had them stack everything on the table and ordered them to pull up their chairs.

"I love Christmas," she said enthusiastically.

"But that's three weeks away," Matt said teasingly. "Why don't we wait?"

"Hey, man," John warned, "cool it."

"First things first," she said, handing each of them a box wrapped in brown paper.

In spite of Matt's feigned casualness, he matched John's speed in destroying the box to get at its contents.

"It's the newest thing on the market," she said as they withdrew two gas lanterns. "They don't smoke like the old kerosene lamps, and they give off white light. Look." She pumped the plunger several times and depressed the built-in flint. A flame erupted inside the glass, and as she modulated the flow of gas, the lantern glowed as brightly as an electric light.

"How about that!" John cheered, proceeding to ignite the second lantern.

"Good," Miss Wilson said. "Now we can take our time."

The large boxes contained down-filled sleeping bags, and the shopping bags produced western jeans, flannel shirts, underwear, cotton socks, leather gloves, and wool jackets. The boys were overjoyed with their "civvies" and eager to tear open the remaining three boxes. She held on to the last package, the only one wrapped in Christmas paper, and permitted them to open the boxes that contained surplus army boots.

The boys glowed with pleasure, but she said, "All these things are really the bare necessities. You will need them to work and survive out here." Then she held out the final box. "This is my special present to you both. This will remind you that there is an outside world waiting for you, and this will keep you in touch until you are ready to enter it again."

"Old newspapers?" John quipped, wanting to make her laugh instead of cry.

Matt snatched the package away from John. "Gimme that, you clown," he snapped in mock disgust. "We're gonna frame this wrapping paper."

"Let's see what's inside before we promise anything," John whispered loudly.

The colored picture on the carton gave away the secret, and John plunged into the package and pulled out a bulky portable radio, encased in black leather, with glistening dials for AM, FM, weather, and shortwave reception. Miss Wilson showed them how to engage the different antennas, and within minutes the room was alternately filled with music, a basketball game, a weather report, and the voice of an airman in Alaska trying to reach his mother in New Mexico by shortwave transmission.

The boys descended on Miss Wilson with tears in their eyes, and the three of them cried, and laughed, and hugged with the final realization that they would indeed make it.

Miss Wilson had to leave on Monday morning. When they had assembled near her car, she waved to her brother and turned to the boys. "I guess I have told you everything that needs to be said. Work hard, and keep up with your daily assignments. I'll try to be back in a month or so, but whether I do or not, stay out of sight until your hair grows back. Policemen have long memories."

She leaned forward and touched each of the boys on the cheek, opened the car door, and sat straight behind the wheel. No one said anything as the car roared to life and started toward the road, kicking up puffs of swirling dust. By the time the dust cleared the car was out of sight, and Earl Wilson had returned to his house without speaking.

Chapter Thirty-five

It had been a busy two days for all of them. They had cleaned the bunkhouse, learned to cook on the wood stove, arranged their furniture, and reached an unspoken truce with Bones. Miss Wilson had structured the situation from the moment they arrived, and they would now be able to cook their own food, wash their own clothes, and doctor their own bruises.

Earl Wilson would purchase their food every two weeks, post general work assignments once a week, and pay them each $30 on the first day of every month. They were well supplied with fuel for the lanterns, batteries for the radio, cold-weather clothing, blankets, linens, household utensils, and school supplies. Everything had been arranged, but suddenly she was gone, and the boys felt empty and insecure.

Matt marveled at the change that had taken place in Miss Wilson after their arrival at the ranch. He had always seen her as a feisty old woman who had managed to maintain a professional distance in spite of her personal interest in her students, so he was surprised to see her trade her orthopedic shoes for work boots and her tailored suits for denim jeans and loose flannel shirts. She had ridden off to town on a shopping spree, and a few hours later she was hauling furniture with the boys, but it all had happened so naturally that they never saw the transition take place.

Before returning to Clearwater, Miss Wilson had discussed the need to change their names. Father Cassidy would provide new birth certificates, school records, and personal histories to corroborate the story that they were orphans assigned to live and work on the ranch, but Miss Wilson warned that the change would not withstand intensive security investigations, so they were not to plan careers in the CIA.

John felt no real compunction about the name change, indicating that his mother had bestowed it on him after giving birth in the Kings Highway elevated station of the Culver line, in Brooklyn. Miss Wilson recommended against changing his first name because there were so many possibilities for confusion—something she remembered from a World War Two spy movie.

John decided to take the name of Williams, and in a gesture of compromise, he retained his first name, except he dropped the *h* and would thereafter be known as Jon Williams.

Matt was intractable in his determination to retain his own name. His return to the mountains, to the ranching life, and especially to the old cabin had brought him even closer to his heritage and sense of family identity—something he had begun to lose over the past six months, something he was now determined to retain.

Matt was more concerned about Ralph and Tony. He asked if it might be possible to have the two join them eventually on the ranch, but Miss Wilson was emphatically negative. "In the first place," she said, "the institution is probably the best place for both boys. Neither one is in any physical danger. Ralph is learning a trade and is being cared for, and Tony is learning to read with that volunteer woman from town."

"But how long do you expect them to be locked up there?" Matt asked angrily.

"Ralph is just about eighteen, and he will probably be released as soon as he can earn a living for himself on the outside. They'll put him into a transitional living program first, and then he'll take a part-time job in town under the direct supervision of his social worker. Believe me," she said, "it is the best thing for him."

"And what about Tony? Do you expect him to stay there for the next eight or nine years, too?"

"Not at all," Miss Wilson answered emphatically. "Mr. Masters has the authority to release any boy whenever he feels the boy is equipped to survive on the outside. My guess would be that they will find a foster placement for Tony as soon as he is capable of reading and succeeding in school."

"If that's so," Matt said challengingly, "why didn't Masters release us instead of arranging for our escape?"

"I did not say Mr. Masters was involved in our little adventure," she said firmly. "But whether he was or not is irrelevant. The fact is that the state director of institutions removed you from Mr. Masters's jurisdiction when the institutional transfer was delivered."

Matt had lost again, and he knew it. In a subdued tone he asked, "Can we at least talk about it again? . . . Ralph and Tony?"

"Of course, but please don't hold out any hope for the impossible."

"Will you at least do this much?" he asked. "Will you at least let them know we're okay?"

Miss Wilson shook her head sadly. "There's just too much at risk here, Matthew. I'm afraid you are going to have to accept the fact that the break must be a clean one. You simply must begin making a new life for yourselves."

Matt knew it would be useless to argue with her, but he refused to accept her advice. Long after Miss Wilson had left the ranch, he continued to dream about reuniting the Fudge Ripples, and he resolved to make it happen.

"What're you thinking about?" Jon asked as he cut into the remnants of the baked ham for sandwiches.

Matt set aside his thoughts of Ralph and Tony and said, "I was thinking we'd better find some horses, so I can teach you to ride. I'm gonna find you one that's so rank he'll have your ass looking worse than your face before you even get into the saddle."

The swelling had begun to diminish, so Jon's smile extended from both sides of his mouth. "Don't bother, man. I'm part of the new breed . . . the first of the *walking* cowboys."

Matt's retort was interrupted by the roar of Earl's pickup, which approached the bunkhouse dragging its muffler and sounding more like an armored tank than a truck. The two boys had started for the door even before the horn sounded outside.

Earl was staring straight ahead, so they assumed he wanted them to get into the truck. The question of whether they should climb into the cab or the back was answered for them by Bones, who had staked his exclusive claim to the truck bed by snarling menacingly at their approach.

Earl drove them along the perimeter of the ranch, which was several miles square. The boundaries were defined primarily by rocks, hills, or trees because the fences were almost nonexistent. Earl had a vague idea of where his cattle might be and pointed out some of the likely locations. He had not rounded up or branded his stock in more than four years, but he estimated he owned 250 to 300 head.

His only source of income had been derived from selling off the few head of cattle that wandered into the corral every winter looking for food. In fact, it was not a ranch at all. It was nothing but a large parcel of real estate inhabited by some wild cows and rangy horses.

Matt's experienced eye assessed the situation accurately. At least twenty acres of this scrub brush country would be required to feed one cow, but it would be difficult to estimate the grazing potential of the ranch unless Earl's cattle were gathered up and contained. It would be impossible to fence the entire ranch, but with a few extra hands and some outlying corrals, they could keep the cattle where they belonged until they were marketed.

Matt tried to discuss his plan, but Earl cut him off. "No more hands. It's *your* job. And you can use the corrals I got." Earl drove the boys back to the bunkhouse and instructed them to check out the corrals and cattle pens on the other side of the hill. "Oughta be five or six horses up there and five or six on the range. They'll need some work."

Matt chuckled at the understatement as the pickup rolled away. Then he clapped his friend on the shoulder. "Let's go, Jon."

"Are you saying 'John' or 'Jon'?"

"What the hell are you talking about?"

"You know . . . with or without the *h*?"

Matt laughed and pulled him by the arm. "We've got work to do, you clown."

It had been so long since ranch hands had lived there that the path from the bunkhouse to the corral was overgrown with sagebrush. As soon as the two boys reached the top of the hill, Matt strode purposefully to the corral, pleased to see that the rails and posts were in place and solid. He was even more pleased when he climbed to the top rail to inspect the horses.

"Look at that," he said appreciatively.

"What?" Jon asked from a safe distance.

The voice was so far away that Matt had to turn around to find his friend standing at the corner of the tack house, obviously ill at ease around the animals.

"Those are great horses," Matt said. "They look like hell right now, but it's real good stock. Come on over," he urged.

"I can see them from here," Jon said. "How come their hair's so long?"

"That's just their winter coat."

"They look like they need haircuts. They look creepy to me."

Matt jumped down from the fence and walked toward his friend. "The way I see it, we're going to have to expand the size of those cattle pens and round up three hundred cattle before June. There's no way we can do that unless you learn how to ride a horse."

Jon's eyes reflected his fear, but he said nothing.

"Let's see what kind of gear we have to work with," Matt said, brushing past his friend and pushing on the heavy tack house door.

The room was dark, but Matt could identify six saddles hanging neatly from pegs on the wall. As his eyes adjusted to the darkness, he located bridles, saddle blankets, and ropes.

Matt emerged from the small shed with a bucket and a kerosene lamp. He handed the bucket to Jon. "There's a windmill on the far side of the corral. Fill this with water, and I'll try to get this lamp working."

When Jon returned, Matt was rummaging through the dimly lit shack for saddle soap, brushes, and oil. He pulled one of the saddles from its peg and began scrubbing away the heavy layer of dust and grime. He inspected the pommel, side bars, and hind bow and found all the leather-covered rigid parts to be sound. Then he pulled on the cinch, latigos, and stirrups before passing the saddle to Jon.

"This one's okay. We'll work on it tonight."

Matt continued to inspect the equipment, rejecting three other saddles because of faulty cinches and dry-rotted straps and stirrups. He finally approved a second saddle and selected the necessary headgear and blankets. He had been so intensely involved in his work that he had failed to notice it was getting cold, but one look at Jon, who was jumping from one foot to the other to keep warm, told him it was time to return to the bunkhouse.

They fashioned a quick supper and worked late into the night, cleaning the leather and rubbing the stiffness out with warm oil. The odor of the leather flooded Matt with good memories, but the entire process was strange and irrelevant to Jon and did nothing to calm his fears.

The old bedsprings screeched in protest as Matt erupted from his nightmare, eyes wide, heart pounding, sweat dotting his forehead and upper lip. The dark room seemed familiar: the glow of embers in the fireplace, the odor of dead coals in the potbellied stove, and dust on the rough-cut pine planks. For an instant he thought he was home again. His breath caught in his chest, and muscles that had been tense for months sagged in momentary relief. It all had been a nightmare. His dad, Clearwater, the es-cape—none of it was real! But as he gathered his wits, and his eyes became accustomed to the dark, he realized that the person under the old quilt in the next bed was John Culver, not Dan McFadden. And that indeed, there *had* been a funeral, a reform school, a Shacky, and an escape.

Matt freed himself from the heavy layers of blankets and sat up. He swung his feet over the side of the bed and flinched when they touched the cold floor. He rubbed his eyes, and the dream that had triggered his panic came back. He was dressed in black and white prison stripes. The bloodhounds bayed in the distance as he struggled through a swamp, negotiating a path through clinging vines, hissing snakes, and bubbling quicksand. An es-caped criminal fleeing from the law.

Matt McFadden—escaped criminal. How was that possible?

He wrapped himself in one of the old quilts and walked to the door of the bunkhouse. It was a clear, crisp night, and the stars sparkled against the blue-black sky.

The words hammered at his mind. ESCAPED CRIMINAL. Suddenly he recalled the night soon after his father had built their first crystal radio. Matt was six and had just started school. He had been doodling at the table on his Big Chief pad when the radio program was interrupted by a news bulletin. Six desperate convicts, armed and dangerous, had escaped from the state penitentiary and were last seen driving a stolen car toward the very mountains where the McFaddens lived.

Dan McFadden grunted and went on with his reading, but young Matt was alarmed. He had seen dangerous criminals in the Saturday morning serials at the Rialto. They were mean and had shifty eyes, and they would cut and shoot people for no reason at all. As the hours passed, every familiar night sound—the big owl spreading his wings in the tree, the old bear sniffing through the garbage—took on a new meaning. Young Matt had tried to sleep, deep under his covers, but the night was alive with knife-wielding desperate men.

The memory of that fearful night was vivid. Matt pulled his quilt tighter against the cold and wondered how many young children were lying awake in fear of the two desperate inmates who had escaped from Clearwater two nights ago. More to the point, how many young children were praying for their capture?

Would those prayers be answered? There were only two certainties: He and Jon had escaped, and there were people out there tracking them down at that very moment.

Tomorrow morning he would tell the old man that they would need rifles if they were to spend their nights on the range.

Earl Wilson provided the boys with a long-barreled shotgun and an old Winchester carbine, and Matt grimly set about the task of teaching Jon to use them. Any thought of breaking horses would be postponed until Matt was certain they could defend themselves against any attempt to recapture them and return them to prison.

Chapter Thirty-six

Matt was determined to start the day right. He awoke early, fed the fire in the stove to take the chill from the room, and set out for the tiny shack, behind the big house, which had once been used for smoking fresh meat. Just as he had anticipated, he found a side of beef and an antelope carcass hanging from metal hooks. The meat was almost frozen, but Mr. Wilson's assortment of knives and saws were so well honed that Matt had no difficulty cutting two large steaks from the beef loin. If Jon was going to spend this day bouncing on and off horses, he at least deserved an extravagant breakfast.

Matt was grinning to himself as he slipped back into the bunkhouse. He was tempted to spoon out some of Miss Wilson's sourdough starter for pancakes, but he realized he would not have enough pans for everything. Instead, he put the coffeepot on the stove and melted a dollop of butter in the heavy cast-iron frying pan. By the time Jon staggered sleepily to the table the steaks were sizzling on the stove.

"That smells good," he mumbled. "We expecting company?"

"No. We've got a busy day ahead of us, that's all."

Jon remembered the horses waiting in the corral. "Oh, yeah. The last supper."

The sun was out, and the sky was blue, but the wind blowing down from the mountains was cold. The two boys hoisted their gear and started up the hill. Jon was stronger than Matt, but he was having difficulty balancing the unwieldy load. By the time he reached the corral Matt was preparing his rope, swinging it through the air to expand the loop and loosen the stiff fiber.

"What are you going to do with that rope?"

"I can't make you ride if you really don't want to, but I've got to start breaking these boneheads."

Jon put his hand on Matt's arm. "You think I'm a chicken shit, don't you?"

"No, Jon. It's just going to take time . . . but you have to be willing to try." Matt knew better. He had seen sons of ranchers and cowhands who could never conquer their fear of horses in spite of their raw courage and persistence, but there was too much at stake to give Jon an easy way out. Without him helping to work the cattle, Mr. Wilson might lose the ranch by summer, and they would have no place to go.

"Okay," Matt said cheerfully. "Let's pick one out. How about that bay with the black mane?"

"What are you going to do?"

"I'll rope him and put a saddle and bridle on him. Then I'll see how he rides. It's simple."

"How the hell do you know that horse will *let* you ride him?" Jon asked contemptuously. "How do you even know he'll stop when you get the rope around him? How do you know he won't just come right at you and step all over your body?"

John was trying to break the tension with humor, but Matt realized his questions were honest. "I don't know if he'll let me ride, but if he throws me off, I'll just get up and try again. And if I rope him and he doesn't stop, then I'll slide behind him on my heels until I can loop the rope around that big post and try to pull him closer." Matt thought for a moment. "What was the other thing you asked about?"

He was now inside the corral, and Jon had his head through the gate. "Run over you. Suppose those horses say, 'Here comes the skinny one. Let's stomp his ass.' "

Matt had never thought about it before. "I don't know," he said. "There just aren't many horses that will charge a man, that's all."

"*Many*," Jon shrieked, spooking the horses. "There don't have to be *many*. There just has to be *one*, you dumb-ass. How do you know which one that is? Does he wear a sign that says, 'Don't rope me 'cause I'm a man charger'?"

Matt laughed and walked slowly toward the cluster of horses as he swung the rope over his head.

Jon's voice was filled with fear and anxiety. "Wait, Matt. I have a better idea. Come back."

Matt dropped the rope and returned to the gate.

"Let's pack our stuff and head for the city. We can get lost there. I know my way around, and no one is gonna mess with us—"

Matt interrupted Jon's plea. "We wouldn't last a week in the city without help. I understand why you're afraid, but I'm not. If we were in the city, I'd be afraid and asking you to come back to the ranch. We're here now, so let's make the best of it."

"You stupid honky. Don't you remember how your own daddy died?"

Matt stopped. He hadn't forgotten how his father had died, but the memory had not created a fear of horses. He had seen his father break a thousand horses and get thrown hundreds of times, but the only time Jon had heard about a man breaking horses was when Matt had described his father's death.

"I'm sorry, man," Jon said quietly. "I'm scared, and I'm making it worse for you. I just don't want you to get bunged up by some damned horse." Then Jon recalled Miss Wilson's words and said, "Remember, all we got is each other."

Matt nodded and turned to retrieve his rope. It was time to stop talking and show Jon how unrealistic his fears were. Dan McFadden had always said Matt could read a horse better than any man he had known. As he advanced on the big bay, he prayed he still had the instinct to pick an easy rider.

The other horses began to prance and scatter, but the bay stood with its ears up and stared at Matt. He stopped swinging the rope and shortened the loop, advancing slowly with his empty left hand outstretched. When he was three feet away, the horse extended its neck and nibbled at Matt's fingers.

"I'll be goddamned," Jon exclaimed happily as Matt continued his advance, speaking gently and trying unsuccessfully to slip the noose over the horse's head. The bay was gentle, but it was no dummy. Whenever the noose came up, it tossed its head back and pranced out of reach.

Matt knew he could be asking for trouble, but he suddenly had an urge to grab the mane and vault onto the horse's back. If he had misread this animal, he would soon be on his butt, but if he was right, he might convince Jon that horses did not eat people for lunch. Seventeen hands of horse was a long way up, but the natural motion was still there, and suddenly Matt was astride.

The brown fuzzy ears flattened and twitched, and the rump muscles quivered, but the bay remained still. Matt wrapped his legs tight and waited for a lunge or a sprint for the nearest gate in an attempt to scrape him off, but nothing happened. That big beautiful horse just stood there and eventually relaxed. As soon as the ears perked up, Matt prodded gently with his knees and walked the bay toward the gate, where his wide-eyed, open-mouthed friend stood staring through the rails.

Matt slid off and handed the lead rope to Jon. "Well, what are you going to name him?"

Jon did not back away, but he was obviously uncomfortable to be standing so close to the snorting monster. "Why should I name him?"

"Because he's going to be yours. From now on you'll be the only one to ride him."

"*Are you crazy?* That's the horse I said looked like he wanted to eat my face, and you march right in there and pick him out for me! Why did you do that?"

Matt laughed and said, "He looked like the gentlest horse in the bunch, and I think he's well trained. So what are you going to name him?"

Jon slowly crawled through the fence and edged up to the horse. "He doesn't belong to me. He's Earl Wilson's horse. Anyway, he probably has a name already." Jon reached out and tentatively touched the bay's fuzzy nose. Then he stroked the forehead and began to smile. The fear was still there, but the thought of owning this big, shaggy animal brought new meaning to their relationship.

"Mr. Wilson may own this horse's papers," Matt said, "but he only owns the body. After you two get to know each other, the horse will be yours. You'll eat together, sleep together, and fight when he doesn't want what you want, and make up when the fight's over. He'll do what you want most of the time, and some times you'll do what he wants if you're smart enough to listen."

Jon continued to stroke the animal's head. "I'm gonna call him Stud."

"*Stud*? You can't call him Stud. He's a gelding."

Jon glared at Matt. "You kept calling it him, and him horses are studs, ain't they?"

"A stud is used for breeding. If you want a working male horse, you have to castrate him so he won't be so wild."

Jon was horrified. "You mean . . . you mean, he's been cut?"

Matt nodded.

"Those dirty bastards," Jon mumbled. He leaned close to the bay's face and said softly, "I'm still gonna call you Stud. No matter what they did to you, I know deep down you're still a stud."

Matt showed Jon how to secure the bridle and set the bit. They placed the saddle over the blanket, and Matt set the cinch. Jon began to get excited as the mangy horse was transformed by the harness into a more recognizable package, but his enthusiasm flagged when it came time for him to mount. He held onto the saddle horn with both hands while Matt guided his trembling foot into the stirrup. When he tried to pull himself up, however, the saddle rocked toward him, and Jon jumped backward, expecting it to fall to the ground. They finally managed to seat Jon by having him climb the fence and lower himself onto the patient horse.

Matt adjusted the stirrups and realized he had no idea how to teach someone else to ride a horse. "Give me the reins," he said. "I'll lead you around a few times." Matt listened to Jon's butt slapping against the saddle with each step. Without looking back, he said, "Keep your butt in the saddle. Relax and go with the horse. When you run, you can lift off, but when you walk or canter, just stay in tight."

Halfway around the corral Stud whinnied and shook his head, trying to adjust to the feel of the saddle. After that the sound of Jon's backside smacking against the saddle stopped, and when Matt looked back to compliment his friend, he found Jon doubled up on top of the saddle with his knees under him and both hands gripping the horn.

"What the hell are you doing?"

"I've seen those cowboy shows, and when the horse throws the bad guy, he always gets caught in that foot thing and gets dragged all over the country. When Stud started to shake back there, I got ready to jump."

Matt was plainly disgusted. "You have to stop fooling around. Look," he said, slapping the palm of his hand against the high stiff back of the saddle. "This is the cantle. You sit back against that real hard if the horse starts to rear, and it'll keep you from falling off."

"Oh, man, why would you even *think* something like that?" Jon said as he gingerly lowered himself into the stirrups. "Suppose old Stud understood what you just said? He's gonna think I'm ready for fancy jumping."

"Oh, nuts, there's only one way to do this. If you're ever going to learn how to ride, you'll have to stay out here with Stud and ride until the crack in your butt feels like it runs all the way to your head!"

Jon seemed to understand the fun was over.

"Hold onto these reins. Don't pull tight, or you'll hurt his mouth. You pull on them when you want to stop. The faster you pull, the faster you stop, but never jerk back on the reins, or you'll cut his mouth and eventually toughen it up so you'll have no way to control him."

Matt spent the next half hour explaining how to neck-rein and how to guide the horse with pressure from the knees. Like most cow ponies, Stud responded well, and Jon learned to signal the horse to start, stop, turn, speed up, and slow down. Then Matt climbed the fence and observed Jon putting the horse through its paces for another half hour.

"One last thing," Matt instructed, "and if you forget everything else but this, you can still be a good rider. Stud *wants* you to be the boss, but he'll test you once in a while just to make sure you are. But being boss doesn't mean you have to hurt him just to show how tough you are. . . . My dad was the gentlest man I have ever known. He was also the best rider there ever was."

Find a Safe Place

Matt spent the next several hours roping and examining most of the other horses. It soon became apparent that they would have to be shod before they would be of any value on the open range, so he decided to find Earl Wilson and discuss the situation.

Jon remained astride Stud during the entire time, mastering the basics of riding, but Matt deliberated about leaving him alone because he was still not able to mount or dismount on his own. He finally decided to carry out his sink-or-swim philosophy of teaching horsemanship by leaving Jon behind with nothing but a warning to remain within the confines of the corral.

Instead of inviting Matt inside the house, Earl Wilson put on his coat and joined him on the front porch. He agreed to bring the farrier to the ranch as soon as possible, and Matt decided to press his luck by discussing another major problem.

"That corral is okay, but it will never hold three hundred head of cattle, Mr. Wilson. We're going to need fence posts and rails to repair what's there and expand the holding pens."

"Figure out what you need to fix up what's already there," Earl said brusquely. "We won't worry about expanding anything until we find out how many cows you can catch."

"Okay, but we're gonna need winter silage and—"

Earl was plainly impatient. "Like I said, boy, don't spend my money for silage until we find out if you can catch anything and hold it long enough to feed." He walked away from Matt, grumbling, "I *oughta* find out if you can ride a damned horse before I pay for a blacksmith."

Matt bristled with resentment. "Don't you worry about me, Mr. Wilson. I can ride any horse you've got, and you'd better get ready to feed your cattle because if there are any still alive out there, we're bringing them in!"

When Matt returned to the top of the hill, he glanced down at the corral. Then he stopped and looked again. From his position he could see every horse in the enclosure, but Jon and Stud were gone. He tried to control his panic and berated himself for recklessly exposing his friend to danger. He ran along the crest of the hill, intuitively assuming that a horse breaking out of the corral would run for the open range.

As he sprinted over the hard ground, his eyes scanned the terrain for Jon's body, and just as he caught sight of the bay tied up outside the bunkhouse, Matt tripped over a rock and went sprawling down the hill.

He heard Jon's laughter even before he could see him, and his panic turned to anger. "Goddammit, what the hell are you doing out here?" he demanded as he approached the bunkhouse.

"Sorry, teach'. I raised my hand to go to the potty, but I guess you didn't see it. But you sure put on a good show."

Matt thought about the spectacle of falling all over himself and started to smile grudgingly. "What made you think that horse wasn't going to throw your ass into the brush and take off for the open range once you let it out of the corral?"

"That's a dumb question, even for you, McFathead. I just had a little talk with Stud, and I said I would treat him good if he let me be boss."

Chapter Thirty-seven: Clearwater

Tony Washington rolled over and stared up at the dim light directly above his bed. He still could not believe that Matt and John had escaped from lockup. He had overheard some of the cottage parents speculating that Masters and Anderson might have set it up to look like an escape, but no one knew for certain. The important thing was that they were gone, and Tony somehow knew they would remain free. With Matt's brains and Jon's cool, the fuzz would never find them.

Tony had spent that first day scanning the fences, thinking they might come back for him and Ralph, but he knew how stupid that would be. Nobody was ever going to come back for them. He had cried that first night, but he recovered, wondering when he would learn to quit expecting anything from anybody. He tried to think about Ralph, but that sad and silent face quickly evoked images of Matt and Jon, so Tony turned his thoughts to the one person that belonged to him alone, Penny Conlin.

Tony and Penny had done so well in their first few sessions that she agreed to continue the reading lessons right through the weekend. The institution was swarming with state policemen and investigators from the warden's office because the escape of two boys from lockup was a spectacular achievement—one that would have required inside help. With Penny there, however, Tony was completely insulated from the confusion. They had progressed quickly through the alphabet and the sounds of each letter, and they were beginning to deal with the pronunciation of vowel combinations.

Penny would purse her lips and say "toy" and "ploy," and Tony would stare at her mouth in abject fascination, completely unable to understand anything except how good he felt when they were together.

Tony continued to spend the two-hour free period with Ralph. Sometimes they would try to shoot baskets, but the tiny boy disliked doing anything in public unless he excelled at it, and the huge mute was too clumsy and uncoordinated to enjoy the game, so mostly they walked by themselves around the abandoned snow-covered yard or sat in the barn while Tony talked for both of them.

For a while Tony vented his anger and disappointment by castigating their two friends who had abandoned them, but Ralph always expressed his disapproval with Tony by hand gestures and facial grimaces that clearly conveyed his displeasure. The gestures were precise and always the same: Ralph would cross his hands in front of his mouth, fingers extended and palms out. Then he would snap his hands down, palms facing Tony and eyes flashing angrily.

"Hey, you always do that," Tony said. "You trying to tell me something?"

Ralph nodded his head curtly.

"Oh, yeah?" Tony said dubiously. "Show me again." His breath was visible in the cold air.

Ralph crossed his hands in front of his mouth and repeated the gesture emphatically.

Tony's face brightened, sensing a new game in the offing. "There! You did it again. It's about them two cop-outs, ain't it? What is it? What ya tryin' to say?"

Ralph's eyes narrowed, and he raised his index finger to his lips.

"Quiet!" Tony shouted and jumped enthusiastically. "You're telling me to be quiet!"

Ralph shook his head and clenched both fists.

"No?" Tony asked disappointedly. "Not 'quiet'?"

Ralph nodded but clenched his fists again.

"Stronger than quiet?"

Ralph nodded again.

" 'Shut up'!" Tony shouted. "You're telling me to shut up, ain't ya?"

Ralph nodded, and the tiny boy jumped out and hugged the older boy's thigh. "You *spoke* to me, Ralphie! And I understood ya!" Then Tony backed away and urged, "Show me again, Ralphie. I'm gonna use that on my boys . . . save my voice. . . . Show me again!" As soon as Tony had perfected the gesture, he said, "Say something else, Ralphie. Do you know any more?"

Ralph shrugged his shoulders and inclined his head uncertainly. He looked around him; then his eyes brightened. He extended both hands, fingers spread and palms down; then he wiggled his fingers up and down.

"I got ya," Tony said, copying the sign perfectly. "What's it mean?"

Ralph leaned over and scooped up a handful of snow. He tossed it into the air, and as it fluttered down, he repeated the gesture.

"Snow!" Tony shouted gleefully. "That's the word for snow!" Then Tony strutted around the yard like a drum major, lifting his knees as high as they would go, repeating the two signs and shouting, "Shut up, snow. . . . Shut up, snow. This is powerful stuff, Ralphie. Show me some more."

Tony's facility for signing was a source of great joy for both boys, and they never missed an opportunity to practice. On Christmas afternoon, however, they were sitting in the barn, and Tony was in no mood for games. He wanted to reminisce about their two friends. "You remember that horse old Matt used to talk about? . . . Jellybean?"

Ralph gestured "Wrong," bringing his fist to his chin with thumb and little finger extended.

"Evergreen?" Tony teased him with a grin.

Ralph pursed his lips in mock disgust and raised his fist to his nose with thumb and pinkie still extended. Then he rotated his fist downward and pointed at Tony, the sign for "You're a silly fool."

"Watch your tongue, Ralphie. If this wasn't Christmas, I'd

be whippin' yo' ass right now." Tony lay back against a bale of hay and muttered, "Juniper . . . that was her name."

Ralph smiled, nodded his head, and, with the index fingers of both hands extended, brought his right fist down onto the top of his left: "Correct."

"Yeah . . . Juniper . . . well, I figure ol' Matt and Big John hitched all the way to Wyoming and got that horse, and right this minute they're ridin' it to New York City. I'll bet ya five Fifi bags against a dirty sock that they'll show up on TV next Thanksgiving ridin' at the head of the Macy's parade."

Ralph's belly jiggled with silent laughter, and he patted Tony's shoulder appreciatively.

Tony was learning to read first-grade books, but no one except Penny and Ralph knew about it. Tony and Ralph regularly retreated to the barn, which was deserted during the free period, and Tony would read. One day Tony recited from a special book that Penny had bought for him. "This . . . is . . . Matt," he read laboriously, watching Ralph's face brighten. "This . . . is . . . Pat. Matt is a . . . boy. Pat is . . . his dog. See . . . Matt . . . run."

The independent reading sessions were usually followed by increasingly tender descriptions of Penny Conlin that made it clear Tony was falling in love.

Chapter Thirty-eight

Tony marched at the front of the column, preoccupied with his thoughts of Penny Conlin. His dilemma was that he was losing interest in his reading lessons, but they were his only excuse for being with her. He was bored with the first-grade reading material because he was getting nowhere learning about tall boys, and their brown dogs, and their red shoes. On the one hand, as soon as he was able to read well enough, he would be separated from Penny; on the other hand, if he failed to show sufficient progress, Penny herself might get discouraged and leave. Why didn't they just let him be with her? What good was reading anyway?

KEEP OFF THE GRASS.

Tony had marched past that sign a thousand times without noticing it. Suddenly it spoke to him. KEEP OFF THE GRASS. He stopped in amazement and was bumped forward by the boys in back of him.

He stumbled a few steps and searched for more talking signs. The column turned the corner near the fence, and there it was. GATE CLOSED EX . . . CEPT FOR EM . . . ER . . . GEN . . . CIES!

Tony trembled with the unfamiliar power of achievement, and his enthusiasm erupted as they approached another of the little signs sticking up from the snow. KEEP OFF THE GRASS. "Hey, you guys," he shouted. "Keep off the grass."

It was forbidden for the boys to talk in line, so Tony's shouts brought Mr. Turpin on the run. "What the hell's the matter with you?"

"Can't you read the sign? It says 'Keep off the grass.' "

"Goddammit, it's winter . . . and we're on the sidewalk! Are you crazy?"

"Don't get uptight, Mr. Turpin, baby. I just wanted to make sure everyone saw the sign . . . just in case." They were approaching the school building, and Tony spied the engraving over the door. The cottage parent fumed as Tony mouthed the syllables quietly, and then the boy shouted, "And, Mr. Turpin, this is the WILLIS PENNINGTON SCHOOL, too."

"Damn you, boy, report to me after school."

Tony struggled to control his emotions throughout the math period. He decided to be cool when he saw Penny, but when the bell finally sounded, he burst from the classroom and sprinted down the hall and into the small office next to the gymnasium. He found her sitting at her desk, and he threw himself into her arms, hugging her around the neck and shouting the good news. "I can read! . . . I can read!"

She was startled at first, but as soon as she comprehended the message, she realized that a great breakthrough had occurred—Tony had just experienced his first transference of classroom learning into the real world—and she returned his embrace and laughed and cried and giggled with him as he sobbed, "I did it! I did it!"

Gary Masters was drawn to the commotion. He stood outside the little office and observed the scene with frowning disapproval. He had already warned Mrs. Conlin that Tony was developing a love relationship toward her, but she had apparently chosen to ignore him. He would have to call her in for another talk.

Penny Conlin fidgeted nervously in the leather chair as she waited for Gary Masters to arrive. Yesterday, when Tony discovered he could read things beyond the pages of his first-grade books, his exuberance had propelled him into her arms, and the superintendent had witnessed the whole scene. It had looked bad, she knew, but Masters had to be made to understand that it wasn't always that way. It had been a beautiful moment . . . electric . . . spontaneous . . . the joy of a young mind awakening. She had to make him understand.

Masters strode into the room with a peremptory "Good morning, Mrs. Conlin." When he sat down and faced her, he realized she had been crying. Her swollen eyes and red nose did little to diminish her beauty, and Masters stared at her silently.

"I'm sorry," she said nervously. "I don't know why I'm like this, but yesterday when you walked into my office . . ." Penny lowered her eyes and shook her head in confusion. "You seemed upset, and I've had this terrible feeling . . ."

"You were right," he said tonelessly. "You're not going to like what I have to say, and I don't like having to say it, but we all have to deal with realities in this place, and that goes for volunteers, too." Masters sat forward in his chair and locked his elbows against the armrests. "I went to the school to find Tony because there was more bad news."

Penny forgot her own tears and stared intently, her face set.

"You know how he is always bragging about his mother, right? Well, it turns out that she's mostly a figment of his overactive imagination. She's been a hooker and junkie for years, but Tony took care of the kids so well no one even suspected how bad the situation was. She completely disappeared about a month ago."

"Poor Tony," she whispered, again on the verge of tears. "What about his brothers and sister?"

"The local judge has just made it official. He severed all parental rights. The other children have been in detention for several weeks, and they will be placed elsewhere as soon as possible."

"Poor Tony," she repeated. "He never talks much about them, but he adored his mother. What will they all do?"

"That's one of the realities I was talking about. In truth, it is highly unlikely that Tony will ever see his mother again . . . *or* his brothers and sister." Masters paused to organize his thoughts. "I think Tony is strong enough to accept that, but when I saw you two the other day, I realized I had a double problem."

"Oh, no," she objected, suddenly coming to life again. "You've got that all wrong."

"I don't think so," he said. "Do you have any idea of the deep feelings Tony has for you right now?"

Penny leaned back and smiled uncertainly. "Of course I do.

We're friends. He likes me as much as I like him. I could never have taught him to read otherwise. He trusts me . . . he likes me and trusts me." She was afraid to express her emotions honestly, and she was having difficulty phrasing credible alternatives. "Okay, more than that maybe," she conceded, shaking her head. "A whole new world has opened up for him. He's . . . grateful perhaps." Penny struggled for the words that would safely convey her true fondness for him and how proud she was of his accomplishment, how warm and loving a boy he was, how vulnerable and giving. As his endearing qualities filtered through her mind, she suddenly understood Masters's concern.

"I guess I never really thought about him in those terms," she murmured, as though Masters were privy to her thoughts. "Everything seemed so perfect . . . just the way it was."

"I'm afraid that won't be enough anymore," Masters said softly. "You have become what Tony has always wanted his own mother to be. Like it or not, you are his own personal walking, talking beautiful fantasy."

Penny straightened in her chair and opened her mouth to object, but the words wouldn't come. Instead, she wearily shook her head in confusion, forced to accept the truth in his words.

"What about yourself?" he asked.

Penny tensed. "Me? What do you mean?"

"In your own mind where do you see this relationship going? What kind of fantasy does Tony fulfill for you?"

Penny was angered and offended. "How dare you! . . . You think I am using that boy! That is absolutely ridiculous."

"Is it? Then are you willing to adopt Tony? . . . Take him home and live with you in that fancy house? . . . That's the way he sees it, you know."

Penny sobbed and pleaded, "Why are you doing this to me? You're treating me like a criminal! All I ever wanted to do was to help."

Masters tried to be gentle and at the same time counter her attempt to change the subject. "We're talking about Tony, and don't you see, Penny, he doesn't think in terms of volunteer relationships . . . or caring on a part-time basis. To him, just like any other kid, you don't care halfway, you don't like just a little bit. The way kids see it, if you become friends, you are friends for a lifetime. If you love, you love for a lifetime. . . . And if you give him anything less right now, you will destroy him."

Penny dropped her show of anger and slumped forward in her chair, finally prepared to admit the truth. "You're right. I do love him. In a way, I guess I *have* been using him, haven't I?"

"Let's just say that you and Tony have satisfied some mutual needs. Unfortunately I can be concerned only with Tony. This thing can't continue. I'm afraid we're going to have to break it off."

"Don't take him away," she said, sobbing. "I love him. I told you."

Masters rose from his chair and paced the room, struggling for a solution. George Conlin was not the kind of man who would accept a black child from the reform school into his home. Not unless it served his own purpose. Twelve years older than Penny, he had married her only to lend credence to his political aspirations. When the voters turned their backs on him, he had retreated to his banking business with a vengeance and completely isolated her from his life. It would never work.

"I'm going to fight you on this, Masters."

The firmness in her voice stopped him. There was a cold determination in her tone that he had never heard before. "There's nothing to fight. Tony is my exclusive responsibility, and I feel—"

"You said yourself that he needs love and security more than anything. Well, I can give him those things, and I will fight you if you try to stop me."

"And what about your husband. Will he accept Tony, too?"

"In time, yes. When he gets to know Tony the way I have, George will accept him. I am certain of it. We will be a family again."

Masters was shaking his head. "Don't you see what you are doing, Penny? You've been using that boy to satisfy your own frustrated maternal instincts, and now you want to use him to patch up your marriage. It's crazy."

"I'll tell you what's crazy." She challenged him angrily. "It's crazy to say that he won't be better off with me than he is here. I'm sure as hell not perfect, and neither is my marriage, but you're absolutely bonkers if you think he will be happier growing up behind bars. How's that for reality, mister?"

Masters was taken back by the change that had come over her. Once forced into dealing openly with her true feelings and the unpleasant consequences, she had mustered her strength and determination. As he studied her face and weighed her arguments, his mind filled with images of Tony's Fifi bags and his dealings with the degenerate barber, Oscar Stone. Then he realized that in six or seven years Tony would have to become another Shacky Wallis in order to survive, and suddenly he was no longer certain about the best course for the boy. Perhaps there was a chance that Penny might indeed be strong enough. If such a possibility existed, however remotely, perhaps he really had no choice.

"This goes against all my instincts," Masters heard himself saying, "but you might be right. Maybe this is going to be Tony's last chance."

Penny had won. She knew it, but it was something other than pure joy that filled her heart as she listened to Masters. She was also frightened. She had come to the superintendent's office fearful of losing Tony. Suddenly she was fearful of winning him. There had not been time to prepare her husband . . . Tony . . . herself. Perhaps this all was a big mistake. Perhaps Masters had tricked her. The confusion and concern were mirrored in her face.

"What's wrong, Penny?"

"I don't know. I mean, what happens now? This is a big step for all of us . . . Tony . . . George . . . me. And what about Tony's schooling?"

"The choices are clear," Masters said firmly. "Tony will either stay right here until he is eighteen, or he will eventually go home as your son. In the first instance, we will find him another reading tutor, and he will go on just as thousands of others have gone on before him. Some make it; some don't. In Tony's case I think he has what it takes to survive."

"And in the second instance?"

"Before I can clear him for adoption, the caseworkers must be as certain as is humanly possible that the fit will be a good one for all concerned. The first step will be to arrange home visitations—maybe afternoons at first. Then, if things go well, some weekends. There will be no commitments on either side until we see how things work out."

"When would this start?"

"Let's not rush things," Masters advised, aware of her uncertainty. "Try to act the same as always. Give yourself time to get used to the idea and to prepare your husband. Don't say anything to Tony until things are set for a visit." Penny was visibly relieved, so Masters grinned and concluded the meeting with "Meanwhile, we'll get some civvies ready, and we'll let his hair grow out a little. You're accustomed to the way he looks, but old George will think his home has been invaded by a Martian."

Chapter Thirty-nine: The Ranch

Jon and Matt had spent more than a month preparing for the roundup. During that time they repaired the corral, the holding pens, and the loading chute. Matt broke six horses, bringing their entire string to seven, but there was one paint that continued to resist Matt's attempts to ride it.

Matt felt seven horses were enough, but his pride would not permit him to give up on that last one. It was the best-looking animal in the string, but after ten consecutive days of bouncing off the hard ground, Matt decided he had had enough. Dragging his bruised body to the corral fence, he asked wistfully, "If that paint was a part of your string, what would you name her?"

Jon thought for a moment and rubbed his chin with the back of his hand. "I'd name her Honky Poon-Tang," he said. "Nice to look at, but dangerous to screw around with."

The boys had not spoken more than a dozen words to Earl Wilson during that entire time. He seemed to have no interest in what they were doing, but two days after the farrier had completed his work, Matt broke two tough horses, and the first shipment of winter silage was delivered the next morning.

They began to wonder why Miss Wilson had not returned as promised, but one evening they found a letter on their kitchen table from her to her brother explaining that two of her students had escaped from lockup while she was in St. Louis, and the authorities had insisted that she remain at Clearwater to assist with the investigation.

Jon's training was almost complete. The boys rode out every day, looking for strays in the immediate vicinity, and they practiced their techniques on two or three cows at a time, herding them into the corral with the same teamwork and gusto required to push thirty head. Whenever he was so inclined, Bones joined the team, circling behind the cattle, nipping at their heels and barking ferociously to move them into the pens more quickly.

Each night the boys completed their assigned schoolwork, cooked their meal, rubbed their bruises and blisters, and fell into bed. If either was lonely, he was too tired to mention it.

Chapter Forty

Cowboys of the high plains consider March the most treacherous month of the year. The days can be warm and sunny, and the early spring flowers begin popping up all over the prairie, but sudden blizzards can blow in with blinding intensity, and ranch hands who are unprepared often never make it home.

Matt had learned his lesson well at a very early age, so as the two boys began to venture farther and farther into the open range to find their stock, Matt's precautions became more elaborate, even to the point of leading a packhorse on an overnight excursion. Jon chided his friend incessantly for slowing them down with so many unnecessary precautions.

They set out in shirt sleeves one morning in early March and traversed two neighboring ranches without spotting any Wilson cattle. By late afternoon, perspiring profusely in the hot sun, they had made their way onto the Taylor grazing lands and began flushing their cattle from the labyrinthal gullies.

The snow started to fall while the sun was still shining. Soon the black clouds blew in, and the spring blizzard struck with full force. They tied up their horses, barely able to see, and covered their sleeping bags with a large tarpaulin. It was a new and terrifying experience for Jon, but as the blizzard raged about them, Matt's only concern was getting stepped on by a blinded cow.

By morning they were covered by more than a foot of snow. They threw off the protective tarpaulin and laughed as the sunshine poured in on their faces along with the wet, cold snow. The two boys came sputtering into the open air and stared into the barrels of three rifles.

"Sit right where you are," one man growled.

The two boys suspected the worst. Their freedom had surely come to an end, but a ray of hope came with the next question.

"What're you two doing here?"

And they were positively exhilarated by the next remark: "What the hell, they're only kids!"

Matt struggled for something to say, trying to remain calm. "We work for Earl Wilson. We've been rounding up his strays."

"Kinda young, ain't ya?"

Another man waggled his rifle toward Jon. "I never seen you around here. Where's your family from?"

"N-no f-family . . . we're new around here," Jon stammered. "We're from an orphanage in Missouri." He could not recall the name and hoped they would not ask. "Mr. Wilson kind of . . . adopted us." Jon felt ridiculous just saying it. "I mean, to work on his ranch."

One of the younger men trudged over to inspect the brands on the boys' horses. "This is Wilson stock," he called out.

The oldest man was still skeptical. "There's only one living thing that can stand to be around Earl Wilson. That's his dog. If you work for that mean old bastard, what's his dog's name?"

"Bones!" both boys shouted simultaneously.

The men lowered their rifles and grudgingly apologized. After they had mounted, the oldest man returned. "Wilson ain't laid an iron on his stock in three, maybe four years, so any unbranded calves you put a rope on had better be with their mamas."

The two boys silently returned to the task of packing up and retrieving the cattle that had scattered during the storm. They drove the cows halfway back to the ranch before making camp. After they had eaten that night, Jon asked Matt what he would have done if the ranchers had not believed them.

Matt was grim-faced and somber. "I would have killed them . . . or anyone else who tried to take me back."

"Me, too," Jon said, and they realized that the experience they had lived through had already killed an important part of their youth.

*   *   *

Two weeks later it happened again. They had spent two days rounding up twenty mangy cows, and they were headed for home when the storm hit. It did not matter which way they turned—the driving sleet and snow seemed to find their faces like smoke from a campfire.

The twenty cows moved slowly forward in a tight cluster, protecting each other from the icy blasts and sharing their body heat. Matt put both hands over his eyes, like a double salute, and finally spotted Jon, a short distance away, on the other side of the herd. His head was tucked into his coat, and his body was humped over the saddle. He had wanted to dig in and weather the storm under the tarp, but Matt had hated the thought of losing the cattle so close to the ranch—waking up to the reality of losing two days' work and having to start the chase all over again.

As the blizzard intensified, however, he regretted his decision. They were completely lost and could not see well enough to identify any landmarks. Matt was no longer fighting the cold. He was fighting sleep, and from what he could see of Jon, his friend had already lost that battle.

Matt wedged his hand between the saddle blanket and the horse to keep it warm. He knew he had to wake up his friend to keep him from freezing to death, but his intentions were lost in the foggy shroud that was enveloping his mind. Crazy thoughts began to slip into his head as the numbness changed to warmth. He giggled half-consciously as he thought the only way he could stay warm on horseback was to set fire to the horse. Suddenly the horse shifted its weight and pinched Matt's hand beneath the saddle. He came awake with a start and kicked his horse toward Jon.

He was surprised to find Jon awake and staring through the tiny tunnel created by the wrapped scarf and blanket. "You ready to dig in?" Jon shouted.

Matt shouted through cupped hands to be heard. "Can't. We've already lost our body heat."

"What then?"

"The horses can find the way. Don't fall asleep." Matt reached over and took the reins from Jon, wrapping them around the saddle horn. "Just keep them moving," he shouted.

The boys kicked, and the horses moved off together through the heavy snow. They had gone no more than twenty steps when they stopped again, and no amount of coaxing could budge them farther.

Jon was yelling something, but Matt was unable to decipher anything above the howling wind except "Smart-ass."

Matt decided he might get his horse started again by leading him. He untied the reins and stepped down into a hip-high snowbank. He fought his way out by leaning forward and lifting his knees high enough to create his own path. Then he lost his balance and stumbled forward, ramming his head into something solid.

He was more surprised than hurt, and in his confusion he pushed at the object as though his goal were to move it from his path. At first he thought he was dreaming again, but the object he was pushing against was flat and man-made, with parallel horizontal ridges.

Jon heard Matt laughing hysterically and concluded that the cold had taken its toll. He jumped from his horse and pushed through the snow toward his friend.

"Can you believe it?" Matt shouted. "We almost froze to death forty feet from home."

Jon reached out and touched the bunkhouse wall. "Out here, I can believe anything," he mumbled to himself.

They both were so completely disoriented that they had to feel their way around the building to find the door. Once inside, they quickly laid a fire with old newspapers, kindling, and bacon fat. They soon had a roaring blaze, and the heat from the old stone fireplace began to melt the snow and ice from their outer clothing.

Matt stared into the flames, entranced, reluctant to consider how close they had come to freezing to death. Jon had depended on his knowledge and judgment in this strange world, just as Matt had depended on Jon at the institution. But Matt had let them down. Jon thumped across the room and opened the door, and Matt was shaken from his self-chastisement by a blast of cold air. "Where the hell are you going?"

Jon was wrapping a dry scarf around his head and across his face. "I'm going to find those horses and blanket them before the saddles freeze to their backs. Then I'll treat them to an extra ration of grain."

Matt threw his gloves to the floor in disgust. "I should have thought of that."

Jon tested their new battery-powered lantern before stepping out into the night. "Maybe it's time I picked up my share of the thinking. You just keep that fire going."

The deep frown on Matt's face was replaced by a smile that crinkled the corners of his mouth. "By God, we just might do it," he thought aloud. "We just . . . by God . . . might make it!"

Chapter Forty-one

By the middle of April Matt and Jon were working together as though they were reading each other's minds. Instead of being able to locate, maintain, and move a herd of fifteen cows, they were bringing in twenty and thirty at a time. Every horse in their string seemed to understand the task and would often react before the reins or knees communicated the command. The old man's dog was also caught up in the excitement of the new activity and had become a valued partner, constantly circling, barking, and nipping to keep the cattle together and moving in the same direction.

Earl Wilson had estimated they would find about three hundred head on the open range, but the boys had already rounded up more than that, and they had seen another hundred coming down from the hills to tear down the neighbors' fences to eat and breed with their registered stock.

The boys rode to the crest of the hill and turned their horses to look down at the old corral. It was brimming with restlessly milling cattle, and a new problem that might be big enough to undo everything they had accomplished was evident.

"One loud fart, and those ugly bastards will bust through that rotten fence like it wasn't there," Jon predicted.

Matt nodded. He had been involved in only two stampedes in his life, and he was not ready for the third.

Their contract with Earl Wilson was clear. The old man had decreed that they could stay at the ranch only if they rounded up every mangy beast he owned and had them ready to load for market by the first week in June. The court had left no alternatives, and there would be no room for appeals or excuses.

Matt and Jon knew where to find the rest of the stock, and since it was early April, there was plenty of time, but there was no room left to hold the cattle. The old corral and holding pens were seriously overcrowded, and Earl Wilson still refused to construct new ones.

It was Jon who came up with a plan. The hills to the south sloped down on three sides to form a large pocket with a relatively narrow opening. It would be useless to drive the cattle into the pocket because the slope of the surrounding hills was gentle enough to permit them to climb up and wander off. "All we have to do is make a vertical cut along the base of those hills, and we'd have steep walls six or eight feet high. Then we'd build a big gate right across that narrow entrance, and we'd have a corral the size of a football field . . .enough room to pen up half the cows in Colorado."

"I agree," Matt said impatiently, "but where would we get the bulldozers . . . and who'd pay for them?"

"We don't use bulldozers."

"We don't?"

Jon was grinning mischievously. "Dynamite."

"That's great." Matt laughed. "Let's send Mr. Wilson down to the corner dynamite shop, or maybe there's a coin-operated dynamite-o-mat in town."

"Don't put me down, man. You're pissing me off."

Their spontaneous arguments had already erupted into more than one fistfight during the winter, and Matt recognized the danger signals. "Okay, okay," he said, attempting to mollify Jon. "I think it's a *terrific* idea . . . too bad we don't have any dynamite."

Jon peered at him skeptically. "You serious?"

"*Sure* I am. So now what do we do?"

"We blow the son of a bitch."

"What?"

"I got the dynamite already. Follow me."

"Oh, shit."

*   *   *

They reined up outside the tack house, and Jon walked briskly into the tiny shed. In contrast with their first visit there, this time it was Matt who stood outside, nervously peering into the dark room.

"Bring me that lantern, will ya?"

"Not on your ass, I won't! Not if you've got dynamite in there."

"Come on, man. The stuff's been in here forever, and nothing's happened yet."

"You don't mean those old wooden boxes with the faded printing?" Matt asked incredulously.

"That's right. I pried open one of the boxes with a hammer, and there it was. That's what got me thinking about it. Here, I'll show you."

The tremor in Matt's voice stopped Jon in his tracks. "Holy God, don't touch that dynamite." Matt's face was ashen, and he did not breathe again until Jon emerged from the shed empty-handed.

"What's wrong, man? You're acting crazy."

Matt's face went from white to red as he erupted in anger. "You crazy bastard! Don't you know the first thing about dynamite?"

"I know this much," Jon hissed, his own anger rising to match Matt's, "if I jammed one of those sticks up your ass, you could stop worrying about the calluses on your butt."

"I mean *old* dynamite. Do you know the difference between old dynamite and new dynamite? Do you know that the nitroglycerin in old dynamite settles into one spot, and you don't need fuses or blasting caps to set it off?" Matt was trembling. "Do you know you could have set off the whole goddamned works by just prying open the box with a hammer?"

The boys stared at each other, their anger abating as they contemplated the latest near miss and wondering how long it would be before another near miss resulted in a full-blown tragedy.

As usual, Jon was the first to find humor in the situation. He grinned and said, "Does that mean you don't like my plan?"

Matt's emotional release was total. It started with a giggle and progressed into peals of laughter that left the two boys hanging on each other for support.

In the quiet darkness of the bunkhouse that night Matt found the solution. "You awake?" he whispered.

"No."

"Maybe we could get the old man to do it."

"Do what?"

"Set the dynamite," Matt said. "He's the one who's had it stored. Maybe he knows how to use it."

"Yeah," Jon said, grinning in the dark.

"Let's go ask him."

"Better wait till morning. He's probably having another party tonight."

They were knocking at his door before breakfast. Neither of them looked forward to having any contact with him. Earl Wilson had resented their presence since that first day when they intruded on his wasting isolation.

The door opened, and he glared out at them under his gray, bushy eyebrows. Matt never understood how Earl could maintain a two-day growth of whiskers without being clean-shaven at least once every third day.

"What now?" he demanded gruffly, in spite of the fact that they had not spoken in more than a month.

Jon nudged Matt, and Matt spoke up. "We have a problem. The old corral isn't strong enough or big enough to hold the cattle that's out there, and we have another hundred to bring in."

"So?"

"Since we can't build a new corral, we thought maybe you could dynamite the walls of that three-sided valley in back of the pens." Matt swallowed hard before continuing. "That would give us one big corral . . . big enough for all the cattle . . . sir."

"I'll make you boys a deal. If you'll stay off my back, off my porch, and out of my sight, I'll mark the holes. Then you drill them, and when you're done, I'll pack the holes and blow the goddamn walls. After that I'll give you your groceries and your pay, and you stay away from me."

*   *   *

The boys stayed close to home for a while, catching up on their studies while they waited for Wilson to mark the holes. Five days later there were tiny red flags staked to the hillside at thirty-foot intervals. When they rode out to inspect the project, they found a long auger and a measuring stick marked at four feet. It took them two days to bore the fifty holes. Then they retreated, taking their string of horses with them to the safety of the bunkhouse.

As soon as Earl Wilson began carrying the dynamite from the shed, the two boys removed themselves and their horses to the greater safety of the distant hill on the rim of the open range. They camped there for four days, until Wilson had the dynamite in place, wired to the plunger, and ready to blow.

"Oh, my God," Matt exclaimed, watching the old man through the field glasses.

"What is it?"

"You were worried about a loud fart setting off those cattle. Do you have any idea how much noise that dynamite is going to make when he leans on that plunger?"

Jon's eyes widened, but before he could respond, the question was answered for them. The ground shook, and three hundred head of cattle seemed to jump three feet into the air. They bellowed in unison and lurched through the old fence as if it were made of cardboard. The brown wave swept across the prairie, and a quarter of a mile away, only Matt, Jon, and their seven horses stood between the stampeding herd and the open range.

They had practiced the stampede drill a dozen times, so each boy knew exactly what to do. They spooked their string of horses before them and rode behind, waving their blankets and screaming for all they were worth. Bones appeared on the scene to help, and by the time the converging forces met the cattle had dissipated their initial fury, and they were turned into a wide arc that led them directly into the mouth of the three-sided valley.

There was so much dust from the explosion and the stampeding animals that the cattle completely disappeared behind the cloud. The boys had no idea whether the herd had been contained in the pocket or not.

The minutes felt like hours, but when the dust began to settle, the presence of the winded cattle inside the enclosure indicated that their scheme had worked. Matt and Jon had the biggest corral in Colorado, and they screamed with joy and threw their hats into the air in celebration of their victory.

Not even Earl Wilson could suppress a grin.

Chapter Forty-two: Clearwater

The rains of late March had melted the snow, and the redbuds on the campus were in full bloom by the second week in April. Tony was exhilarated by the advent of that particular spring because he sensed that he was on the verge of a new life. His unhappy past had conditioned him to accept the futility of hope, so he dared not permit himself to express his feelings openly, but they were there all the same, and something good was about to happen.

"That's kinda beautiful, Ralphie. Show me again."

Ralph was demonstrating the sign for "spring." His left hand covered his right fist; then the right fist pushed upward, fingers spreading as they appeared.

"It looks like a flower popping out of the ground, don't it?" Ralph nodded happily and guided the younger boy's hands. Tony had become completely insensitive to the crippled left hand he had once kept hidden, and he practiced the sign carefully until he had it perfected. "Wait'll I show Penny," he said enthusiastically. "Help me pick some dandelions for her."

Gary Masters had taken a calculated risk, but he had seen it as Tony's last chance for the brass ring. The weekend passes to the Conlin house had become a regular thing, and his judgment appeared to have been vindicated by the glowing reports he was receiving from Penny and the boy. What they failed to tell him, however, was that George Conlin had stalked from the house in anger and disgust on the day of Tony's first visit and had subsequently removed himself whenever Tony was scheduled to reappear.

In contrast with Tony's euphoric happiness, Penny's life was in total disarray. The only two people who failed to see the tiredness in her face and the torment in her eyes were her husband, because he had stopped caring, and Tony, because he was blinded by his love for her.

Masters saw it immediately. Her shoulders slumped, and her eyes seemed not to focus. She had come to him as an attractive and vivacious thirty-year-old only six months earlier, but she had deteriorated into a dispirited and defeated shell. When she spoke, her voice reflected her weariness. "You knew George would never accept him, didn't you? You knew Tony could never live with us. Why did you say those things to me? Why did you hurt me like this?"

Masters was stunned. "It was wrong of me to let this happen," he said. "It was foolish. I knew better. I thought—hoped, I guess— that if you really loved him—"

"I *do* love him. Don't you understand? He fills a very important part of my life, and I fill an important part of his life. But someday George and I might have a child of our own. If that happened, where would Tony fit in?"

Masters stopped grieving for the woman and struggled to choke back the anger that was rising within. "All right. All right. Don't say another word. I had no right to get hung up on a fairy-tale finish, and I had even less of a right to let you get involved." He paced the room restlessly, angrily grinding the fist of one hand into the palm of the other while Penny sat outwardly impassive but inwardly struggling with her own confused feelings of guilt and despondence.

"I'm sorry," she said tonelessly. "I only wanted to help."

He stopped pacing and returned to face her, his anger finally abated. "I believe that," he said. "And in many ways you've helped him a great deal. You just tried to do more than you were capable of. You've opened a new world for him. . . . I just hope we haven't killed him in the process."

"Oh, God," she moaned as her feelings began to break through. "How can you say that?"

Masters recognized the symptoms of an emotional upheaval, and he tried to calm her with gentle reasoning. "Every one of my boys has grown up with rejection. They judge their own self-worth by the way others see them. Your feelings toward Tony instilled in him a sense of acceptance—"

"And now my 'rejection' will kill him," she shrieked. "Is that what you're saying?"

"Not at all," he objected. "What I am trying to say is that we must not let this appear to be a flagrant repudiation. If possible, we should try to terminate your work with him by degrees over the next couple of weeks, try to let him down easily."

"Terminate! Why can't we go back to the way it was? Why does it have to be all or nothing?"

It was Masters's turn to be confused. "But I thought—"

"All I said was we couldn't *adopt* him. He still needs me, and I need him. Why can't it be the way it was?"

Masters's indignation swelled, but he struggled to control himself. When he finally spoke, his voice trembled. "What Tony needs is a permanent relationship. What you need is for him to fill temporarily an empty space in your life that will someday be taken by someone else . . . just as soon as you and your husband decide you have made enough money to slow down and have a kid of your own."

Penny jumped up and screamed, "That's not true! It's not that way, and you know it!" She turned before Masters could move and ran from the room.

He sat down heavily and buried his face in his hands. It had gone all wrong.

Penny ran down the back stairs of the administration building and directly to her room in the school building. She had hoped to clean out her desk and avoid seeing Tony until her mind cleared, but he burst through the door with a toothy smile and a bouquet of dandelions.

When he saw her face, he dropped the flowers and stood transfixed. "What happened? Who did it?" Then he walked forward and reached out to touch her tearstained cheek, but she turned her head and stepped around him to close the door.

She needed time to think, to put her priorities straight. She would never give him up. But perhaps she needed more time to sort things out. Perhaps Masters might lighten up after a few days. The important thing now was to avoid doing or saying anything that might make things worse.

Penny gently framed the boy's face in her hands and spoke in a clear, controlled monotone. "Tony, I was crying because I won't be seeing you for a while. I've just spoken with Mr. Masters . . . he said it would be all right . . . I care for you very much, but . . ." She couldn't go on. The boy's big eyes were pleading for understanding, and when she saw them filling with tears, she completely dissolved. Sobbing out of control, she quickly embraced him and ran from the room.

Tony stood in shocked silence, unable to move, unable to believe what had just happened. What had he done to cause this? Had he teased her too much? True, she had scolded him lightly, but he thought she had liked it. *What else could it be?* He had learned to read, and his hair was growing out. Suddenly a terrible conclusion dawned on him, and he flopped into the chair. Penny had just come from Masters's office. *He must have told.* Masters had told her about Oscar Stone and the Fifi bags. Now she thought he was dirty, and he would never see her again! She didn't understand! He had to do it to survive! He needed to find her and tell her he wasn't dirty and bad.

Tony dashed from the room, screaming, "It's the Fifi bags, ain't it? Wait for me. I won't do it no more."

The boys in the gym stopped to watch the screaming boy, and Shacky motioned from the bleachers to Walt Pate. Walt closed in with several others to quiet Tony, but he misread their intentions, and when he saw them coming at him, he dashed into the hall, shouting for Ralph.

After a wild chase they cornered him in the men's room. The boys tried to calm his hysterical panic, but to Tony they were the final hostile obstacles between himself and Penny, and he was determined to destroy them. He lowered his head and charged into the group, painfully butting Walt Pate in the stomach. Then fists began to fly, and the tiny boy was flung into the air. He came down with sufficient force to smash the back of his head against the porcelain commode with a sickening thud.

Ralph lumbered down the hall in a panic. His momentum carried him into the door with a crash that tore it from the upper hinges. He began tearing bodies from the back of the crowd and hurling them into the hallway. He knew only that Tony was in there and in trouble. Ralph's frenzy was complete when the voices closest to Tony shouted, "You killed him!" and "No! It was an accident!"

When he finally reached Tony, he stared down at the broken body in horror and disbelief. Tony's eyes were closed, but his mouth was still set in grim determination. Blood flowed onto the tile floor from both ears. Ralph fell to his knees, gently lifted Tony, and rocked back and forth while tears streaked his face and his body convulsed with muted sobbing.

One of the teachers rushed into the room and tried to take the limp body from Ralph, but the hate and anger radiating from the mute boy frightened the teacher away. Ralph walked from the building with his friend in his arms, and no one else attempted to interfere.

Through his tears Ralph saw Gary Masters sprinting across the quadrangle, and he stopped. Masters pulled up ten yards away and walked the rest of the way, shaking his head, crying, and mumbling, "Oh, no. Dear God, no."

Ralph held out Tony's body. Masters accepted it and turned away slowly as the mute boy dropped to the ground, pounding the earth in grief.

Rich Anderson arrived only seconds later. He pressed his ear to Tony's chest, then quickly reached under the boy's collar, searching for a pulse. "Put him down. Quick!" Rich ordered sharply, trying to break through Masters's daze.

Gary Masters wondered vaguely what Anderson was doing. The intercom message had been definite. "There's been a fight. Tony Washington is dead." Then the sight of Ralph carrying Tony's body . . . *Surely* . . .

"Goddammit, Gary, snap out of it! This kid needs help!"

*　　*　　*

The neurosurgeons had been operating for more than an hour before Gary Masters fully recovered his composure. He and Rich Anderson set up shop in a nearby recovery room to plot their strategy. "The first thing we need to do is to get Ralph and bring him here," Masters said. "If he gets to tearing that cottage up, he'll fill the goddamned hospital with bald-headed kids."

"I'll call and have security pick him up," Anderson suggested.

"There aren't enough cops in this entire town to bring him in if he doesn't want to come," Masters said. "He likes you. You'd better go out there and talk to him. And don't say anything about Tony until we know if he's going to make it."

Anderson found Ralph in the barn. He had dissipated his initial fury on the bales of hay that lay strewn about the place, and he was sitting and rocking in the darkest corner when Anderson approached. Rich knelt beside the boy and gripped his shoulder without speaking. Soon he shifted his weight and sat with his shoulder touching Ralph's in the darkness.

"I'd like you to take a ride with me, Ralph." The boy's body jerked from side to side, and Rich knew he was shaking his head. "Tony's not here," Rich persisted. "Mr. Masters needs you. He asked me to come and get you." A few moments later the two rose without speaking and walked to the car.

As soon as Ralph was settled into a room on the hospital security ward, Anderson rejoined Masters. "Any word yet?"

Masters shook his head and looked at his watch. "It's only been two hours. They said it would be a lot longer."

"Did you call the office?"

"Yeah, but they don't know much. There was a fight, but no one knows what it was about for sure. Apparently Tony ran out into the gym, yelling something about those damned Fifi bags, and some of the older boys took off after him. That's all we know."

Anderson was concerned. "Do you think Shacky set him up? If the kid was threatening their supply, Shacky might get mean . . . just on principle."

"Could be," Masters said. "One thing's for certain. They all think Tony's dead, and until we find out for sure what was going on—whether someone was trying to kill him—let's keep it that way."

"What about the staff?"

"No one," Masters repeated. "I don't want anyone to know."

"Ralph?"

"We'll see about Ralph."

The operation lasted more than six hours, but as the chief neurosurgeon walked from the operating room, the spring in his step foretold the good news. Masters's heart jumped to his throat, and he gripped Rich Anderson's forearm for support.

"He's going to make it." The surgeon smiled. "Tough as twelve-gauge wire."

Masters was speechless.

"He'll be hearing bells for a month, but with his hangover that won't matter much. He'll feel more dead than alive for a couple of weeks."

Gary Masters heard himself laughing insanely while Anderson pounded him on the back. Somewhere in the confusion a voice said, "I'll look in on him in the morning. You two could use some sleep."

They barely had time to clean up and change clothes before it was time to return to work. Rich drove them to the truck stop outside town for a hearty breakfast and a private strategy session.

"The way I see it, we have two problems," Masters said. "First we have to find out what happened to Tony, and why. I have a feeling it has something to do with Penny Conlin . . . maybe one of the boys got jealous . . . maybe Tony decided to turn pure and cut off their Fifi bags . . . or it could have been a straight power play by the older boys to take Tony out and put in their own leader."

"Any of those sound feasible," Rich said.

"Yeah, but the fact is that Tony could be laid up for a couple of months. That means we have plenty of time to figure things out before we have to send him back."

Rich looked worried. "It also means there will be a totally new power structure by that time, and Tony might find himself right back in the hospital or worse."

"Like I said, we have time to figure that out." Masters shrugged. "The thing that bothers me right now is Ralph. That's our second problem. Right now he thinks Tony is dead. As soon as the shock wears off, he could do a lot of damage to someone."

"But you wouldn't keep that a secret from him, would you?" Rich asked. "That would be cruel. They were tight."

Masters shrugged and said, "Let's talk about that. Ralph was eighteen last February. Technically speaking, we have no legal hold on him. If we send him back to the school and he tears up the place, what do you think will happen to him?"

"Wouldn't that depend on you?" Rich asked.

"Ordinarily it would. But Ralph is classified as profoundly retarded."

Anderson was shocked. "You're kidding! By whom?"

"Probably some social worker who figured if you can't talk, there's something wrong with your mind. The important thing, though, is that's his official classification, and if he steps out of line, they'll pack him off to the state hospital without so much as a hearing."

"Well, that settles it then," Rich said with finality. "We have to tell Ralph that Tony's alive."

"That won't solve our problem. He still might try to even the score. Worse yet, if and when Tony gets back, Ralph is going to be his full-time—and very vulnerable—protector. You saw how easy it was for Shacky to get Jon and Matt committed to the adult penitentiary; it'll be a piece of cake for him to get Ralph shipped off to the state hospital."

Rich was shaking his head. "What's the answer then?"

"The only thing we can do is to get Ralph out of there right away . . . like in the next couple of days. We won't even send him back to the school. We'll process him right out of the hospital."

"But if we tell him that Tony's still alive, he won't go, will he?"

"I doubt it," Masters said. "But I don't think we can take

that chance. I think we should tell him only as a last resort. Let's just get him out of here . . . as far and as fast as possible."

"Where will he go? You can't just turn him out on the highway."

Masters grinned conspiratorially. "Maybe Miss Wilson will have some ideas."

When Verna Wilson entered the hospital room, she thought Ralph was dead. He had refused to eat or drink for three days, and when intravenous feedings were prescribed, he calmly tore the tubes from his arms and pulverized the heavily taped bottle between his hands. Miss Wilson touched his hand, but he did not respond. He lay unmoving on top of the covers, staring blankly at the ceiling. Only after she found his pulse did she ask the guard to leave them alone.

"Ralph," she said softly, "I have something to tell you. I should have told you a long time ago. Matt wanted me to." She examined his eyes closely for any reaction—some spark of recognition at the mention of Matt's name—but there was nothing. "I don't know if you can hear me, son, but Matt and Jon want you to know that they are well and happy . . . and they want you to come live with them."

Miss Wilson took a step backward, fearing that Ralph had surrendered his will to live and was already beyond help. Suddenly she gasped and brought her clenched fists to her mouth to suppress a wrenching sob. Ralph had not moved a muscle. He continued to stare blankly at the ceiling, but a tear rolled down from the corner of his eye.

Gary Masters put the machinery into motion immediately. Ralph was four months beyond his eighteenth birthday, and the superintendent was solely responsible for determining whether such a boy was sufficiently equipped to survive on the outside. Masters certified him as a competent auto mechanic and submitted the release to the director of institutions, knowing full well that the state would welcome an excuse to get rid of the boy.

Ralph failed to respond as quickly as they had hoped, however. He had begun to eat, but he seemed unable to shake the depression of losing Tony. "I think we have to tell him," Miss Wilson suggested. She herself had only just learned the truth.

"Not yet," Masters ordered. "We'd never get him out of town. Let's get him moving around more. Make him take lots of walks . . . any kind of exercise." Then he included Rich Anderson in his warning: "Just make sure he gets nowhere near that intensive care unit. Do you both understand?"

Masters's prescription turned out to be the magic pill. At first Ralph resisted the routine, only grudgingly accompanying Miss Wilson and Rich on short walks around the floor. Soon, however, he was walking around without being prodded, and in a few days he had the run of the hospital.

One day, outside the cafeteria, he overheard two nurses giggling about the antics of that cute little boy in intensive care, and a few hours later, following another quick tour of the hospital, Ralph's mood improved dramatically, along with his appetite. By the time his official release arrived he was back to his old self.

Miss Wilson and Rich were congratulating Masters on his perspicacity, but he himself was skeptical. "I don't know. I've never been that smart before. Are you both absolutely certain he didn't find out about Tony?"

There was no question in Anderson's mind. "No way that big moose could have sneaked into intensive care without being seen. You've been up there. Have you ever seen any tighter security in a hospital?"

Masters had to agree. He had been permitted to visit Tony twice a day and each time had been required to show his credentials at the entrance to the ward. "Okay, you convinced me," he conceded with a smile. "I'm brilliant. . . . Now let's get that boy out of here before we push our luck."

Chapter Forty-three

Masters purchased a bus ticket for Ralph to a small town fifty miles southwest of Clearwater City. Miss Wilson followed the bus out of town and picked him up there to ride the rest of the way with her. It was an unnecessary precaution because the search for Matt and Jon had long since been abandoned by the authorities, but Masters refused to permit anything to go wrong so late in the game.

They drove through the morning and late into the afternoon. Miss Wilson regaled Ralph with the stories of his friends' adventures and accomplishments, and he devoured every bit of them. On occasion he would ask her to repeat some of the stories, gesturing primitively to convey his meaning. Then he would laugh silently as the events unfolded again.

After they had started down the western slope of the mountains, Miss Wilson fell silent. She had written her brother to say she was bringing Ralph, but she could not anticipate what his reaction would be. She had tried to soften the impact by suggesting that it might only be a short visit, but her instinct told her otherwise. She had also enclosed a note for Matt and Jon, telling them of Tony's accident and of her intention to bring Ralph to the ranch as soon as he was ready to travel. She had written the letter before she had learned of Tony's survival, and she was later instructed to keep the secret from Matt and Jon.

It was a warm June afternoon, and they had driven much of the way with their windows down. As they neared the house, however, Miss Wilson rolled up her window, and Ralph did the same, apparently thinking the swirling dust was making her uncomfortable.

She stopped in front of the porch, smiled at Ralph reassuringly, and pressed once on the horn. Her reason for closing the windows became immediately obvious as the familiar figure of Bones came howling from the garage, falling all over himself as he turned the corner, and finally throwing himself against the windshield and sides of the car, snapping his jaws, as if he were going to eat the vehicle and its two passengers.

Matt and Jon had seen the dust of the approaching car from the loading pens, and they were galloping over the hill even before they heard the horn. From a distance they saw Bones going through his ferocious routine; then, to their horror, they saw Ralph's door opening.

"No, Ralph! Shut the door!" Matt shouted in vain.

The two riders spurred their mounts, hoping to divert Bones from the attack, but by the time they had swung into the front yard Ralph was standing next to the car, hugging Bones around the front shoulders while the dog licked his face.

The three boys hugged and slapped at each other wildly while Bones contended with Matt and Jon for a place close to Ralph.

When Earl appeared on the front porch, he ignored his sister, who had become a regular visitor in the past six months, but he scowled ominously at the new young man.

Verna Wilson was apprehensive. "Now, Earl, Ralph will be no trouble at all, you'll see. In September Matt and Jon will be in school all day, and you will need someone to look after things for you."

"Can't afford no more hands."

"Balderdash! When I was here last, those boys had four hundred head ready for market. We're practically *rich*."

Matt and Jon pulled Ralph to his feet excitedly, and they alternately asked questions about Clearwater, described the ranch, and tried to shoo the dog. They avoided any mention of Tony. Ralph was nodding, smiling, and gesturing animatedly, but Earl noticed that no sound was coming out.

"What's wrong with him? . . . Tetched?"

"No, Earl. Ralph's a mute. He's very bright, but he cannot speak."

Earl's eyes narrowed as he peered at the newcomer with keener interest. "Big kid."

"Ralph is the strongest boy I have ever known!" she said with a hopeful smile.

"You say he can't talk?"

"That's right," Miss Wilson said, sensing victory.

"He kin stay."

Early the next morning Verna Wilson asked her brother to show her the loading pens. She had listened to the sweet sounds of hundreds of bawling cows throughout the night, and she was eager to see the results of the six-month roundup.

The boys heard the old truck bouncing up the hill, so they left their breakfast to be there when Miss Wilson viewed the new cattle compound for the first time. Earl must have been telling her about the dynamite just as they arrived on the scene because the blood had drained from her face, and she was staring at him in angry disbelief.

"You crazy old bast—" she breathed contemptuously. Then she turned on the boys and scolded them more civilly. "That was a *terribly* risky thing to do."

The cattle trucks began arriving the following day. The boys had herded almost 600 head, and Earl had contracted to ship 450 to market. The two Wilsons watched as Matt and Jon expertly cut out the cattle and drove them to the loading chute. Ralph stood at the entrance to the chute to wrestle the reluctant cows into the barriers by hand.

Earl was impressed by the boy's strength. "You sure he can't talk?"

"I *told* you so," she said.

"Got any more like him?" he asked with a twitch of his lips.

"Why, Earl Wilson! I do believe you just made a joke."

Chapter Forty-four: Clearwater

Penny Conlin was incensed. "You act like God almighty around here, making up your own rules as you go, but that was the cruelest stunt I have ever heard of."

Gary Masters joined his hands on top of his head and leaned back in his chair, smiling. He had managed to suppress the truth about Tony's condition for almost two weeks—until Ralph was safely out of town and Tony was out of danger. Tony had asked about Ralph, and he seemed strangely satisfied with the simple response that Ralph had been sent home. No further questions, no regrets, and it bothered Masters that the boy had not shown more remorse. Perhaps there had been some brain damage after all, he thought.

Tony was more insistent about seeing Penny, however. Masters and Anderson tried to prepare the boy to deal with the inevitable truth that there would be no future for him in the Conlin household, and he quickly dispelled their fears about brain damage by assuring them, "Aw, shoot, I knew I could never be their kid. They're the wrong color."

Penny had finally read the truth about Tony in the *Clearwater Sentinel*, and in less than an instant she crossed the line from profound mourning to outraged, bellowing indignation. She had burst into Masters's office without being announced, and she was ventilating her pent-up grief and guilt with unbridled fury when he raised his hands in mock surrender and laughed. "I give up! Truce! As soon as you calm yourself, I will take you to see him."

She was instantly mollified. "You will? I can see him? This isn't another trick, is it?"

Masters laughed again. "No, he wants to see you. He's been asking for you all week."

When they arrived at the hospital, Tony was holding court in his semiprivate room. The old man in the next bed was laughing painfully, holding his stomach to keep the stitches from bursting, and three nurses bustled about, trying to bring order to the room, while Tony regaled them with funny stories that were fluently punctuated by the signs Ralph had taught him.

Masters walked in first, and Tony whooped, "Hey, everybody, here's the main man. He's the"—the boy raised both hands to the sides of his head and curled his fingers—"superintendent," he interpreted. "Get it? This is the sign for 'boss man.' " Then he raised his hands and repeated the gesture, adding some irreverent finger waggling and mooing sounds for laughs.

When he saw Penny in the doorway, his smile disappeared, and he dropped his hands. She stared at the bandages encasing his skull and gasped as tears formed in her eyes.

Tony's voice was very soft, and he was no longer performing for laughs when he said, "And this is my . . . friend." Instead of hooking his index fingers together, which was the sign for "friend," however, he clenched his fists and crossed his forearms over his chest—the sign for "love."

Chapter Forty-five: The Ranch

Miss Wilson had suggested that Ralph might take over the responsibility for regularly driving to town to purchase supplies for the boys, so he immediately unloaded his tools—a standard parting gift from the reform school automotive program—and went to work on the old pickup. He installed new jets in the carburetor, cleaned the plugs and points, and set the timing. Except for the roar of the mangled muffler, the old truck performed beautifully.

At Ralph's insistence the boys chipped in to buy materials to remodel the bunkhouse. First they finished insulating the rafters; then they covered the ceiling with Sheetrock. One day Matt and Jon returned from a four-day trip across the range to find that Ralph had installed privacy walls partitioning their bedrooms. But there were four bedrooms instead of three, and they teased him about preparing for unexpected company. Three weeks after he had arrived, Ralph had transformed the shabby bunkhouse into a comfortable and attractive four-bedroom bungalow.

Matt was uncomfortable that first night, and he didn't know why. As soon as he heard Ralph's heavy breathing, he whispered, "Jon . . . you awake?" Their rooms had no ceilings or doors, only six-feet-high walls, so Matt had no trouble hearing the muffled response.

"Damn right."

"I can't sleep either. How come?"

"You ever had your own bedroom before?"

Matt started to laugh at the ridiculous question; then he separated fact from fantasy and sat up in surprise. "No, by God. I've never even *slept* in a bedroom before. Have you?"

"Only that one with the mattress on the floor and bars on the window. Go to sleep."

For the first time since escaping from Clearwater, Matt had to conjure the image of the old fireplace to put himself to sleep, but it wouldn't come. Instead, Tony's face came to him. The three boys had avoided talking about his death, but it was never far from the surface of everything they did. Poor Ralph was having the hardest time letting go. He had built four bedrooms instead of three, and he had repaired and refinished a fourth chair for the kitchen table. Suddenly Matt chuckled aloud.

"What?" came Jon's annoyed response.

"I was just thinking about that first day when that big kid carried Tony out of the administration building. Remember how he was screaming, 'Zombies'?"

Jon chuckled in spite of himself. "Yeah. That was a long time ago. Now *please* let me go to sleep in my own private bedroom."

Less than a year had passed on the calendar, but Matt agreed: *That was a long time ago.* Matt fingered the scar around his neck and wondered about Charlie and Juniper. Would he ever see either of them again? As he finally drifted off to sleep, it occurred to him with considerable satisfaction that someday he *might* see them, but it was not absolutely necessary . . . not anymore.

Ralph had not attempted to ride, but he took a special liking to the horse that Jon had named Honky Poon-Tang. *Nice to look at but dangerous to mess around with.* Matt had never been able to break Honky Poon-Tang, so whenever he and Jon rode off with their string, the beautiful paint was left behind or worse still, was relegated to the ignominious role of packhorse. Ralph identified with its plight, and he never missed an opportunity to feed it oats from his hand. Before long it would trot over to the fence whenever he approached the corral, and it permitted him the license of scratching its nose and rubbing its ears.

Matt made the mistake of assuming that the ornery old paint had mellowed in the two months since it had last bucked him off. He saddled it confidently, patronizing Ralph with "You watch how I do this, Ralph. I'm gonna break her for you, so's you can ride with us when you feel like it." Ralph was pleased and excited, but Jon straddled the fence with a sneering grin.

"Better get out of the way, Ralph. More than likely that horse is going to be giving you Matt instead of the other way around."

Ralph turned questioningly to Jon just as Matt seated himself in the saddle, so he missed his two-second ride.

"You're getting better." Jon laughed as Matt crawled through the dust and Ralph scampered over to help.

Matt stood and brushed himself off with considerable embarrassment. "Maybe you can do better." He challenged Jon. "You gave her her name, so why don't you try to give her some manners, too."

Jon watched Ralph comforting the horse and had an inspiration. "Maybe you're right. I oughta take care of this before she really kills you." He climbed down from the top rail and said loudly, "Bring her over here, Ralph. No, pick up the reins and lead her. . . . That's right." Ralph stirred up more dust than the horse as he shuffled across the enclosure leading the paint. "Just take her around the corral a couple of times," he instructed, watching the two of them walking contentedly.

When he was finally certain that Ralph and the horse were on friendly terms, Jon showed Ralph how to lead it by the halter. Jon picked up the reins and gingerly climbed into the saddle as soon as Ralph had a firm grip. "Just hold on tight," he urged. "And don't let go, even if she starts jumping. You understand, Ralph? . . . Please?"

The paint felt Jon's weight and twitched violently, but it did not buck. It stepped forward, then stopped and shook its head while Jon begged Ralph not to let go of the halter. "Scratch her nose or something. Get her mind off it," he hissed nervously. Then the horse started forward again, with Jon on its back, calmly following Ralph's lead.

Within a week Honky Poon-Tang was Ralph's horse.

Miss Wilson returned for the Fourth of July weekend. She was pleased with the bunkhouse renovations, but her most pleasant surprise was Ralph. He had been there only a month, but he sported a deep tan, he had slimmed down considerably, and most of all, he was riding a horse.

The boys were grilling lamb burgers for dinner. The surrounding ranchers had finally come to accept them as competent cowhands, so Matt and Jon were often called upon to do the neighborly thing whenever a barn needed to be raised or a corral repaired. In return they were paid in fresh lamb, and they were getting sick of it.

"I never thought I'd be looking forward to antelope season," Matt complained. Ralph rapped him on the shoulder in mute protest. "That's easy for you to say." Matt laughed. "You haven't been eating lamb since last March."

"I love fresh lamb," Miss Wilson volunteered. "I'll show you some great ways to fix it." Ralph looked at her disapprovingly. "What's wrong?" she asked.

Jon answered for him. "He hates anyone slaughtering animals for food."

"Especially those cute lambs," Matt said teasingly.

"Right," Jon added. "So now we have a special rule. Ralph eats only the animals that die from natural causes."

Miss Wilson continued to drill the boys on their studies while Ralph rooted them on silently. She promised to be back in August for one final session before the beginning of school, but she proudly pronounced them every bit as learned as the grades on their forged transcripts indicated. They would enroll as high school juniors, and she assured them they were well prepared.

"It's not too soon to be thinking about college," she said that evening. "There are four or five good junior colleges within a hundred miles of here. They are not too expensive, and I will be able to help with—"

"Thanks a lot," Matt interrupted. "We've been talking about that already. Especially what Coach Cole told me that night in the gym at Clearwater." Miss Wilson looked puzzled, so Matt explained. "About football. He said the best way for us to get to college was to play sports. And all the people around here say we're plenty big enough."

"That's the understatement of all time," Jon interrupted. "We had to go down and register at the high school about three weeks ago, and you wouldn't believe how small those kids are." Jon was then six feet two inches tall, and Matt stood a half inch shorter. Both were broad-shouldered and muscular, and compared to other boys their age, they were two tough, hard men among children. "Tell her what you said about how we looked, Ralph."

Ralph smiled broadly and made the signs for white flowers; then he pinched his nose between his thumb and index finger, screwing up his face as the boys laughed and slapped each other in glee.

"I don't get it," Miss Wilson said with a tentative smile. "A smelly flower? You looked like smelly flowers?"

"No," Jon explained. "When Ralph saw us standing with those other kids at the high school, he said we looked like two skunks in a daisy patch."

In the week that followed Miss Wilson's departure, Ralph was completely preoccupied with fixing up the old pickup. He changed the plugs and points, the oil and filter, and he greased every fitting; he packed the front bearings and flushed the radiator, but nothing he did could compensate for the noise of the torn-up muffler. Not satisfied with the way it sounded, Ralph rummaged through the garage until he came up with a piece of metal large enough to fashion a patch. It was a 1926 West Virginia license plate in surprisingly good condition. He measured it against the hole in the muffler and started pounding it against a log to mold it into the proper shape.

"Hold it, Ralph. What the hell are you doing with that thing?" Jon asked excitedly. Ralph slipped it over the torn muffler to demonstrate his plan, but Jon shook his head emphatically. "No way, buddy. That belongs to the old man. Miss Wilson told us to keep our hands off. See the date—1926—West Virginia? The old man bought his first car for his honeymoon. That's the license plate. He's saved it ever since. He'd kill you if he saw you messing with it."

Ralph was deeply contrite and pounded the plate back into shape immediately.

"I saved your life, Ralphie," Jon said, teasing him. "Remember, you owe me."

Chapter Forty-six: Clearwater

The time had come for Gary Masters to make his decision. Tony had been in the hospital for seven weeks and was climbing the walls for action. He still wore his bandages like a helmet, but the doctors were ready to release him. Masters's problem lay in the fact that Shacky had already installed Tony's successor and now enjoyed a monopoly on the sale of Fifi bags. Shacky had passed the word that Tony would return only in a subordinate role, and if he objected too strenuously, they would have him back in the hospital before his bed got cold.

Rich Anderson was puzzled. "What gets me is that he doesn't seem to give a damn. All he asks is that we let him stay in the hospital for another week."

"Yeah, I can't figure it out," Masters said. "First he wants out and can't stand another day in there; then he asks for another week."

"It's all part of his act," Anderson said. "He's scared to go back but doesn't want to admit it. He says he needs a full eight weeks of rest; then he can whip the world."

"I know, but I still can't figure it out."

Masters got his answer at a staff meeting that evening. A telephone call interrupted the conference, and as he listened, his face turned gray. When he hung up, he said slowly, "Tony Washington escaped from the hospital tonight."

Rich Anderson jumped to his feet. "When? How? Have they searched the building? He couldn't just walk away!"

"He didn't," Masters said. "One of the nurses saw him riding off in an old pickup. She said it was falling apart. He won't get far."

"Did she get the license number?" Anderson demanded excitedly, not knowing whether to be happy or sad.

"No," Masters answered. "She was confused. She said it was a West Virginia license . . . 1926."

Miss Wilson slapped her forehead and fell back into her chair. "Oh, my God." Masters and Anderson stared at her without speaking, suddenly suspecting the truth. "You know"—she laughed—"If Ralph weren't officially classified as profoundly retarded, he might be a prime suspect."

Gary Masters leaned back in his chair and smiled the smile of a contented man. "You know, for the past six months—ever since Matt dismantled Shacky—I have been feeling personally responsible for those four boys . . . I just realized it. . . . I suppose that's the main reason I've been hanging on here. Tony was the last of the loose ends, wasn't he?"

Miss Wilson and Rich Anderson exchanged apprehensive glances as the smiles disappeared from their faces.

"Rich, what do you think George Hacker will say when he hears about Tony's escape?" Masters was up and pacing the room, but he was grinning mischievously.

Rich shrugged. "He won't like it."

"The word is 'pissed,' my friend." Masters was practically dancing with joy, clapping his hands gleefully. "And what I wouldn't give to see it."

"Calm down, Gary. This could mean your job."

Masters walked to the table and slapped a small key down in front of Anderson. "You're missing my point," he said with a broad smile. "That's the key to the strongbox in my lower-left-hand drawer. When you open it, you will find two letters: One is my resignation—type a date on it and mail it to Hacker—the other one is addressed to the FBI. I wrote it after we got that shipment of wormy meat; then I updated it after Hacker sent down the institutional transfer for Matt and John. It lays out the whole stinking mess we've got here, and it's going to send a lot of slimy politicians scurrying for cover." Masters picked up the key and pressed it into Anderson's hand. "Mail them both!"

Anderson came out of his chair with a protest. He looked toward Miss Wilson for support, but she was smiling with pleasure. "Where the hell are you going?" he finally managed as Masters headed for the door.

"I said that Tony was the last of the loose ends. I'm just going to make sure it's been tied up right."

The highway west was practically deserted, so Masters pushed his Camaro to the limit. He had thought it might take half the night to catch up with Tony and Ralph, but as he sped past one of the many rest areas off the highway, he caught a glimpse of an old pickup. He made a U-turn as soon as he could and returned for a closer inspection. As he cruised past the rest area again, a huge figure of a man was pouring gas from a can into the tank while a tiny elf in a white turban danced around him teasingly.

Chapter Forty-seven: The Ranch

At first Matt and Jon were worried that Ralph had been in an accident. He had left for town before dawn and hadn't returned. They made some calls from the Morgan Ranch, but by that time the stores had closed. They debated about calling the highway patrol, and when they saw no alternative, they finally did so. There had been no reported accidents in the area. The last call they made was to the gas station on the highway, and Fred Stansfield confirmed that Ralph had filled the tank the night before, along with a fifty-gallon drum and three five-gallon cans.

"Wherever he's heading, he's got lots of gas to get there," Jon mumbled.

Matt agreed and I added, "I just hope he's got enough to get back."

The following day, their anxiety turned to depression as they forced themselves to deal with the possibility that Ralph might have deserted them. They spent the night at the Morgan Ranch, where they were helping round up strays, but their hearts were not in it.

They returned home near dusk, pushing their mounts as they approached the Wilson place. Matt reined up at the top of the hill overlooking the bunkhouse and corral and sighted the truck. "He's back!" Jon galloped past him without slowing, and the two of them raced down the hill at breakneck speed.

Ralph was standing in the door as they approached, but something was wrong. He usually came out to greet them, but this time he just stood there. When they were close enough to see the expression on his face, they pulled up and dismounted. He seemed about to cry. They moved forward, shouting, "What's wrong, Ralph?"

Ralph simply shook his head sadly and turned his back on them. Matt and Jon stopped and looked at each other in concern. Suddenly Ralph turned back to them with a big grin and scooped Tony to his shoulders.

Matt and Jon stood stunned as Ralph stumbled through a patch of waist-high grass, carrying Tony aloft. "Hey, you dumb cowboys, look who's here!"

The sound of Tony's voice convinced them he was real, and Matt and Jon sprinted forward to embrace their two friends. When the dust settled, and the four of them lay exhausted on the ground, Tony asked, "What happened to all the buffalo? What kind of a place is this anyway?"

Ralph jumped to his knees and held out both fists, one facing upward and one down. Then he moved them to his right and rotated his fists—"A safe place."

From the top of the far hill the man in the dusty Camaro watched the reunion through his tears. Then he started his engine and slowly picked his way across the rough ground toward the narrow road.

EPILOGUE

1984

The characters and events in this story are real. Some were portrayed as accurately as memory permitted, and some were composites of the professional experiences of the authors.

Walter Pate was released from Clearwater just prior to his eighteenth birthday, and he was arrested three weeks later on a charge of armed robbery. He was sentenced to twelve years in the penitentiary. We know only that he dropped out of sight after his parole, five years later.

Shacky Wallis left Clearwater on a work-release program soon after Tony's escape. He went to work as a janitor at a major university in the midwest, a job he has kept since that time. As Gary Masters had predicted, Shacky changed drastically when there were no more boys to intimidate. He still swaggers around with a severe limp, but he is otherwise a pathetic sight. His front teeth do not fit properly, and he wears an outrageous orange hairpiece that attempts to match what is left of his faded red hair. He continually sneers at people, but instead of striking fear, as they once did in Matt and the other boys, his sneers are a point of ridicule. Shacky is a social recluse and a complete misfit who is now content merely to exist.

Earl Wilson died the year after our story ended, and Verna Wilson returned to the ranch permanently. She is still there and has willed the ranch to Ralph, who has managed the place for the past eight years. He lives in the old house with her, his wife, the former Loretta Morgan, and their three children.

Find a Safe Place

Tony Washington spent the rest of that summer on the ranch, but he was never comfortable with rural life, so he set out to find his mother two months later. The other boys never heard from him again, but if Tony held true to the statistics relating to similar cases, we may fairly well assume that the realities of his childhood neglect caught up with him, and he probably returned to his earlier behavioral patterns on the fringe of society.

Gary Masters continued to fight the good fight elsewhere for several years following the boys' reunion. He won a national reputation for his work, appearing on several network television talk shows, but when he finally realized that the public was unable to relate to the plight of incarcerated children, he turned to a different career and prefers that we not violate his anonymity.

Matt and Jon did indeed play high school football, and they played it well. Both were named to the all-state team in their senior year. Jon then accepted a football scholarship to a major urban university in the Northeast. Upon graduation he was admitted to law school under a minorities' recruitment program. Although he had a less than spectacular undergraduate record, he excelled as a law student, and he is now a distinguished attorney in Chicago, where he lives with his wife, Marcie, and two sons, Matt and Wilson.

Matt McFadden decided to attend one of the local community colleges on a football scholarship in order to remain closer to the ranch. He later transferred to the Unviersity of Colorado on an academic scholarship, and he went on to medical school. In 1979 he completed his residence in pediatrics and accepted a position at a major children's hospital and research center in the Rockies.

The people and events we have written about are not unusual when you consider that more than a million children are incarcerated in the United States every year. Of that number, at least half are not even accused of a crime. Like Jon, Matt, Ralph, Tony, and countless other nonoffenders, the children are locked away because there are no parents to care for them and no other place for them to go.

If you close this book doubting the truth of what you have read, we have failed in our task. Three of the children in our story have succeeded, but literally tens of thousands more, from six to eighteen years of age, who are capable of the same success, are now languishing behind bars, even in your own state.

Think about the waste.

About the Authors

ALEXANDER LAZZARINO and E. KENT HAYES, the former an attorney and the latter a criminologist specializing in juvenile offenders, have devoted their careers to helping disturbed children through the Menninger Foundation in Topeka, Kansas. Their cases have ranged from twelve-year-old child murderers to teenagers who just don't fit in and have nowhere to go but correctional institutions. Their first book was *Broken Promise*, published by Putnam in 1978, and was also made into a television movie of the same title.